CONSERVING NATURE'S DIVERSITY

Conserving Nature's Diversity
Insights from biology, ethics and economics

Edited by

G. CORNELIS VAN KOOTEN
University of British Columbia
Wageningen University

ERWIN H. BULTE
Tilburg University

A.R.E. SINCLAIR
University of British Columbia

LONDON AND NEW YORK

First published 2000 by Ashgate Publishing

Reissued 2018 by Routledge
2 Park Square, Milton Park, Abingdon, Oxon OX14 4RN
711 Third Avenue, New York, NY 10017, USA

Routledge is an imprint of the Taylor & Francis Group, an informa business

Copyright © G.C. van Kooten, E.H. Bulte and A.R.E. Sinclair 2000

All rights reserved. No part of this book may be reprinted or reproduced or utilised in any form or by any electronic, mechanical, or other means, now known or hereafter invented, including photocopying and recording, or in any information storage or retrieval system, without permission in writing from the publishers.

Notice:
Product or corporate names may be trademarks or registered trademarks, and are used only for identification and explanation without intent to infringe.

Publisher's Note
The publisher has gone to great lengths to ensure the quality of this reprint but points out that some imperfections in the original copies may be apparent.

Disclaimer
The publisher has made every effort to trace copyright holders and welcomes correspondence from those they have been unable to contact.

A Library of Congress record exists under LC control number: 00132608

ISBN 13: 978-1-138-72674-1 (hbk)
ISBN 13: 978-1-138-72669-7 (pbk)
ISBN 13: 978-1-315-19126-3 (ebk)

Contents

List of Tables vii

List of Figures viii

List of Contributors ix

Foreword xi

1 Introduction: Conserving Biological Diversity 1
   G. Cornelis van Kooten, Erwin H. Bulte, A.R.E. Sinclair

2 The Loss of Biodiversity: The Sixth Great Extinction 9
   A.R.E. Sinclair

3 Biodiversity: Concerns and Values 16
   G.G.E. Scudder

4 Is Conservation Achieving its Ends? 30
   A.R.E. Sinclair

5 The End of Conservation on the Cheap, Revisited 45
   Robert L. Pressey

6 Threat to Biodiversity: The Invasion of Exotic Species 68
   *Emina Krcmar-Nozic, G. Cornelis van Kooten,
   Bill Wilson*

7 Economic Perspectives on Preservation of Biodiversity 88
   R. David Simpson

8	Biodiversity: Forests, Property Rights and Economic Value *Roger A. Sedjo*	106
9	Economics, Endangered Species and Biodiversity Loss: The Dismal Science in Practice *Erwin H. Bulte, Daan P. van Soest, G. Cornelis van Kooten*	123
10	Biodiversity and Ethics: Religion, Science and Economics *G. Cornelis van Kooten*	143
11	Implications for Democratic Theory: A Normative Analysis *Lesley Jacobs*	160
References		170
Index		199

List of Tables

Table 1.1: Threatened and Endangered Species as of March 31, 1999 3
Table 1.2: Total US Federal plus State Expenditures on Endangered Species, 1989-93 4
Table 1.3: Neoclassical and Ecological Views of Sustainability 7
Table 5.1: Areas of Remaining Native Vegetation in LP (low-priority) and HP (high-priority) Landscapes, Eastern 60% of New South Wales 54
Table 6.1: Estimated Numbers of Exotic Species in the United States 73
Table 6.2: Costs of the Gypsy Moth Invasion, United States and Canada 80
Table 6.3: Impacts of the Dutch Elm Disease in the USA and Canada 81
Table 6.4: Projected Timber Losses from Forest Pests due to Imported Logs from Siberia and Russian Far East, 1990-2040 83
Table 6.5: Classification of Measures to Prevent Bio-invasions 85
Table 8.1: Forest area change in developed countries, 1990-1995 108
Table 8.2: Comparison of 1980 and 1995 Forest Cover 109
Table 9.1: Annual Benefits of Primary Forests, Atlantic Zone, Costa Rica 127
Table 9.2: Optimal Forest Stocks to Hold in Humid Costa Rica (hectares) 129
Table 9.3: Protecting Elephants in Zambia and Kenya: Optimal Stocks . 136

List of Figures

Figure 3.1: The Ecosystem Cycle 27
Figure 5.1: Environmental Coverage of Reserves in NE New South Wales 47
Figure 5.2: Distribution across Major Tenures of Remaining Native Vegetation with High Priority for Conservation in New South Wales 55
Figure 6.1: Growing World Trade, 1963-1996 72
Figure 6.2: Value of Canadian Imports, 1994-1998 75
Figure 8.1: Demand and Supply of Wild Genetic Resources for Pharmaceutical Use 113
Figure 8.2: Demand and Supply of Biodiversity as a Life Support System 115
Figure 9.1: Marginal Value of Land in Agriculture, Two Valuation Functions 128
Figure 9.2: Economic Losses and Number of Species 133

List of Contributors

Dr. Erwin H. Bulte is Assistant Professor in the Department of Economics, Tilburg University, and in the Department of Economics and Management, Wagengingen University, both in the Netherlands. (e.h.bulte@kub.nl)

Dr. Lesley Jacobs is Associate Professor of Law & Society and Philosophy, York University, Toronto, Ontario, and was previously 1997-98 Liberal Arts Fellow, Harvard Law School, Cambridge, MA. (ljacobsglaw.harvard.edu)

Dr. Emina Krcmar-Nozic is a senior research associate with the Forest Economics and Policy Analysis (FEPA) Research Unit, University of British Columbia, Vancouver, BC. (ekrcmar@interchange.ubc.ca)

Dr. Geoff Scudder is Professor Emeritus in the Department of Zoology, University of British Columbia, Vancouver, Canada.

Dr. Roger Sedjo is Senior Fellow with Resources for the Future, 1616 P Street NW, Washington, DC, 20036 USA. (sedjo@rff.org)

Dr. Robert Pressey is a biologist at New South Wales National Parks and Wildlife Service, PO Box 402 Armidale NSW 2350 Australia. (bpressey@ozemail.com.au)

Dr. David Simpson is a Senior Fellow with Resources for the Future, 1616 P Street NW, Washington, DC, 20036 USA. (simpson@rff.org)

Dr. Anthony R. E. Sinclair is Professor of Zoology and Director of the Centre for Biodiversity Research at the University of British Columbia, Vancouver, Canada. (sinclair@zoology.ubc.ca)

Dr. G. Cornelis van Kooten is Professor of Natural Resource Economics in the Faculties of Forestry and Agricultural Sciences, and Co-director of the FEPA Research Unit, University of British Columbia, Vancouver, Canada, and in the Department of Economics and Management, Wagengingen University, Netherlands. (gerrit@interchange.ubc.ca)

Dr. Daan P. van Soest is Assistant Professor in the Department of Economics, Tilburg University in the Netherlands. (D.P.vanSoest@kub.nl)

Dr. Bill Wilson is Director, Industry, Trade and Economics, Pacific Forestry Centre, Canadian Forest Service in Victoria, British Columbia, Canada. (bwilson@pfc.forestry.ca)

Foreword

It is only appropriate that a book on the conservation of the earth's biological diversity is published in the final year of the millennium (the new millennium actually begins in 2001). The past decade has seen unprecedented interest in, and concern about, the loss of species and human-caused destruction of ecosystems through, among other activities, tropical deforestation. Is this interest ephemeral? Are other events or crises likely to overshadow concern about biodiversity? Is the problem over-rated and likely to disappear on its own, for whatever reasons (e.g., as world population levels off, as developing countries become richer, as ethical viewpoints change)? Is there even agreement on the extent of the biodiversity-ecosystem loss problem and what might be done to resolve it?

This book seeks to answer some, but certainly not all, of these questions. The authors of the various contributions to this volume approach loss of biological diversity and ecosystem degradation from various disciplinary, experiential and ethical perspectives. Even within a discipline there is disagreement about the processes or causes of biodiversity loss, its importance, and what to do about it, but such differences are more pronounced across disciplines. This is readily seen by a careful reading of the various chapters that make up the volume. It is unlikely, therefore, to expect an easy resolution of issues related to biodiversity.

Yet, there are strands of agreement, places where the language of one discipline is understood by that of another. For example, biologists and economists remain divided, for the most part, about what the historical evidence on species loss means and how meaningful it is to project future species loss on the basis of the species-area relation. If these points are overlooked, and they can be, there appears to be remarkable agreement on human nature and the role of governments and markets, although such agreement is not always fully understood. Once a decision is made to protect certain ecosystems, agreement on how best to do so also appears to be forthcoming. Only the technical details need to be resolved, but this is a minor aspect of the larger problem.

The purpose of this volume is not to find common ground (although some is found), but rather to investigate and present the alternative inter- and intra-disciplinary viewpoints.

The original impetus for this volume came from a November 1997 workshop on the "Conservation of Biodiversity: Merging Biological, Ethical and Economic Theory" held in Vancouver, Canada, and sponsored by the Peter Wall Institute at the University of British Columbia. At the workshop, it became abundantly clear that disagreement about many issues remained. This led to further exploration of issues by the authors of the current volume.

The editors wish to acknowledge financial support for this project from the Sustainable Forest Management Network at the University of Alberta, and the Forest Economics and Policy Analysis Research Unit and the Centre for Biodiversity Research at the University of British Columbia.

Finally, this volume could not have come to fruition without the help of several people. The editors wish to acknowledge the contributions and technical support provided by Louise Arthur, Cynthia Suh, Connie Ho, Irene Wingate and Emina Krcmar-Nozic. It can only be hoped that this collection of papers will begin readers on the trek towards merging the ideas from a variety of disciplines involved in the protection of the globe's valuable resources.

1 Introduction: Conserving Biological Diversity

G. CORNELIS VAN KOOTEN, ERWIN H. BULTE,
A.R.E. SINCLAIR

Loss of biological diversity (or biodiversity) is considered one of the greatest threats facing humans today, subsuming such environmental problems as tropical deforestation and global demise of the fishery. The three primary and proximate causes of extinction of known species are over-exploitation, introduction of exotic species and habitat conversion. A possible future threat to biodiversity is global change as caused by ozone depletion and the greenhouse effect (Smith et al. 1995). Thus, it is humans, one way or another, who "decide" on which species will survive and which will not.

In an earlier volume, Swanson (1995) examined four underlying reasons for the loss of biodiversity. First, human societies choose the amount of biodiversity to retain along a development path, but such paths have been haphazard, likely leading to greater loss of biodiversity than desired. Second, there has been a failure to create appropriate institutions for internalising the public good nature of biodiversity (i.e., biodiversity provides benefits to everyone, not just the individual decision maker or country). Third, inappropriate government policies have encouraged destruction of ecosystems, including the fishery (e.g., Harris 1998). Governments have purposely permitted ecosystem demise in pursuit of other objectives (Bromley 1999). Finally, it is argued that humans are self-interested, pursuing economic goals that are in fundamental conflict with other species. More broadly, it can be argued, on the one hand, that economic development is the main factor leading to the loss of species, while, on the other, that poverty is the root cause. Swanson (1995) concludes that no one cause dominates, but that there is a grain of truth to all explanations for the demise of nature.

2 *Conserving Nature's Diversity*

This volume goes further than just the economic side of the debate, looking rather for a broader consensus about conservation of biodiversity. In this volume, we examine biological, economic and ethical issues pertaining to the preservation of biodiversity. As might be expected as a result of the enormity of such a task, only fragments of the various aspects of debate in these divergent fields are presented. Nonetheless, they do provide an indicator of the possibility of reaching a consensus about the problem and the need and design of appropriate policies to prevent further loss of biodiversity. In this chapter, we provide a perspective on the debate and an overview of the fundamental points of the various authors of the collection.

Decline in Biodiversity: What is Being Done?

Both Sinclair (Chapter 2) and Scudder (Chapter 3) point out that global society could potentially lose a million or more species in the first decade of the new millennium. This constitutes some ten percent of all known species of plants and animals. Such projections are based on a relationship between number of species and the area they occupy. The species-area function requires information about the extant number of species in a particular area, the rate of land conversion (assumed to equal habitat loss), and the parameters of the function. (In Chapter 9, Bulte et al. rely on the species-area relation to make predictions of potential species loss.) Unfortunately, not only are data on existing species unknown, but the exact nature of the species-area relation is somewhat speculative, having been estimated only from limited observations from small islands and perhaps not even applicable to continental areas or even large islands. Although projections of species loss are speculative, there is no denying that species are being lost and that many others are threatened or endangered.

The United States is the only country that has passed legislation to protect endangered species, namely, the Endangered Species Act of 1973, which is currently up for re-authorisation. As part of this legislation, a tally is kept of species that are threatened or endangered, including foreign ones (Table 1.1).

The data indicate that there are 1,181 threatened and endangered species of plants and animals in the USA, and that recovery plans are in place for 75% of these. There are also 560 foreign species of plants and animals on the list, but this is clearly an underestimate of the actual number of threatened and endangered species outside the USA, and the US number may itself be an underestimate. The reason is that it costs money to identify species and get them listed, and more money is available for doing this in the USA than outside it.

Table 1.1: Threatened and Endangered Species as of March 31, 1999

Group	Endangered USA	Endangered Foreign	Threatened USA	Threatened Foreign	TOTAL	with Plans
Mammals	60	251	8	16	335	49
Birds	75	178	15	6	274	77
Reptiles	14	65	21	14	114	30
Amphibians	9	8	7	1	25	11
Fishes	70	11	40	0	121	88
Snails	18	1	10	0	29	20
Clams	61	2	8	0	71	45
Crustaceans	17	0	3	0	20	12
Insects	28	4	9	0	41	27
Arachnids	5	0	0	0	5	5
Animal Subtotal	**357**	**520**	**121**	**37**	**1,035**	**364**
Flowering plants	540	1	132	0	673	494
Conifers	2	0	1	2	5	2
Ferns & other	26	0	2	0	28	26
Plant Subtotal	**568**	**1**	**135**	**2**	**706**	**522**
TOTAL	**925**	**521**	**256**	**39**	**1,741**	**886**[a]

[a] There are 519 approved recovery plans as some cover more than one species.
Source: US Fish and Wildlife Service as reported by Shogren and Tschirhart (1999)

Funds are required not only to identify and list species, but also to develop and implement recovery plans. For the period 1989-93, the federal and state governments in the USA spent more than $1.5 billion on endangered species (Table 1.2). Of this amount, more than half was spent on 60 endangered mammal species, and more than 77% on 135 mammal and bird species that are endangered.

While more than 60% of endangered species are plants (568 species), less than 1.5% of expenditures were allocated to protect them; 79 snail and clam species received only 0.6% of expenditures. Clearly, expenditures are biased towards high-profile species, namely, mammals and birds, and to a lesser extent fishes and reptiles.

In addition to government expenditures, conservation of endangered species may involve substantial costs for private landowners.

Often conserving species boils down to safeguarding natural habitats, and the usual way to achieve this is to impose restrictions on land use. As these restrictions may be costly and infringe upon landowner's rights to use their land as they please, society faces a tradeoff when it pursues the lofty goal of biodiversity preservation in practice (Mann and Plummer 1995).

Table 1.2: Total US Federal plus State Expenditures on Endangered Species, 1989-93

Taxonomic Group	Expenditure ($ millions
Mammals	809.1
Birds	388.6
Reptiles	68.9
Amphibians	1.4
Fishes	227.9
Snails	1.4
Mussels	8.7
Crustaceans	0.7
Insects	14.3
Arachnids	3.1
Plants	22.2
TOTAL	**1,546.3**

Source: Shogren and Tschirhart (1999)

The forgoing discussion illustrates two points. First, species are threatened and endangered, and they are disappearing. For example, Ricciardi and Rasmussen (1999) provide the first estimates of extinction rates for North America's freshwater animals. They find that, since 1900, at least 123 freshwater animal species have been recorded as extinct, and that common freshwater species, from snails to fish to amphibians, are dying out five times faster than land species and three times faster than coastal marine mammals. In North America, at risk species account for 49% of the 262 remaining mussel species, 33% of the 336 crayfish species, 26% of the 243 amphibian species, and 21% of the 1,021 fish species. It is non-native species that pose the most serious threat to indigenous freshwater animals, with even sport fish transplanted from one lake to another capable of taking over an ecosystem by driving less aggressive native fish toward extinction. The subject of exotic invasions is discussed by Krcmar-Nozic et al. (Chapter 6).

Second, it costs money to protect species and, as a result, it is necessary to uses funds as effectively as possible. One way to do this is by creating national parks, wildlife refuges, wilderness and other protected areas that make it possible to protect the habitat of several endangered and threatened species at the same time. Again, it is not possible to protect all potential habitats and choices must be made. However, as Pressey (Chapter 5) points out, globally, we have protected species that are less valuable, both from a commercial and biodiversity standpoint. By protecting (poor-quality) public land, we practise conservation on the cheap. He illustates this with examples from Australia. The disappearance of the golden toad and other amphibians in Costa Rica has been attributed to climatic changes, and many losses have been recorded in national parks and nature reserves, indicating pervasive threats even in protected areas. Sinclair (Chapter 4) addresses this concern, arguing that money, enforcement and vigilance are required to ensure that there is no encroachment on protected areas and to guarantee that species will indeed be protected in parks and other nature reserves.

Biodiversity Paradigms

There are interdisciplinary as well as intra-disciplinary disagreements about the role of natural versus reproducible capital in sustainable development. Two viewpoints pertaining to sustainable development can be identified—the ecological view that natural capital needs to be maintained intact and the neoclassical view that holds that the sum of natural and reproducible capital needs to be sustained, that it is possible to substitute some reproducible capital for natural capital. These are often labelled as the strong and weak views of sustainable development.

Strong sustainability argues, first, that some natural resources are essential for production, and their loss would constitute a catastrophic event (see Chapters 2 and 3). Second, even for production processes where natural capital is not yet an essential ingredient, substitutability declines as resource stocks are depleted. Finally, there are no substitutes whatsoever for many natural resources, especially biodiversity, because of its unique character. The implication is that such critical natural capital should be conserved, regardless of the opportunity cost of so doing. The ecological view is clearly influenced by developments in biology and ecology. Concern about the demise of natural (biological, meteorological) systems is a common theme in the biology-ecology literature, and is at the heart of the strong sustainability perspective. The ecological view often supports some form of population control, regulations and/or incentives to prevent loss of species, agreements to limit trade in threatened and endangered species, subsidies or sanctions to prevent tropical deforestation, constraints on free trade, and other similar interventionist policies.

The neoclassical paradigm is the antithesis of the ecological view that natural capital imposes severe constraints on growth—that economic collapse might be brought about by ecosystem collapse. The neoclassical view is that, as biological resources become scarce, their relative values will rise, which leads to greater investments in their conservation. These points are made by Simpson (Chapter 7) and Sedjo (Chapter 8). The neoclassical view is that the elasticity of substitution between natural capital and reproducible capital is high. Further, this view argues that loss of species is exaggerated and that species loss does not result in ecosystem dysfunction, and possibly not a loss in genetic diversity (Nee and May 1997). It is possible to substitute some species for others. In Chapter 9, Bulte et al. explicitly argue that an economist's approach to conservation of nature and biodiversity is likely consistent with further conversion of natural capital into alternative assets that are useful to society at large. They illustrate this point with several case studies.

The "typical" ecological position thus prescribes conservation of natural capital, even at considerable cost, while the position of some economists is more favourably inclined towards further development. It is the link between past evidence and future projections that is likely to be most contentious between the two positions, although interpretation of past evidence may well be a source of controversy in some cases. For example, based on current and historic trends, ecologists generally maintain that population growth is *the* major threat to the environment and sustainable development, while neoclassicals are optimistic that population growth is slowing sufficiently that it will no longer be a problem in the future. Rather, they may claim, it is poverty that needs to be addressed. However, it is clear that decisions with respect to biodiversity conservation are not to be based exclusively on the issue whether it is possible to substitute away from natural capital (and biodiversity) in production, or not. In addition to this rather technical matter, such fundamental matters will be motivated by what is the "right" thing to do. In other words, we are encroaching upon the (perhaps slippery) terrain of ethics, which is the subject of Chapters 10 and 11. A summary of the main positions of the neoclassicals and ecologists with respect to sustainable development more generally (as opposed to only biodiversity) is provided in Table 1.3.

Table 1.3: Neoclassical and Ecological Views of Sustainability

Neoclassical	Ecological
1. Focus is on what happens at the margin, because it is at the margin that decisions are made. The scale of the economy relative to the resource base is irrelevant.	1. Focus is on large-scale ecosystems and possibilities for irreversibility. There are scale effects—certain "triggers" could set in motion large-scale ecosystem processes that result in irreversible loss in ecosystem functioning.
2. Economists employ steady-state models that assume equilibrium.	2. Models in ecology focus on resilience and non-equilibrium dynamics.
3. The value system employed is utilitarian.	3. A value system must come from outside ecology as ecology does not have its own.
4. Monetary values are used to measure and "value" changes in environmental quality.	4. Monetary valuation is generally opposed, especially as it is applied to decisions affecting threatened, large-scale ecosystem productivity.
5. Prices play an important role signalling scarcity and, as a result, encouraging substitution and technological innovation. While unpredictable and difficult to measure, technological change has been shown to be a powerful factor in the past and will continue in that role in the future.	5. The role of prices and technological change is downplayed. Prices do not reflect reality because of the existence of externalities. Technological change is unpredictable and unreliable for solving future problems.
6. Discounting and present values are used.	6. Discounting is generally opposed, and the emphasis is on future generations.
7. The current generation owes the future opportunities equal to its own, which means maintaining a non-declining aggregate capital stock. Adequate investment needs to be maintained to compensate the future for the use (or degradation) of certain resources.	7. Safeguarding the functioning of large-scale ecosystems figures prominently in satisfying concerns about intergenerational fairness. Preservation of variety of ecosystem functions (with aesthetic services featuring prominently) is what matters for the future.
8. Attempts are made to measure the well-being of various generations and then compare them (referred to as teleology, implying the making of decisions for the future generation).	8. The rights of future generations trump the mere enjoyments of current generations, enjoyments that come at the expense of future well-being. This is a rights-based theory, or deontology.
9. The Safe Minimum Standard of Conservation allows tradeoffs (see Chapter 10).	9. The Precautionary Principle permits less scope for balancing costs and benefits.
10. Property rights of individuals feature prominently, with government's role specified as that of setting and enforcing the "rules of law," and, where justifiable, relying on the State to correct externalities.	10. Individualism is seen as a source of environmental degradation. State intervention is needed to protect ecosystems.

Source: van Kooten and Bulte (2000)

It is the different viewpoints that lead one to be optimistic about species loss and biodiversity, and the other to be pessimistic. Reconciling these "opposite" positions poses a tremendous challenge for the development and implementation of policy related to biodiversity, and economic policy more generally. It cannot be done as long as long as "... the current strategy of asserting, defending, and applying opposed, monistic systems of value in exclusive disciplinary contexts is continued" (Norton and Toman 1997, p. 565).

While an interdisciplinary approach might resolve some of the issues, it may not be able to resolve those related to world or ethical viewpoints as opposed to theoretical approaches. Van Kooten (Chapter 10) and Jacobs (Chapter 11) consider these ethical issues in greater detail. Van Kooten goes somewhat further by examining ethics in the context of a new economics that seeks to bring into mainstream economics social, psychological and political considerations. He points out that any attempt to find a common ethic on which to base concerns about biodiversity is likely to fail, but that it is still possible to reach agreement on an appropriate policy approach. It is the policy role that needs to be emphasised.

Given interdisciplinary disagreements between biologists, economists and ethicists, and even intra-disciplinary disagreements, what is to be done about biological diversity? The first step is the one taken in this book, and that is to get the various disciplines to talk to each other, to start looking for common ground. For their part, biologists need to be more forthright about how they measure biodiversity and loss of species. They need to be more cognisant about the worldview they hold and how it may differ from that held by those in other disciplines, all the while recognising common touchstones upon which interdisciplinary insights can be built. Although economic models generally begin with an unrealistic view of human behaviour (an area where improvements are certainly needed), they nonetheless provide powerful insights into the required means for protecting biodiversity, insights that can be harnessed by those seeking to conserve biodiversity. To these one needs to add the insights from ethics, so that, by working together and talking to each other, it will be possible to minimise the loss of nature's diversity. This volume is a start in that direction.

2 The Loss of Biodiversity: The Sixth Great Extinction
A.R.E. SINCLAIR

Interest in biodiversity and the number of species in our environments has increased markedly in the last two decades of the twentieth century, coincident with an increasing anxiety over the extinction of species as habitats are lost to human exploitation. Rhetoric, however, has often jumped far ahead of the facts. It is, therefore, useful to review what we know of extinction processes. Major reviews of extinctions can be found in Raup and Sepkoski (1984), Scudder (1993), Pimm et al. (1995a), Lawton and May (1995) and Pimm (1998).

A History of Human Exterminations

Species may be disappearing at unprecedented rates due to human intervention but this is not just a phenomenon of the past few decades. Humans have been exterminating species for as far back as we can detect. First, let us consider the history of human populations as they spread around the world. Modern humans came from Africa and spread across Eurasia some 200,000 years ago. Our evidence for human invasions starts after that, the earliest occurring in Australia, somewhere around 50,000 years ago according to evidence from charcoal deposits. North America was invaded over the Bering Strait about 15 thousand years ago. From Indonesia, humans spread over the Polynesian Islands, some 3,000 years ago, reaching Hawaii 1,500 years ago. Other invasions occurred in Madagascar about 1,500 years ago, and finally in New Zealand about a thousand years ago.

The extinction of the large marsupials in Australia coincided with the arrival of humans. It was the largest marsupials that went extinct, species such as the elephant-like marsupial *Palorchestes* feeding on trees, the giant kangaroos and the group known as the Diprotodonts, animals the size of rhinos. These were the species that were particularly prone to human extermination. In Europe, the very large species such as the Irish elk, mammoths, and woolly rhinos disappeared with the arrival of modern humans displacing Neanderthal man during the ice ages. The arrival of humans in North America coincided with a spectacular increase in the frequency of extinctions beginning some twelve thousand of years ago. Again it was the large mammals that disappeared from North and South America, species such as the mastodons, mammoths, giant ground sloth and glyptodonts (two-meter long, giant armadillos). These very large species, such as mastodons, living in the slow growing low productivity conifer forests, would have had both low populations (a few thousand) and very low reproductive rates. If humans had simply killed some of the babies, this would have caused their extinction. Furthermore, humans may well have altered habitats through fire and so indirectly caused extinctions. Thus, overwhelming evidence suggests these extinctions were human-related.

The Pacific islands provide evidence of extensive eradication by Polynesian peoples before contact by Europeans (Steadman 1995; Pimm et al. 1995a). These islands were progressively colonised from west to east starting some 4,000 years ago and finally north to Hawaii some 1,500 years ago. On each island they found many tame and often flightless birds which they ate to extinction. The evidence comes from fossil bones (e.g., Olson and James 1982). On the Hawaiian Islands, 43 species are known only from their bones; by various calculations some 101 species are thought to have been exterminated by early colonisers. Presently only 136 Hawaiian bird species remain and of these only 11 species have large enough populations to allow long term survival (Pimm et al. 1995a, Pimm 1998).

In New Caledonia a meter-and-a-half long turkey-like bird was hunted to extinction some 1,700 years ago, at the same time as a primitive crocodile. Their remains are found in the aboriginal food middens. Thus, recent evidence shows that the first inhabitants of the Pacific islands systematically eradicated island birds (Steadman 1995) and exterminated fully twenty percent of the world's bird species. Throughout the Pacific, therefore, we see the same story.

In Madagascar, a few hundred years ago the giant ostrich-like "elephant birds" (the biggest birds in the world) disappeared along with giant lemurs as a result of hunting. In New Zealand some 12 species of large flightless moas, birds similar to those on Madagascar, were killed off by the Moa hunters (predecessors of the Maoris) about a thousand years ago.

In modern times, during the 1600s, we see the disappearance of the Aurochs, the progenitor of the domestic cattle, despite efforts by the Kings of central Europe to save that species. The Stellar's sea cow, a manatee, discovered by the Russians on British Columbia's coast in 1714, was extinct by 1740. The whalers and sealers killed off the Great Auk, a flightless seabird living off the Atlantic coast of Canada last century, the last one being recorded in 1844.

The process of extermination continues today with native peoples of Greenland and Canada causing the decline of the Common Murre, a seabird related to the Great Auk. Freshwater mussels in North American rivers comprise some 297 species in two families (Williams et al. 1992). They live in riverbeds and are sensitive to sedimentation, changes in nutrient contents of the water and pollution. Most species have early larvae that parasitise fish. The spread of agriculture and human habitation in the past 100 years has resulted in high sedimentation, run-off of fertiliser, sewage effluent and industrial pollution. Many of the fish species on which the mussels depend have disappeared. In short, habitat in nearly all rivers has been destroyed. Some 21 species have gone extinct and another 120 are on the verge of extinction (Pimm 1998).

The southern tip of Africa supports a special type of flora, called "fynbos" a relict of ancient habitats when Africa was part of the great southern continent, Gondwana. There are many plant and animal endemics associated with the fynbos. Of about 8,500 flowering plant species, 36 have become extinct in the past century and another 618 are currently threatened, that is, likely to become extinct in the next few decades. Conversion of the fynbos to agriculture, combined with the spread of domestic exotic plants, are the main causes of extinction (Pimm 1998).

In general, therefore, we find that all peoples, both aboriginal and colonial alike, have systematically exterminated species as far back as the archaeological record allows us to look. This record tells us about large species because they are easily found in the fossil record. There are many other species, about which we have much less knowledge, that have also become extinct.

Background Rates of Extinction

I have illustrated high extinction rates from different groups of organisms to show that extinction is not confined to the few higher vertebrates. To interpret these extinctions, however, we need to know what would be expected from normal non-human causes of extinction, the background rate of extinction.

Extinction is part of the evolutionary process. Over geological time major groups of organisms have evolved, diversified into subgroups and each in turn diversified. The geological record of diversity shows five major extinction events in the past 600 million years (Sepkoski 1992). Nevertheless, extinctions of species have proceeded at a slower rate between the major episodes of extinction. The current estimate of species in the world is roughly 50-100 million (Pimm 1998). The geological record suggests that the average longevity for a species ranges between 5-10 million years. These figures allow us to estimate that our present-day extant species represent only 2-4% of all species that have lived in the past 600 million years (May et al. 1995). Furthermore, over 90% of all extinctions occurred, not in the five major extinction events, but in the intervening times (Raup 1986, 1992).

As an example, if we take a sample of one million species and each species lives one million years then one would expect one extinction every year. With this type of calculation we can estimate the background rate of extinction over the fossil record. For all fossil groups the estimate is 0.2 - 2.0 extinctions per million species per year (E/MSY). Some groups, such as marine invertebrates have relatively low rates (0.2 E/MSY), others such as mammals have somewhat higher rates (1.0 E/MSY) (May et al. 1995; Pimm 1998). To put this into context, there are about 10 thousand species of birds in the world today. With a background rate of 1.0 E/MSY, and the longevity of a species of one million years, we would expect to see one extinction every one hundred years.

Present-day Extinction Rates

Using the observed extinctions from the mussels we see that 21 extinctions from 297 species in 100 years is equivalent to 707 E/MSY. In general, estimates for global extinction rates for various groups of organisms fall in the range of 20-200 E/MSY. When we compare these with the expected background rate (0.2 -2.0 E/MSY) we see that present-day human-induced rates are ten to one hundred times higher than during pre-human times.

Causes of Extinction

By far the greatest cause of extinction comes from the loss of habitats (Griffith et al. 1989). Loss of tropical forest is the most highly publicised aspect of this (and is discussed in Chapter 4 in the context of habitat renewal). However, virtually all other native habitats have suffered loss to various extents with hyper-arid (desert) regions being a possible exception (Sinclair et al. 1995). Rivers are impounded, coral reefs destroyed by dynamite, natural grasslands are ploughed. There are few disturbances that increase the whole community, most disturbances result in the loss of rare species and the increase of populations of common, often exotic species.

The second most important cause of extinction arises from the introduction of exotic species. Many of these are accidental, as with noxious weeds and insect pests, a consequence of the increased human travel and trade (see also Chapter 6). Others, however, are deliberate. In freshwaters, the stocking of exotic fish for sport, or (rarely) for food, has caused at least 18 extinctions of fish species in North American rivers. Catastrophic changes in the fish biodiversity of Lake Victoria, East Africa resulted from the introduction of Nile perch (Pimm 1998). Islands in particular are prone to the effects of exotics, and so this cause is prevalent in the Pacific region. In Australia, the deliberate introduction of the European rabbit (*Oryctolagus cunicules*) and red fox (*Vulpes vulpes*) in the 1800s has been the primary cause of extinction for 18 mammal species, exacerbated by concomitant habitat loss (Burbidge and McKenzie 1989; Short et al. 1992; Sinclair et al. 1998).

Lesser-known causes are due to "knock-on" effects. Species that are co-evolved with another, such as plants with specialised insect pollinators, will go extinct if one of the pair goes extinct. When the last passenger pigeon (*Ectopistes migratorius*) died in the early 1900s so also did two of its obligate parasites, two louse species (Stork and Lyal 1993). Parasites are particularly prone to such co-extinctions.

Centres of Extinction

Extinctions do not occur uniformly or randomly across the globe. Instead, we see a pattern where extinctions are concentrated in certain areas, and these areas, it turns out, are centres of endemism. These are areas where there are relatively high numbers of unique species with very restricted ranges (Pimm et al. 1995b). Such species are prone to extinction as a result of habitat loss because they do not have a wide enough range to accommodate the loss. They may be extirpated immediately from a given loss of habitat, such as forest clear-cut, or the remaining population may be too small to survive. In general, endemics have smaller ranges, and lower densities than widespread species, and so are intrinsically prone to habitat loss.

Predicting the Future

From much experience biologists have found an empirically defined relationship between the number of species and the area they occupy. This relationship has allowed us to predict how many species will be lost for a given proportion of habitat loss, and given the rates of habitat loss, how long that will take. For example, if we have 90% of a habitat, we should lose 50% of its original species (MacArthur and Wilson 1967). Pimm (1998) shows that this relationship makes reasonably good predictions for the loss of bird species whose range was restricted to the hardwood forests of the eastern United States. These forests were reduced to 1-2% of their original extent during the 1800s. The species-area relationship predicted that 17% of the 28 forest-restricted species should have become extinct, or approximately 5 species. In fact, four species did go extinct (passenger pigeon, Carolina parakeet (*Conuopsis carolinensis*), ivory billed woodpecker (*Campehilus principalis*), and Bachman's warbler (*Vermivora backmanii*)).

    In general, the species-area relationship makes different predictions of extinction rates depending on the degree of endemism. The most restricted species (say endemic to single islands or patches) have the highest rates, inter-archipelago endemics (endemic to groups of islands) the next highest, while non-endemics (widespread species) have the lowest rates. This is in general agreement with the observed pattern of centres of extinction discussed above.

Conclusions

Recent political interest in biodiversity has occurred because of its loss. The term biodiversity has become more familiar since the 1992 Biodiversity Convention in Rio. We are essentially concerned with changes in the ecosystem—the decline of populations, extinctions, and how to prevent them. We are concerned with whether we preserve species, or sub-species and races, or even genotypes—different genetic groupings. Ultimately, we must be concerned with the preservation of habitats because those are where all species live. Unless there are sufficiently large patches of habitat, the species they support will decline to extinction. The processes of extinction are well known and can be summarised into three major types—random events due to sudden changes in weather (extreme winter cold, droughts, hurricanes, fires, floods are examples of events that can wipe out small populations), competition from other more abundant species and predation.

The reason why we are so concerned about these questions is that we are this century losing species at about 100 times the rate that has occurred over the past one million years. Indeed, this rate is similar to that in the five major extinction events in the history of life on our planet, including the extinction of the dinosaurs—this is the sixth great extinction in world history.

3 Biodiversity: Concerns and Values

G.G.E. SCUDDER

To most people, biological diversity, to use the full term, means animal and plant species, the members of the two kingdoms of living organisms recognized by Linnaeus (1735). Some might recall that Haeckel (1866) recognized four kingdoms, and they would then include microbes and protists. Finally, those that follow Cavalier-Smith (1987, 1991) would acknowledge a suite of kingdoms, and a wide diversity of both prokaryotic and eukaryotic organisms.

However, to biologists, biodiversity means more than just organisms. Scientists now accept that the term biodiversity encompasses biological composition, biological structure and biological function (Noss 1990). Noss (1990) recognises that these compositional structural and functional concepts apply at the regional-landscape, community-ecosystem, population-species, and genetic levels. Thus the term biodiversity is now all inclusive, and involves all the living world, and what goes on within it.

There is an increasing concern world wide about the loss of biodiversity (Wilson 1988; Reaka-Kudla et al 1996), and this topic is now high on the public agenda. It brought the nations of the world together at the Earth Summit in Rio de Janeiro in 1992, and culminated in an International Convention on Biological Diversity.

The international concern involves primarily the loss of species, for the most part now caused by loss and fragmentation of habitat (Ehrlich 1988). The rate of loss is increasing to such an extent that many believe there is an impending crisis with respect to the diversity of life on earth (Wilson 1985; Myers 1987).

Loss of Species

There is ample evidence of human induced extinction of species in the past (Blockstein and Tordoff 1985; Burney 1993; Klein 1992; Miller et al. 1999; Olsen and James 1982; Steadman 1991, 1995; Stuart 1991). Scientists have documented 484 animal and 654 plant species extinctions since the 1600s (Adler 1995). It has been estimated that the current rate of extinction may be 1000 to 10,000 times the natural background extinction rate (Wilson 1988; May et al. 1995; Powledge 1998). For example, it seems likely that at least half of the original species in Madagascar have already disappeared or are on the point of doing so, and that some 50,000 or more species may have been eliminated in the past 25 years in western Ecuador (WCED 1987).

The estimates of population extinction are far greater than those of species extinction (Mlot 1997). Hughes et al. (1997) have calculated that on average, each species is composed of 220 populations, totalling 1.1 to 6.6 billion populations globally. They estimate that in tropical forests, some of the Earth's richest habitats, 1,800 populations are lost every hour—some 16 million per year. Such estimates may appear astronomical (Mlot 1997), but, if correct, have serious consequences for future human well-being.

At the present time, at least 5,366 animal and 26,106 plant species are at significant risk of extinction in the foreseeable future (Adler 1995). One quarter of the world mammal species is at risk of extinction, together with 11% of the birds, 25% of amphibians, and 34% of fishes (Holden 1996). Almost 10% of the world's tree species are in danger of extinction, some of these being in a critical state, with only a single remaining tree known (Williams 1998).

In the past, the probable cause of extinction for many birds and mammals was hunting and the introduction of alien species (Groombridge 1992). Many of the now endangered mammals have been brought to the brink of extinction by over-hunting, poaching and similar activities (O'Brien 1994; Rabinowitz 1995; Myers 1987; Berger and Cunningham 1994).

Loss of Habitat

Although almost any stress, physical or biological, can cause extinction, loss of habitat, particularly the clear-cutting of tropical forests, is said to be the largest factor contributing to the loss of species (Steadman 1991). Emphasis has been placed on the tropical rainforests, because although they cover only 7% of the earth's land surface, they are thought to contain more than 50% of the total species on earth (Myers 1988b; Lovejoy 1997).

At least 40% of all the tropical forest has been destroyed in the last 50 years (Caufield 1982; Myers 1995a), and is being destroyed at an ever-increasing rate. Once destroyed, this rainforest will likely not regenerate (Shukla et al. 1990).

Oedekoven (1980) has documented the loss of tropical forests in the State of São Paulo in Brazil, showing that by 1973, only 8.3% remained intact. Shukla et al. (1990) have noted that if current rates of destruction continue, the Amazonian tropical forests will all disappear in 50 to 100 years. Nepstad et al. (1999) have shown further that present estimates of annual deforestation for Brazilian Amazonia actually capture less than half of the forest area that is impoverished each year.

Such tropical deforestation is not confined to Amazonia (Aldhous 1993; Skole and Tucker 1993; Sinclair et al. 1995). Green and Sussman (1990) used satellite imagery to show the loss in Madagascar, and demonstrated that by 1985, 66% of the original rainforest had been destroyed, with some 50% removed between 1950 and 1985, at an average rate of 1.5% per year.

The rate of tropical deforestation varies around the world (Caufield 1982; Skole and Tucker 1993), with an average of 0.6% annually in South America, about 1.5% in Central America, and 1.6% in South East Asia (Aldous 1993). Caufield (1982) reports figures as high as 10% annual deforestation in Nigeria and the Ivory Coast.

Globally, forests once covered more than 40% of the earth's land surface, but their expanse has been reduced by one-third (Myers 1995). Many different forested areas have been disrupted and destroyed at rates comparable to that reported in the tropical rainforests (Aldous 1993). Temperate rainforests in particular are under siege (Feeney 1989; Norse 1990; Sierra Club of Western Canada 1993; Sinclair et al. 1995).

Losses of mangroves and wetlands indicate that these habitats are in more danger than forests (Sinclair et al 1995; Tolba et al. 1992). Significant areas of rangeland or grassland have been converted to agriculture or pastureland, or degraded, with desertification within some drylands totalling 75% or more (Tolba et al. 1992). Cropland and pasturelands now occupy at least 36.6% of the land area of the world (Morris 1995).

Habitat Fragmentation

Not only has there been a massive loss of habitat in recent times, but much of what remains is becoming increasingly fragmented, with dramatic impact on biodiversity (Burkey 1995; Kruess and Tscharntke 1994; Laurance et al. 1997, 1998; Reid et al. 1996; Skole and Tucker 1993; Wilcove and Whitcomb 1983). Habitat Fragmentation, defined as the conversion of a large continuous patch of habitat into smaller, isolated or tenuously connected patches surrounded by a matrix of other habitat types (Wiens 1989), affects species and communities in a number of different ways (Estades and Temple 1999). The consequences of fragmentation depend on factors such as the duration since fragmentation, fragment size, distance between fragments, shape of fragments (Saunders et al. 1991), matrix (Barrett et al. 1994; Wiens 1994), life cycle (Hanson and Urban 1992), with responses being both species and scale dependent (Jokimäki and Huhta 1996).

Large undisturbed areas in the size range of one to several thousand km^2 are needed to prevent a veritable rush of extinctions in extinct prone species (Terborgh 1974). However, the probability of providing undivided, unchallenged, and undisturbed space for species that require 10^4 or more km^2 of land to maintain minimal viable populations are essentially non-existent except in the most inhospitable climates and terrains (Schonewald-Cox and Buechner 1991).

Ecosystem Disturbance and Degradation

Earth's ecosystems are now human dominated (Noble and Dirzo 1997; Vitousek et al. 1997). Human activities have put us on a collision course with the natural world (Stern 1993). The legacy of human activity now controls many modern ecosystem characteristics (Turner et al. 1990; Foster et al. 1999).

Although some human impacts, such as industrial accidents, have had sudden, dramatic and newsworthy impacts on local ecosystems, other human impacts are more cumulative and have had far-reaching and larger scale effects (Dodson et al. 1997). These cumulative human activities are linked to an unprecedented litany of environmental problems (Cohen 1995). These include deforestation, shortage of firewood, overgrazing, loss of top soil, desertification, siltation of rivers and estuaries, dropping water tables, shrinking wetlands, toxic poisoning of drinking water, oceanic pollution, acid rain, erosion of the ozone layer, global warming, loss of wilderness areas and loss of species (Davis and Bernstam 1991). International public opinion rates acid rain, global warming, ozone depletion, species loss and loss of rainforest as very serious world wide environmental issues (Bloom 1995), that are not really being addressed in an effective way.

Humans are now outstripping geological processes in their power to sculpture the face of the globe (Monastersky 1994). Nearly all of the most productive land around the world has been under some form of cultivation for many centuries, and sometimes thousands of years (Huston 1993). Agriculture is widely recognised as being one of the most significant human alterations to the global environment (Matson et al. 1997). Agriculture and forestry have tested the resilience of nature, and have adopted technologies that have prompted ecosystem degradation (Altieri et al. 1983; Noble and Dirzo 1997) and nitrogen overload (Moffat 1998).

Land conversion and intensification have altered the biotic interactions and patterns of resource availability in ecosystems, and have had serious local, regional and global consequences (Matson et al. 1997). The demise of the Aral Sea is perhaps the most notorious ecological catastrophe of human making (Stone 1999), but comparable man-made ecological disasters can be found in many areas of the world (Kaiser 1999; Malakoff 1998).

Humans have introduced numerous chemicals into ecosystems often with disastrous results. The story of DDT and other pesticides is well known (Pimentel and Edwards 1982). In fact, some 70,000 synthetic chemicals have been injected into the environment, for the most part with minimal testing (Myers 1995).

Humans, intentionally and inadvertently, have introduced a wide variety of species to ecosystems in which they do not belong (Elton 1958). Such alien species introductions have resulted in ecosystems that now not only differ radically in structure from those originally present, but are substantially different in function (Richter 1997). Some ecologists believe that such alien invaders have had much more impact on ecosystems than have pollutants, climate change, or other manifestations of global change (Schindler 1991).

Human influence on the planet has increased faster than human population (Cohen 1995). It has been calculated that nearly 40% of the potential terrestrial net primary productivity is used directly, co-opted, or forgone because of human activities (Vitousek et al. 1986).

By 2050 the world's current population of 5.6 billion will have grown to between 7.8 and 12.5 billion (Roush 1994; Cohen 1995), after which it is expected to decline. Ecologist's findings suggest that a near 50% increase in world population, allied with a doubling of gross world product per person, will create substantial additional stresses on both local and global ecosystems (Vitousek et al. 1986; Daily et al. 1998). There is no convincing evidence that a stable human population with newly acquired affluence, will treat the environment better than affluent populations have in the past (Stern 1993). Thus ecosystem disruption, loss and degradation of habitat, and loss of species, which have clearly been the result of human activity in the past (Terborgh 1974), are likely to continue and expand in the future.

Concerns and Consequences

The concerns and consequences are easy to envisage in many cases, but there are likely to be some surprises, because so little is known about the workings of the living world. In general, biodiversity is important in five contexts: societal values, medical and scientific benefits, economic benefits, ecosystem services and ecosystem function.

Societal Values

Many believe that it is ethically or morally wrong to cause species to go extinct. The public acknowledges that, once a species becomes extinct, unique genetic information and evolutionary history (Nee and May 1997) is lost forever. The public also has more intangible values related to national identities, manifested by the wildlife shown on flags, stamps and currency.

Medical and Scientific Benefits

There is a great deal of chemical biodiversity in the natural world (Patrick 1997), now so important to mankind. Nearly 50% of the medicine prescribed in North America was derived from wild species, mainly plants (WCED 1987). Well-known examples include aspirin from willow which dates back to the time of Hippocrates (Lovejoy 1997), digitoxin from foxglove, and more recently taxol, for fighting ovarian and other cancers, from the Western Yew (*Taxus brevifolia*). The commercial value of these medicines and drugs in the USA now amounts to some $14 billion a year (WCED 1987) worldwide, and including non-prescription materials plus pharmaceuticals, the estimated commercial value exceeds $40 billion a year (WCED 1987).

There are new discoveries every day, often in unexpected areas. For example, the US National Institute of Health is putting $4.3 million into research on St. John's wort (*Hypericum perforatum*), as it appears to contain a potent anti-depressant chemical (Holden 1997). In the past, this plant has been regarded as a weed that had to be eliminated, and major efforts at biological control were launched for its eradication (Holloway 1964; Huffaker 1967; Harris and Maw 1984). A similar new discovery is the anti-microbial steroid, squalamine, from the dogfish shark (Stone 1993).

First Nations know these values in their use of native plants in traditional healing. Modern plant breeding involves plants and more recently genes taken from the wild (WCED 1987; Raeburn 1995). All modern biotechnology is based upon discoveries about what is happening in the living world. The polymerase chain reaction, an important tool in modern biotechnology and molecular biology, works because of an enzyme discovered in a bacterium found in the protected hotsprings of Yellowstone National Park (Lovejoy 1997).

However, as argued in this volume by Simpson (Chapter 7), Sedjo (Chapter 8), and Bulte et al. (Chapter 9), it is marginal values that matter, not absolute or average values. At the margin, the value of species is nearly insignificant.

Economic Benefits

The economic benefits of biodiversity in the form of natural resources are easy to measure, because ecosystems convert energy into biomass that is directly used in commerce. These commodities include fish from aquatic ecosystems, timber from forests and crops from agricultural lands.

To cite two examples, Pauly and Christensen (1995) using data for 1988-1991 from the UN Food and Agriculture Organisation have shown that the mean total world fish catch is about 943 million tons a year. Mosquin and Whiting (1992) have shown that, in Canada in 1988, the value of cut-timber in industry shipments was $49 billion.

Ecosystem Services

Natural ecosystems provide a number of ecosystem services, which are critical to human survival. Many of these are not conventionally valued in the market place usually being regarded as "externalities" (Nash 1991). Many of these have been listed by Costanza et al. (1997) and include: maintaining the hydrologic cycle; regulating climate; maintaining the gaseous composition of the atmosphere; generating soils; storing and cycling nutrients; pollination and biological control.

It has been estimated that the economic value of bee pollination in agricultural crops in the USA is $20 billion annually (Levin 1983) and $1.2 billion in Canada (Winston and Scott 1984). The total world value of bee pollinated crops is estimated at $200 billion a year. Natural pest control services alone are estimated to have an economic value ranging from $54 billion to $1 trillion globally (Daily 1997).

The total value of ecosystem services are estimated to average some $33.3 trillion annually (Costanza et al. 1997), 35% being terrestrial based and 64% marine ecosystem based. However, this $33.3 trillion annual value is regarded as too high by others (Roush 1997), and too low by still others (see Chapter 9). Conventional economists point out that this is about double global output (GDP) of $16 trillion. They state that the estimate is based upon willingness to pay calculations, so how should the earth's inhabitants possibly pay more than their total income? They thus conclude that this $33.3 trillion figure is totally meaningless in the context of economic decision making. It is just these arguments that lead to the undervaluing of ecosystem services. As Daily (1997) points out, these services are invaluable (see also Chapter 9).

It seems improbable that the earth's ecosystems are not invaluable. But, just as in the case of species, such values are meaningless because humans never need to decide to eliminate all ecosystems at one time. Rather, decisions are made about converting a particular forest stand to agriculture, or to catch another ton of fish; decisions are made at the margin.

Ecosystem Function

An ecosystem is essentially a complex of organisms (often including humans), interacting with one another, and with the environment in which they live. Such ecosystems and their communities are composed of species in complex food chains or food webs, with every link being vital for structure, function and integrity. In such food chains and food webs there are bottom-up controls (resource limitations) (Chen and Wise 1999) and top-down controls (limitations by predation) (de Ruiter et al. 1995; Polis and Winemiller 1996).

Large vertebrate predators are obvious examples of top-down control species in ecosystems. Therefore, loss of these dominant species can cause large degradations of the ecosystem functions in which they are prominent.

There are several models or hypotheses of the possible relationship between biodiversity and ecosystem function (Vitousek and Hooper 1993). Each model or hypothesis makes a different set of predictions in terms of function.

At one extreme is a linear model that asserts that each species has a vital role and function in the ecosystem. This has been called the rivet hypothesis (Ehrlich and Wilson 1991). Each species is viewed to be like a rivet in an airplane wing. Each is vital for the wing to hold together and function. Rivets may be removed one by one, but the effect is not noticed until one too many is removed. Then the wing falls off, the equivalent of the ecosystem collapsing. Thus it follows that in an ecosystem, each species is essential.

Ehrlich (1993) says that ecologists generally accept the viewpoint expressed by the "rivet popper" analogy, and believe that a policy of continually exterminating populations and species eventually will dramatically compromise ecosystem services. However, it remains impossible to specify when "eventually" might be. For an alternative view concerning this metaphor, see Budiansky (1995, pp. 182-83)

A second model asserts that there are certain species that are crucial for ecosystem structure and function (Mills et al. 1993). This is the basis of the keystone hypothesis developed by Paine (1966, 1969) from research on the role of the sea star (*Pisaster ochraceus*) in the Washington rocky inter-tidal ecosystem. Such keystone species have a prominence in ecosystem function that is much greater than would be expected on the basis of their relative abundance within the ecosystem (Power 1995).

Keystone species have now been detected in a broad array of ecosystems, taxa, trophic levels, and ecological processes (Power et al. 1996). They occur in all of the world's major ecosystems, and are not always of high trophic status (Powers et al. 1996). They can exert effects, not only through the commonly known mechanisms of consumption, but also through such interactions and a processes as competition, mutualism, dispersal, pollination, disease, and by modifying habitats and abiotic factors (Bond 1993; Mills et al. 1993).

Although there is a lack of a well-developed protocol for identifying potential keystone species (Powers et al. 1996), comparative experimental studies have shown that not every ecosystem has keystone species (Menge et al. 1994). Furthermore, even in those that do, they may not always maintain a keystone role either in time or space (Menge et al. 1994; Power et al. 1996).

The third model with respect to biodiversity and ecosystem function asserts that not all species in ecosystems are essential for ecosystem function and integrity (Lawton and Brown 1993). This is the redundancy hypothesis (Walker 1991), which proposes that species have overlapping roles in communities, such that the loss of one species is compensated by an increase in number or activity of another.

Ecosystem processes often have considerable redundancy built into them (Lawton and Brown 1993) and some species appear functionally redundant. For example, Ray and Grassle (1991) state that there is redundancy in marine ecosystems.

Although theories about the relationship between biodiversity and ecosystem processes and function have had a long history in theoretical ecology (Elton 1958; MacArthur 1972; May 1973; McNaughton 1977; Pimm 1984), there is still considerable debate, and limited experimental testing of hypotheses. So far, neither evolutionary theory, nor empirical studies have presented convincing evidence that species diversity and ecosystem function are consistently and causally connected (Grime 1997).

So far experimental field studies (Tilman 1996a; Tilman and Downing 994; Tilman et al. 1996, 1997a, 1997b, 1998) and Ecotron experiments (Naeem et al. 1994, 1995; Naeem and Li 1997; Lawton et al. 1998) have been somewhat limited in scope and complexity. Although they suggest that some minimum number of species is essential for proper ecosystem function, and that to some extent the more biodiversity present the more productive, stable and resilient is the ecosystem, there is still no firm basis for making conclusions about ecosystem function based on diversity (Huston 1997). It is not possible to quantify the number of species needed for a functional ecosystem (Woodward 1993). The mathematical theory surrounding these issues is still lacking (Tilman et al. 1997b).

Nevertheless, there is strong evidence to show that productivity and nutrient cycling in terrestrial ecosystems are controlled to an overwhelming extent by the functional characteristics of the dominant plant. Also, evidence indicates that ecosystem function depends upon an essential complex of different functional groups, and that there are obvious irreplaceable species and functional types.

Diversity is functionally important in ecosystems, because it both increases the probability of including species that have strong ecosystem effects, and because it can increase the efficiency of resource use (Chapin et al. 1997). If the species complement is not at the maximum the ecosystem can include, then the dynamic richness is reduced (Woodward 1993). This reduced richness then lays the ecosystem open to invasion and disruption. It seems likely that high biodiversity is vitally important in structurally diverse ecosystems such as layered forests, and in ecosystems that experience drastic fluctuations on a seasonal or longer time scale (Grime 1997).

Consensus at the moment suggests that all hypotheses about the role of species in ecosystems are partially correct. It seems likely that all elements of biodiversity are involved in ecosystem function over the long-term. Although some species may not be essential at a particular place or time (Naeem 1998), they undoubtedly have a function, that may become critically important at some stage of the ecosystem cycle, or when there are large environmental changes or perturbations.

Long-term Ecosystem Function and Integrity

Once formed, an ecosystem has a certain amount of integrity, that is, the ability to adjust to and survive when subject to various perturbations. However, this self-organising or self-stabilising ability has limits, and at any time the ecosystem may move beyond its normal stable state (Graham and Grimm 1990; Kimmins 1996a).

Ecosystems are not in a permanent stable state. They continually undergo a birth, growth, maturity and death process, what Holling (1986) refers to as the exploitation, conservation, release and reorganisation cycle (Figure 3.1; drawn after Holling 1986).

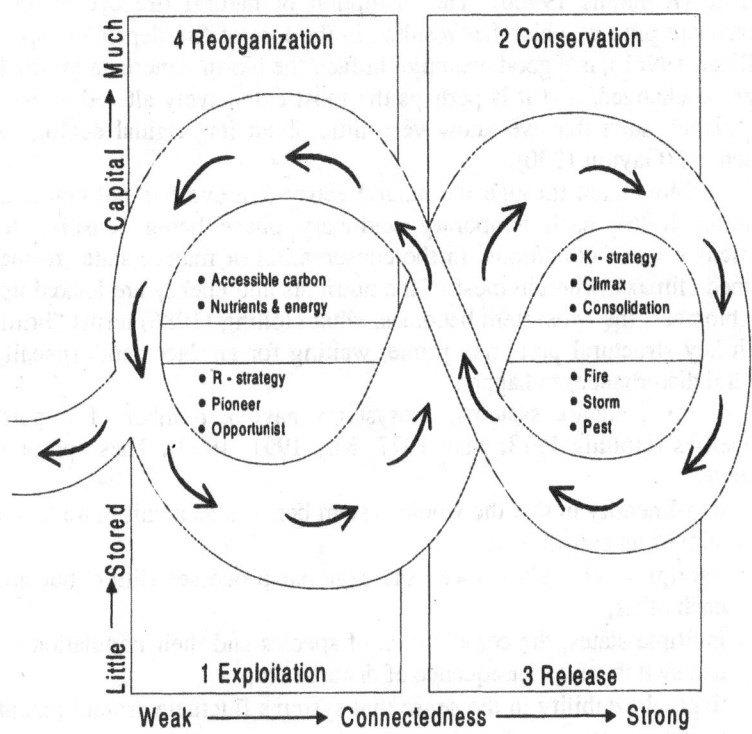

Figure 3.1: The Ecosystem Cycle
The arrows show the speed of the flow of events in the ecosystem cycle, where arrows close to each other indicate fast change and arrows far from each other indicate slow change. The exit for the cycle at the left of the figure indicates the stage where a flip into a greatly modified ecosystem is most likely.

Essential components of the cycle are natural disturbance events, a vital process influencing both biological diversity and ecological function (Sousa 1984). Normal disturbance events vary with each ecosystem, encompassing such processes as individual treefall in tropical rainforests

(Hubbell et al. 1999) and windthrow, fire and pest outbreaks elsewhere (Kimmins 1996b).

Humans have altered natural disturbance regimes, causing such disturbance-driven ecosystems and disturbance-dependent ecosystems to change (Kimmins 1996b). The disruption of natural fire cycles on the Wisconsin prairie, which has resulted in the loss of fire dependent species (Tilman 1996b), is a good example. In fact, the North American prairie has been so changed, that it is perhaps the most extensively altered biome on the planet, such that we know very little about its original ecology and functions (Gayton 1990).

Movement through the natural ecosystem cycle is not continuous (Holing 1986), each temporary stationary phase being sensitive to a particular set of conditions. In the conservation or mature state (formerly termed climax), wherein most of the nutrients and energy are locked up in the biomass, the ecosystem becomes, what Holling (1986) terms "brittle", with key structural parts risk prone, waiting for an "accident" (usually a natural disturbance) to happen.

As complex systems, ecosystems have a number of important properties (Holling 1973; May 1977; Kay 1991, 1993). These properties include:

- non-linearity in that the whole system behaves as a unit more than the sum of its constituents;
- multiple scales since local and regional processes differ, but affect each other;
- multiple states, the combination of species and their population sizes can switch, as a consequence of disturbance;
- dynamic stability in the sense that systems fluctuate around potential stable points;
- resilience in that within a range of environmental perturbations they maintain their characteristic species assemblages although they show fluctuation;
- fragility as measured by the limits that a system can tolerate perturbations; and
- catastrophic behaviour, the ability to exhibit sudden change if perturbations move the system beyond the limits that determine the systems' fragility (Regier 1992).

These properties emerge because ecosystems are thermodynamically open systems that are never in equilibrium (Kay 1991, 1993; Kay and Schneider 1992). They are also self-organising, and as such, may have abrupt changes when a new set of interactions and activities emerge among the components and in the whole system. The form that this self-organisation takes is not predictable.

It follows that, at a specific geographic location, there is the potential for a number of different ecosystems, communities and species to exist, in addition to the present set. With extreme disturbance or change, a given ecosystem can "flip" into a new regime. While such change occurs naturally associated with major events such as climate change, they can also occur as a result of human activity. Evidence for this is available in the Mediterranean (Thirgood 1981), the New Guinea highlands, and the Scottish moors, and is likely to occur in the Amazon (Shukla et al. 1990). Given sufficiently heavy-handed use, much of the forested land in British Columbia, could be ericaceous heath (Kimmins 1996b).

Conclusion

A recent food chain flip involving Killer whale predation on sea otters has occurred in Alaskan waters (Estes et al. 1998), although the causes are complicated (Kaiser 1998) and may involve more than just anthrogenic changes in the offshore oceanic system as suggested by Estes et al. (1998). Since it has been predicted that in the future there will be conflicts over increasingly scarce resources (Stern 1993), such ecosystem impacts and ecosystem changes can be expected to increase in the future. Already humans are inexorably fishing down marine food webs as larger and more commercially valuable species disappear, creating impoverished and vastly different ecosystems (Pauly et al. 1998). The human species must soon realise that nature is not infinitely productive and resilient.

4 Is Conservation Achieving its Ends?
A.R.E. SINCLAIR

The world is facing today the greatest loss of biodiversity in the history of the human species, and this loss is occurring through our exploitation of biological production. Estimates put our expropriation of biological production at around 40% (Vitousek et al. 1986), production that would normally go to other species. The consequences for other species are either smaller habitat patches or lower population densities, both leading to smaller population sizes and hence greater risks of extinction. Biologists consider that such extinctions are detrimental to the long-term survival of our planet and they have responded by attempting to save species and habitats. The sense of urgency has catapulted the conservation movement into a crusade. In this frenetic environment few people have stopped to consider carefully whether their activities are the most appropriate or indeed even correct. Hence, I ask here whether our conservation practices are actually achieving our objectives namely maximising our chances of preserving habitats and the species they support. The answer will not be self-evident; it will depend on the values and priorities for the future.

Society's Lack of Memory for Nature: Need for Ecological Baselines

Society's memory for their environmental surroundings is short, usually about 30 years, roughly equivalent to a working life. People remember things as they were in their twenties when they first become aware of their surroundings. Consequently, the reference point against which we can measure change is always changing itself. Thus, society has little institutional memory for its environment and so it does not notice these changes taking place. For example, Scotland is known for its beautiful rolling hills covered in heather. However, these heather moorlands are largely an artefact of the clearances that took place some two hundred years ago. At that time Scotland was covered in forest and would have looked much like Norway or Sweden today with pine, birch and aspen forests. The Scottish forest was cleared in the 1700s to graze sheep and, apart from a few small patches, virtually all of the forest has gone. People like Scotland as they now find it, they do not appreciate that the highlands are ecologically degraded, trapped in a peat moorland and unable to return to forest because the soils have changed. The main point is that people have long forgotten what the highlands in their natural state were really like.

The great flightless birds of New Zealand, the moas, died out only a few hundred years ago. Indeed, there is some evidence that one of the last moas was seen in the late 1800s. These moas shaped the forests with their heavy browsing; and many plants show adaptations to protect themselves from moa feeding. Yet society has no firsthand knowledge of this dominant force in New Zealand habitats, the knowledge was never passed on.

If we cannot appreciate what the world looked like a mere 100 years ago, what hope is there of understanding that the forests of Costa Rica or the Yukon were shaped by the great mammoths, mastodons and woolly rhinos a mere 10,000 years ago; and, like New Zealand, some plants still have adaptations that encouraged mammoths to feed on their seed pods.

In general, two important points emerge from a review of history. First, humans have been exterminating species for as far back as we can determine. Species that cannot tolerate human depredation and habitat destruction go extinct. The rest coexist with us. With every advance in technology another set of species is exterminated, unable to tolerate the new weapons. Modern extinctions are merely the continuation of extinctions caused by the first peoples to visit our lands. Second, society has little or no "memory" for what is lost or even for what is natural; we have no appreciation for times past.

The Task for Conservation

There are some 50 million species of organisms in the world. At the current rate of species loss, a million of them will be exterminated in the next ten years (Diamond 1989; Soule 1991; Ehrlich and Wilson 1991; Raven and Wilson 1992; Smith et al. 1993). Clearly, we cannot save them all, so we have to make decisions as to which to save or let go. In general, society makes such decisions on the basis of politics, emotions or convenience. Thus, decisions are made according to what is feasible in different countries, what is large, glamorous and obvious (the so-called charismatic species), or what happens to take the fancy of local conservation groups. These are criteria that are arbitrary, opportunistic and whimsical.

Conservation organisations, both government and non-government, use these charismatic species to raise funds for their preservation, and they hope that smaller species will be saved as a consequence. These large species are called umbrella species. One example of an umbrella species is the spotted owl (*Strix occidentalis*) of western North America. This species requires large areas of mature conifer forest, and it is assumed that such large areas will be suitable for many other species. Other examples are the giant panda (*Ailuropoda melanoleuca*) in China, the tiger (*Panthera tigris*) in India, and elephant (*Loxodonta africana*) in Africa. Unfortunately, there is no evidence that such species actually result in either more species being saved from extinction, or even the right species being saved.

Another concept is the "indicator species," one whose fate provides an early warning about the well-being of the system as a whole. Ostensibly the idea of umbrella species sounds reasonable. Such species attract public attention and conservation organisations, both government and non-government (e.g., as the World Wildlife Fund, the International Union for Conservation of Nature), use these large, charismatic species to raise funds for their preservation and hope the smaller species will be saved along with them. However, the concepts of umbrella species, flagship species and indicator species remain untested despite much conservation policy being based on them (Landres et al. 1988).

The conservation of endangered species is through crisis management. Decisions are opportunistic: we do what we can at the time in terms of funds, people and politics. Allocation of funds is *ad hoc* and subjective. Environmental pressure groups demand attention for their own pet projects without regard to whether these are the highest priority projects or even necessary ones.

Classical examples of the subjective approach to conservation planning are the confrontations so prevalent in the 1990s on the west-coast of Canada, the south-east coast of Australia and the North Island of New

Zealand over the logging of old-growth forests. Each valley is the scene of a confrontation between environmentalists and logging companies. This is the First World War approach of trench-by-trench warfare. There are no natural "stopping rules" to the fight, for once one valley dispute is settled, the next is in contention. Given this, it is logical for a company to put up a stand at the first valley, not the last. The environmentalists do not appear to appreciate that confrontation is enormously expensive in terms of time, money and people, with no assurance that such valleys are the ones that ought to be saved. They are the "feel good" valleys, but they could be the wrong ones because they have not been chosen on an objective basis. Thus, neither side does well out of this and as a result many, if not most, present day conservation actions are inappropriate or out of context.

Since we do not have enough resources to save the million or so species destined for extinction in the near future we must optimise the distribution of limiting resources such as time, land and funds to save the most species—to maximise conservation. Time is vital because with every passing year more is lost; land and funds are limiting because there is a finite amount available, the more assigned to one place means the less set aside in another. There is an opportunity cost because there is a limit to what society is willing to pay. We must be sure, therefore, that the areas we spend time and money on are our highest priority.

Three Levels of Problems in Conservation

To avoid our current *ad hoc* approach to setting priorities for areas of conservation we need a long-term conservation policy. Such a policy can only develop from an understanding of the types of problems involved. There are three levels of problems that need to be addressed by biologists and policy makers. The lowest level, third-order problems, are very specific and I touch on these first because they are the ones most conservationists look at.

Third-order Problems

Conservation ecology focuses at the level of individual populations, species, areas, or networks of populations or areas. These questions focus on practical problems such as (i) the decline of populations, (ii) population viability analysis, (iii) fragmentation of habitats, (iv) connectivity of habitat patches, (v) the degree of dispersal shown by a species, and (vi) the shape of reserves or reserve networks. These are the current favourite subjects of academic researchers.

Governmental and non-governmental organisations focus on the preservation of particular endangered species or habitats. These efforts aim primarily to describe the status of species or areas, as, for example, the population size of a rare species or the degree of human encroachment on a threatened habitat. Usually, such species belong to the higher "charismatic" vertebrates, and the higher their profile the larger the organisation that deals with them.

Third-order questions beg a number of more general questions. For example, on what basis are particular species chosen for protection? Or, why should one area be preserved over another? As a world community, we have neither the resources nor the political will to save all species (as was clear from the Earth Summit conference in 1992 at Rio). We are therefore faced with hard decisions concerning which species we should attempt to save and which must be abandoned (Soule et al. 1986; McNeely et al. 1990; Vane-Wright et al. 1991).

Second-order Problems

Species Triage. Given limited resources and time, we are obliged to adopt "Species Triage." This term originated in the Crimean War where doctors were trying to save lives with insufficient resources and had to decide who needed the most attention. The concept is used here in the context of saving species or habitats: some species or areas can be left unattended because they can tolerate human encroachment, others are too far gone to warrant an extensive investment of time and resources because extinction in the near future is certain. A third group of species or areas are those which are possible to save with some help.

How do we decide where to focus our efforts and scarce resources, on which species and habitats? The present *ad hoc* approach, although sometimes politically expedient, is highly unlikely to optimise our use of time and land in ways that maximise the number of species saved. Therefore, we need to develop a method for the optimal partitioning of effort and resources to maximise conservation on a world basis. It is most probable that the habitats and species currently receiving most of the resources and attention may not be the appropriate ones (Pressey and Tully 1994). Optimisation procedures for deciding how to allocate resources become increasingly important as fewer resources are available for conservation. This problem is most important in developing countries, such as many of those in Africa, where annual rates of increase in human populations average close to 3% (Sinclair and Wells 1989).

Choosing Sites for Conservation. A start has been made in developing a global programme of conservation for species (Noss 1990; Tisdell 1990; Vane-Wright et al. 1991; Faith 1992) and reserves (Margules 1989; Margules et al. 1988, 1991). I review the approaches that have been made in identifying which species need protection and the location of reserves.

Gap Analysis and Hotspots. The first step in deciding where to place protected areas employs "gap analysis." Gap analysis is the standard approach (Kiester et al 1996) used to identify which species or habitats are included or excluded from protected areas. The problem is that it provides no mechanism for deciding which of the many excluded species or habitats should be included first.

The next method identifies biodiversity hotspots, or areas containing the greatest number of species. Priorities can be set on the basis of species numbers in an area (Saetersdal et al. 1993; Sisk et al. 1994), the number of endangered species (Dobson et al. 1997), the degree of threat (Beissinger et al. 1996) or a combination of these criteria (Kershaw et al. 1995). This approach has been used to set policy for the Amazon forest (Myers 1990; Rylands 1991). Although it makes some attempt at setting priorities it does not look for optimum solutions to resource allocation. Hotspots have been documented in Britain for a number of biological groups (Prendergast et al. 1993), including birds, butterflies, dragonflies and primitive plants. Hotspots for birds were on the south coast, butterflies in the centre and east of England, dragonflies in other areas of the south, and liverworts in Scotland. If we were to assign protected status to all hotspots for all groups, an unworkably large area would be required. The same picture emerges for hotspots in British Columbia (G.G.E. Scudder, pers. comm.). The hotspots for bryophytes (mosses) are mainly on the Queen Charlotte Islands, whereas, for vascular plants (the more advanced plants), they are largely on Vancouver Island. The highest diversity of endemic insects and other invertebrates is in the Okanagan valley of southern BC. In general, hotspots do not overlap.

Thus, setting priorities for conservation areas on the basis of hotspots does not narrow our options sufficiently. In addition, this approach is uneconomical because it over represents common species while often completely missing rare species, as was demonstrated when the method was applied to British birds (Williams et al. 1996). It does not give us the best distribution of land to represent as many species as possible. Thus, the hotspot approach is inefficient (more resources for fewer species), it is unworkable for more than one category of species, and it cannot incorporate social and economic values. Conflicting objectives are currently handled by round table bargaining and compromise. Such methods do not necessarily lead to the most cost-effective result for society or to the protection of maximum biodiversity.

Complementarity. An alternative approach is complementarity (Margules et al. 1988; Vane-Wright et al. 1991; Pressey et al. 1993). It starts by taking the areas with the rarer species first, and then, as more resources are made available, adding areas with the next rarer species. If there is a choice, it adds in the areas with the most species. This proceeds stepwise until all species are included or resources are exhausted. Each new area that is added complements the set of reserves (the priority set) that is already saved. Hence, duplication is held to a minimum and all species are represented. In addition, other criteria can be used to make decisions where choices are available.

Pressey et al. (1994) have developed the concept of "irreplaceability" as a measure of how much choice there is when a site is chosen. For example, if there is only one site where a species is found then this site is irreplaceable (100% irreplaceable) if it is lost, so it must be included in any set of reserves. If there are two sites then there is one choice that can be made (50% irreplaceable) and so on.

Complementarity and irreplaceability have now been tried in Australia, where the method was invented, on wetlands and forest patches (Margules et al. 1988; Pressey and Nicholls 1989; Nicholls and Margules 1993; Pressey 1994, 1997), in Britain on birds (Williams et al. 1996), in South Africa on reptiles (Lombard et al. 1995), and in Oregon on vertebrates (Csuti et al. 1997). In each case, complementarity was more efficient than hotspots, by as much as five times (i.e., five times as much can be saved for the same cost). This is an approximate optimality procedure designed to maximise the conservation of biodiversity for the least cost. Its great advantage is that it allows an objective approach to setting the priorities for which habitats, species or other categories should be conserved, using all information including biological, social and economic values.

The complementarity procedure uses a variety of habitat and biological information and different weightings for land use, economic value and social values. Priority areas do not necessarily imply reservation or set asides, but they do identify areas within managed forests or other land use categories that deserve special attention with respect to the protection of sensitive species and for the restoration of habitat. Biological, social and economic data are used in two ways. First, a set of areas is identified in which all species or habitats, or biological communities, are represented at least once, twice (or more), or in which a nominated proportion of habitat area (e.g., 10%, 15%) is present. Alternatively, given a predetermined proportion of habitat to be protected (say 12%), the method finds that combination of land units that maximises the number of habitats and species. This combination then becomes the priority set.

The first stage formulates the data in a computer database as in a Geographical Information System. The most common types of data utilised are:

1. spot locations for rare species;
2. distributions in the form of grid cells for widespread species, habitats or community assemblages;
3. geographical distributions of physical and chemical environments, including geology, soils, climate, *et cetera*, whichever are available; and
4. data on land use, human population characteristics, economic values and social values (e.g., aesthetic, traditional values of First Nations).

The complementarity approach now needs to be used on a global scale. This has been demonstrated for a few groups such as owls and milkweed butterflies (Vane-Wright et al. 1991).

Owls are appropriate because of the spotted owl controversy in the forests of western North America (Wilcove 1994). The most important area for owls is somewhere in Central America. The first site in North America would be ranked eleventh in importance, and this represents the burrowing owl. The spotted owl is represented in Central America. We do not have to worry, on this basis, about spotted owls anywhere along the West Coast. We are not off the hook, of course, because profits from logging the West Coast should be used to purchase and maintain forests in Central America, if appropriate offsetting investments to preserve owls are to be made—a strong sustainability assumption. Indeed, the tropical forests should be secured for owls before the temperate forests are logged, not afterwards. In fact, the majority of owl species are in Southeast Asia, and we should be spending our profits from logging there, not in North America, for conservation.

The same analysis for milkweed butterflies (family *Danaidae*) shows that Southeast Asia is also the most important area for this group. A similar global assessment for bumblebees shows that an area in China has highest priority, followed by an area on the Canadian Shield. This shows not only that we should set aside a protected area for bumblebees in Canada, but the necessity of analysing conservation requirements on a global rather than a local (national) basis.

First-order Problems

Protecting Conservation Sites. The next question is, how do we protect habitat? Traditionally, we have set up reserves and then protected them in order to prevent losses of habitat and species taking place outside the reserves. For example, tropical forests are declining rapidly in all countries, and the amount of loss is directly related to human population pressure (Sinclair et al. 1995; see also van Kooten et al. 1999; van Kooten and Bulte 2000). Vancouver Island shows the same rate of loss for its temperate forest, but it is not caused by population pressure.

If reserves are the solution to preventing loss, we should expect habitats and species to be safe within them. However, evidence on the fate of reserves does not support this assumption. For example, Strathcona Provincial Park on Vancouver Island was set aside some 50 years ago to protect temperate old-growth rainforest. Between 1954 and 1990 most of the valleys containing the large trees have been excised from the park and logged. In their place, areas of mountain-top comprised of snow and rock have been added to replace them. This is a blatant attempt to obscure the fact that a reserve has been eroded for economic and political reasons. However, Strathcona is not an exception, all Parks and Reserves around the world are experiencing gradual attrition. We are losing our protected areas bit by bit. If we have lost this much in about fifty years, how much will be left after the next two hundred or five hundred years? That is the time span we must think about. At the present rate of attrition we will have lost all of our reserves by the end of that time. Society will not object because, as pointed out earlier, it has little memory for change. There is, therefore, nothing to stop this loss.

Serengeti National Park in Tanzania is at the top of the UNESCO World Heritage list of sites established in 1972 at the Stockholm conference. If we cannot prevent attrition in Serengeti we cannot prevent it anywhere.

Serious poaching for rhino horn in Serengeti started in 1977 and by 1980 all rhinos had been exterminated from the Park. Between 1977 and 1988 some eighty percent of elephants were killed and the rest were saved only with the ivory trade ban in 1988. Wild dogs, some of the rarest carnivores in Africa, numbered over 100 in the 1960s in Serengeti but all are now gone. Some 40% of the lions died in 1993 as a result of canine distemper contracted from domestic dogs. Canine distemper has spread as a result of the exploding human populations with their infected domestic dogs around the periphery of Serengeti; it appears that domestic dogs first made contact with wild dogs, then hyenas, and most recently lions. Such population declines are forms of attrition because they compromise the natural workings of the ecosystem. The natural area in the Serengeti region has decreased by about 50% since the beginning of this century. The legally protected area started in the 1920s and built up to the 1960s and 70s. It levelled out and then declined somewhat as portions were removed, as in Strathcona Park. More significantly, the natural area is now less than the legally protected area. At the present time there are areas inside Serengeti Park with no large mammals left alive, they have been removed by poaching. Thus, we must recognise that we cannot protect even the most important conservation areas in the world (Sinclair et al. 1995; Sinclair and Arcese 1995).

Renewal: Replacing Lost Habitat. It is a delusion to think that a reserve will prevent the eventual loss of habitats and species. Within a reserve we lose as much as if no reserve had been present. The only advantage of a reserve is that it takes a little longer to lose everything. The reserve allows us to buy time to do something about the attrition. Are we using this extra time to do something about this attrition? To counteract the loss of habitat requires an addition to the reserve to balance the loss. We have to add to the reserve new habitat and new area. If we replace lost area with new area at the same rate, we can end up with some constant amount. This amount is called the "habitat constant." The reason, therefore, for having a reserve is not to protect habitats *per se*, but to buy time so that we can replace what is lost (Sinclair et al. 1995).

Are we replacing lost area or renewing lost habitat? Not only is there no renewal, but the policy has not even been considered. Unless we implement a policy of habitat renewal, reserves will not achieve their ends and our descendants will have nothing left. At the present time we are so desperately responding to crises of extinction that we have not had time to examine our current long-term conservation strategies.

40 *Conserving Nature's Diversity*

This conclusion is not good news to either conservationists or resource users. Conservationists do not want to be told that merely setting up a reserve is not going to save anything. Logging companies do not want to find that, in order to cut down a hundred hectares of old-growth forest within a reserve, they must first grow a hundred hectares of old growth forest, not replace it afterwards—and that takes two hundred years. If governments or companies are not prepared to do this, then reserves will not save anything.

How Much Habitat Should be Protected?

Having decided on the priority of habitats and species, the next decision concerns the amount of each habitat that needs to be put aside. British Columbia, for example, has assigned a maximum of twelve percent of the land area. Where does the twelve percent figure come from? McNeely and Miller (1984) reported that 4% of the world's habitats had been put aside in reserves. The Bruntland report for the United Nations (World Commission on Environment and Development 1987) recommended that three times this amount should be protected. This figure, or something similar, has become the politically accepted target. Apart from its biological irrelevance, the 12% figure is difficult to apply. It cannot simply be 12% of what we have presently remaining because that is biologically meaningless. Further, to what habitats do we apply the 12%? Some habitats are very small—do we save 12% of these?

This question was examined by comparing the amount of tropical forest presently remaining as a proportion of the original area of forest in 17 Asian countries (Sinclair et al.1995). If one starts with the original untouched amount of forest then one takes 12% of that. However, if half of the forest remains, then twenty-four percent, not twelve percent, must be reserved; and if only twelve percent of forest remains, then 100% must be set aside. This produces a 12% threshold curve. Comparing the amount of forest reserved in these 17 countries relative to this curve, only two countries did better than the 12% curve. Almost all of the countries are far below the curve. Thus, to achieve 12%, they must actually grow more native forest and cease logging altogether.

In North America the 12% threshold is also not achieved. In British Columbia, for example, 12% is applied to large areas so that common habitats are over represented, and endangered or threatened habitats are under represented. The areas of high diversity for invertebrates are in the South Okanagan valley of British Columbia where there are some 300 species of arthropods, many of which are endemic (Scudder 1991). In addition, the area supports a number of important vertebrate species such as the sage thrasher (*Oreoscoptes montanus*), burrowing owl (*Athene cunicularia*), and tiger salamander (*Ambystoma tigrinum*). This area is largely grassland and semi-arid sagebrush (*Artemesia*). Large tracts of conifer forests take up almost all of the 12% (indeed, well over 12% of conifer forests have been reserved), but this habitat does not represent the habitat of the endangered birds, salamanders and insects. Nowhere close to twelve percent of the grassland habitats, where these rare species occur, is reserved. British Columbia is failing to live up to its own arbitrary legislation.

I have used the 12% figure for the sake of discussion. However, is 12% of a habitat sufficient to ensure long-term survival of species? Analysis of the minimum amount needed to ensure survival, using the complementarity approach shows some forty to eighty percent of the habitat must be protected for rare and endangered species (Margules et al. 1988). For some of the rare habitats, such as the remaining bunch grass in the Okanagan, all of it must be protected. Thus, we must be considering protection for much larger proportions of habitat to avoid extinction.

Global Climate Change and the Location of Protected Areas

Assuming that sufficient reserve area is obtained and renewal is applied, we must then ask, where do we place reserves? The obvious answer is to place them where the animals or plants occur. At first sight this makes sense. However, global climate change is altering the world biomes. Whether the climate gets colder or warmer is the subject of debate, but change is going on. The problem is that when the climate changes, the species making up our communities change their geographic locations at different rates. We know this from changes in species distributions that have taken place after the last ice age 12,000 years ago. Following the ice age, forest communities in the US Southeast moved northwards with the warmer climate. However, the various tree species moved at different rates so that species living together 12,000 years ago had different ranges by 6,000 years ago (Davis 1986). Thus, a reserve placed at present times to protect a community could easily lie outside the new range of the community under a warmer climate. Hence, reserves must be placed *now* in areas where we anticipate species to move because, by the time that they are needed, the areas will no longer be available. Furthermore, several such areas will be required because the species making up the community will be moving into different areas. So far no efforts have been made to place reserves for future conservation.

Loss of Biodiversity and Ecosystem Function

Biologists are currently concerned that a loss of species will alter the ability of our ecosystems to function. The problem is difficult to study because ecosystems have thousands of species—in the soil, in the vegetation, and in the animals supported by them—and this complexity prevents us predicting what will happen from loss of species. One might be able to predict what would happen when A eats B, but one cannot predict what would happen two or three links down a longer line of species. One can understand each link individually, but not the outcome of a sequence of links. In fact we know so little about this aspect that we really have to start from scratch and devise new ways of studying the question.

One approach is to look at ecosystems that have already been changed extensively, as have those in New Zealand, Australia or Hawaii, where many exotic species have been introduced. For example, several plant species of the group called *Hibiscadelphus* in Hawaii have gone extinct because the birds that pollinated them, a group of endemic honeyeaters, themselves went extinct. Another example is that of *Calvaria*, a plant on the island of Mauritius in the Indian Ocean. It had not been known to germinate for more than a century. The dodo, a giant flightless pigeon, and the size of a turkey, had probably eaten the seeds of *Calvaria*. This bird went extinct in the 1700s due to human hunting. Temple (1977) fed *Calvaria* seeds to turkeys and when the seeds were defecated they germinated. The loss of the dodo, therefore, caused the ecological link to be broken and so other species were endangered.

These examples illustrate how species are co-evolved, one species depending on another. Before we allow species to become extinct we need to deduce the long-term effects on other species and on ecosystem function. The problem is that for most systems we do not know what those links are because they are so complicated.

The presence or absence of single species can upset even very complex habitats. Take the house mouse as an example. In North America mice are a nuisance but they are not a serious problem. In Australia, however, house mouse populations expand into plagues (Singleton 1989); such events do not occur in North America or Europe and we need to find out why there is this difference in the ecosystems.

As another example, Asian water buffalo were imported to Australia in the early 1800s. Between 1830 and 1970 the population expanded and completely altered the swamps and woodlands of tropical Australia. Pathways created by the water buffalo drained fresh water from large areas and let in brackish water from the sea. Such major changes in hydrology have killed large areas of woodland in northern Australia. Similar changes do not occur in Asia where water buffaloes occur naturally. Thus, we need to compare altered systems as in Australia or Hawaii, with unaltered ones to understand how biodiversity loss will affect our planet.

Is Conservation Achieving its Ends?

I started by asking whether conservationists are achieving their goals of saving the maximum amount of biodiversity. The answers appeared obvious but in fact there are some extremely difficult problems to deal with. At the present time, conservationists have been confronted with an accelerating rate of species loss. Their response has been to do what is possible for each extinction crisis. Areas for protection are currently decided by what is left out of reserves (gap analysis) or by which area contains the greatest number of species (hotspots). These approaches will result in an inefficient use of valuable resources, with money and land area being allocated to species that do not warrant them while others are left with little help. Other protocols such as complementarity or newer optimisation procedures can represent more species with greater evenness of resources and for less cost.

Conservation has traditionally protected biodiversity by setting up reserves. There is ample evidence to show that all reserves in the world are presently in a state of decline as a result of attrition from human interference. Reserves serve only to slow the rate of decay compared to areas that are unprotected, they do not protect biodiversity forever as is commonly conceived. Reserves merely allow us to buy time to reverse the attrition through a policy of adding in habitat to replace the lost portions, a process of habitat renewal. So far no policy of habitat renewal has been contemplated and time is being lost. Unless such a policy is instituted we will lose as much biodiversity as if no reserves had been set up.

Globally there appears to be a consensus that around 12% of land area needs to be protected. In some jurisdictions, such as British Columbia, this is a legislated target. However, this target has little biological relevance and is likely to be insufficient for most endangered and threatened species. Over 50% of special habitats may be required to prevent extinction.

The location of reserves has been decided entirely on present distributions of species. There has been no consideration for future range changes due to global climate change. Consequently, many of our current protected areas will be inappropriate in about 50 years time. We must assign protected area status to future range *now* because such areas will not be available in the future.

In general, conservationists have not paid sufficient attention to these problems. Most conservationists work in the field and not enough have stood back to ask the question: are we doing the right thing? Some conservation biologists, probably those in academic institutions, should be doing more to explore these issues and advising government field staff on the priorities of conservation. These priorities must be made on a global basis and not on a country by country basis. To achieve this role, an intergovernmental committee, similar to that advising on Global Climate Change (the Intergovernmental Program on Climate Change) should be set up.

5 The End of Conservation on the Cheap, Revisited
ROBERT L. PRESSEY

In 1992, an article (Adam 1992) appeared in a little-known journal dedicated to nature conservation in New South Wales. Although local in scope, this article touched on issues of global significance that are even more important in 2000. Among its major points were four that are explored further here in a wider context. First, the main approach to nature conservation in New South Wales has been strict reservation. Second, pre-existing public land, because it involves no acquisition costs to the Government, has been overwhelmingly important as a source of new reserves. Third, a result of this "conservation on the cheap" is a very imbalanced pattern of conservation, not only geographically but in relation to particular vegetation types and species. Fourth, redressing this imbalance will require new ways of doing business in conservation, not only because the supply of cheap public land is finite but because many of the highest priorities for conservation are elsewhere. This new approach will need much more money for nature conservation on private land (whether the land is acquired outright or managed cooperatively with the present owners), much better data on biodiversity (and more money to pay for the necessary surveys and analyses), and resolution of several important ethical issues about the use of public funds, oversight of management of private land, and the responsibilities of individual landholders in achieving goals set not always by themselves but often by other members of society.

This chapter expands on these four points to show that "conservation on the cheap" (Adam 1992) did not end in the early 1990s. It is still alive and well and living in ... well, in most places. All over the world, areas dedicated to nature conservation have been drawn dominantly from land with least potential for commercial and, in some places, subsistence uses. Understanding this phenomenon—its causes and consequences—is important if we are to be effective in retaining the largest possible sample of natural variety on the planet.

The chapter begins with brief accounts of the concentration of formal conservation management on land with least value for other uses, both in New South Wales and in other parts of the world. It then outlines some of the biological implications of this approach to nature conservation and the reasons why it has been, and apparently continues to be, prevalent. It finishes with a brief discussion of one of the important measures necessary to make conservation decisions more effective than they often are—conservation on private land.

Conservation on the Cheap in New South Wales

By 1992, when Paul Adam's article—the title of which has been borrowed for this chapter—was published, the bias inherent in the New South Wales reserve system was already recognised. Strom (1979a) referred to public land as the major source of reserves and described the public land estate as "the most rugged, the least desirable for agriculture or the most inaccessible" land. Other authors, drawing on field experience and summarising historical information, also reached the conclusion that reservation was mostly applied to land with limited potential for commercial uses (Lunney and Leary 1988; Lunney and Moon 1988; McMichael 1990; Recher 1990; Reed 1990; Whitehouse 1990). Subsequent regional analyses of natural environments or vegetation types have been able to quantify biases in the types of land covered by reserves (Braithwaite et al. 1993; Pressey et al. 1996; Keith and Bedward 1999) and this has now been done for the whole State (Pressey et al. submitted a). The recent quantitative studies are important because they provide hard, conclusive data and powerful graphical techniques to support the earlier, more intuitive conclusions. "Conservation on the cheap" is increasingly an established fact in the minds of scientists and bureaucrats in natural resource agencies, not just a claim by disaffected conservationists.

Quantitative analyses of patterns of reservation in New South Wales have also elaborated on the theme of cheap conservation. A study of the north-east of the State (Pressey et al. 1996) illustrated that, at the end of 1994, reserved areas, as percentages of each of the environments in the region, are far larger in the more rugged(S3) and/or less fertile(F1) areas (Figure 5.1a) showing proportion of total area reserved.

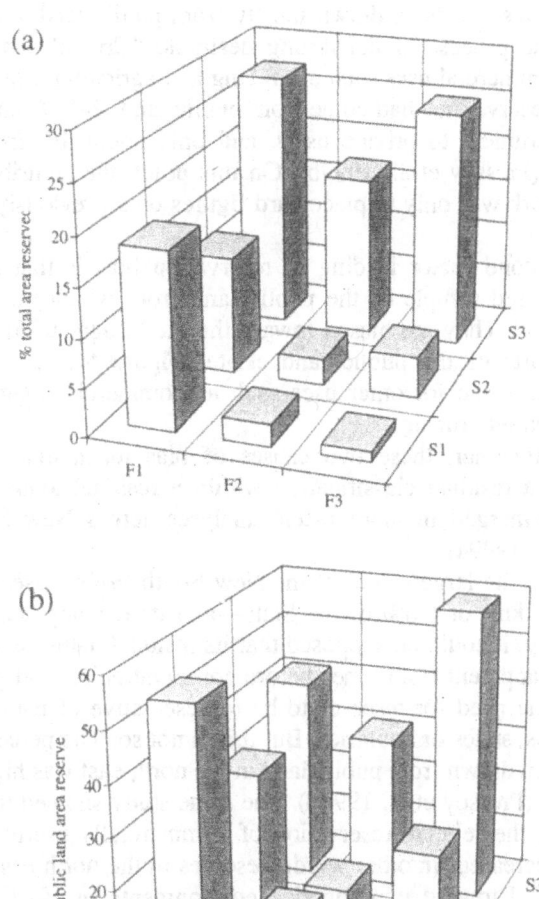

Figure 5.1: Environmental Coverage of Reserves in NE New South Wales[1]

The study attributed this pattern to two factors. First, as already known, reserves had been drawn mostly from public land which was left over from the process of converting desirable "Crown" land to private tenure for commercial uses such as grazing and agriculture. In 1994, about 72% of the reserve area had come from public land, 24% from land leased by the Government to private users, and only about 4% from privately owned land (Pressey et al. 1999b). On this point, the contribution of the north-east work was only to place hard figures on a previously established fact.

A second factor leading to reservation bias is that reserves are actually a biased sample of the public land from which they have been largely derived. They are biased toward the most rugged(S3) and/or least fertile(F1) parts of the public land estate (Figure 5.1b), the remainder having higher value for other uses such as commercial logging in State forests and leased grazing.

Put together, these two causes of bias mean that conservation reserves are a residual classification within a residual tenure. The same pattern has emerged in more recent analyses across New South Wales (Pressey et al. 1999a).

Given the large extent of the New South Wales reserve system—about 52,800 km^2 or 6.6% of the State—and its development over more than a century, it could be supposed that its residual nature is an historical artifact, still apparent from times before conservationists and governments understood the need for reserves to be representative of natural variation across regions, states or countries. But this is not so. The percentage of the reserve system drawn from public land in the north-east was higher in 1997 than in 1994 (Pressey et al. 1999b). The same study showed that, over the same period, the relative reservation of commercially useful land across the region decreased. In other words, reserves in the north-east were more strongly biased toward unproductive environments in 1997 than Figure 5.1a shows in 1994. The recent Statewide figure of 85% of the reserve system derived from public land (Dick 1997) would now be higher with the reservation of about 360,000 ha of public forest in 1998.

Another possible argument against the analyses in Figure 5.1 is that formal nature conservation in the north-east is relatively recent, beginning about a century after development for agriculture and grazing. So biases would be expected because these commercial uses pre-empted nature conservation in the most productive country. But this only partly explains the unevenness of the reserve system. If reservation is expressed as a percentage of the remaining vegetation in each environment (Pressey et al. 1996, 1999b), two things become clear.

First, reserves are still strongly biased toward steep, unproductive land and, second, the environments that are poorly reserved relative to widely accepted conservation targets (e.g., Anon. 1995; JANIS 1997) are generally those with most potential for agriculture and urban development. Reservation continues to focus on the cheap lands while the remaining, unused opportunities for conservation action on the flat, productive parts of the region steadily diminish as native vegetation continues to decline there. The pattern is very similar across much of the State (Pressey et al. 1999a).

The second argument against these interpretations could be mounted: by limiting the analyses to strict reserves, the potential contribution of various off-reserve measures is ignored. Again, this only partly applies. It is true that effective off-reserve initiatives are increasing in New South Wales and that they are encouraging conservation management of important remnants of native vegetation, including some with substantial commercial potential if cleared (e.g., Prober and Thiele 1993; Lambert and Elix 1996; Lunney and Matthews 1997; Young and Gunningham 1997). It is also true that these initiatives are supported to varying extents by funds from the State and Commonwealth Governments. Nonetheless, these are localised bright points against a less exciting background. Of the many factors shaping this background, four are notable.

First, formal off-reserve measures such as zoning and other classifications are just as strongly biased to steep and unproductive land as strict reserves, at least in the north-east (Pressey et al. 1996).

Second, ongoing declines in the real State conservation budget will mean less capability in investigation, management and research for private lands.

Third, the State Government is currently struggling to deal with its legislative requirements for new approaches to managing native vegetation across tenures. At present, there is a lack of agreed, strategic goals and an absence of explicit, effective protocols for identifying conservation priorities and then affording them appropriate protection. If these difficulties are resolved, however, the situation could improve dramatically.

Fourth, and related to the previous point, the various effective initiatives for conservation on private land have not been gathered into an overall strategy for the future of the biodiversity of the State.

Conservation on the Cheap in the Rest of the World

There is considerable evidence to show that conservation on the cheap is not some peculiarity of New South Wales. The same general pattern has been documented in other parts of Australia (Webb 1966; Ride 1975; Harris 1977; Kirkpatrick 1987; Hall 1988; Saunders et al. 1996) and in many parts of the world, including New Zealand (Mark 1985), Canada (Henderson 1992), Britain (Leader-Williams et al. 1990), several countries in Africa (Pullan 1983; Rebelo 1997; Barnard et al. 1998), Malaysia (Aiken 1994), and the United States (Beardsley and Stoms 1993). Doubtless, many other examples exist but have not been published in the primary literature. The perception of reserves as valid only while they remain residual is illustrated glaringly by revocations of reserved areas when they proved valuable for mining, logging, grazing or agriculture (Harris 1977; Runte 1979; Mercer and Peterson 1986; Aiken 1994).

Cheap conservation has perhaps been described most provocatively and controversially in the United States. Runte's (1972) article titled "Yellowstone: it's useless, so why not a park?" was presumably intended to spark debate. This aim was achieved spectacularly by his subsequent book (Runte 1979) with its chapter on the "worthless lands," prompting harsh criticism (e.g., Cox 1983; Sellars 1983). Three of the main points made by the critics are worth noting, but not because they refute the argument that reserves are generally residual to commercial land uses.

- The term "worthless" was applied too narrowly by Runte, being primarily concerned with major issues of national development (mining, timber, grazing, agriculture) and not with the potential for personal or company profits.
- Some park areas in the United States have very high contemporary values as real estate but nonetheless retain their integrity.
- Many parks in the United States were the subjects of battles between conservationists and commercial interests, demonstrating considerable economic worth at the time of establishment.

These criticisms serve to qualify, rather than refute the generalisation that reserves are residual (and see Runte 1983). First, patterns of reservation (such as those in Figure 5.1) are largely the outcome of many decades of government policy on major commercial land uses, not decisions about individual enterprises. Second, reserve systems, at least in First World countries, might now be well defended from potential encroachments, but individual reserves generally had little or no value for agriculture at the time of establishment. Many also had limited value for other uses. Third, in broad geographical context, the conservation battles that demonstrate forgone commercial values of some of today's reserves have largely been on the margins between good agricultural land and those areas too steep or infertile for any significant commercial use. Logging has been an important and well-publicised competitor for reservation in these marginal areas (e.g., Vincent 1992; Franklin 1995; Dargavel 1998). In broad context, the achievement of conservationists has been to extend nature conservation further into marginal areas than it would otherwise have gone, rather than taking it substantially onto good agricultural land.

There is little published information on which to base a judgement about the present global trend in cheap conservation, so the following points are impressions gained from discussions with conservation planners working in other countries:

- The establishment of conservation areas in the less productive parts of regions and countries is continuing apace while large areas of native vegetation in the more exploitable landscapes continue to be used and cleared for commercial purposes, including foreign exchange;
- As a counterweight to this trend, albeit presently a small one in terms of sheer extent, various initiatives are underway to conserve remnants of nature in privately-owned, productive landscapes (e.g., Miller 1996; Knight 1999);
- Many of these initiatives are not nested within integrated national or global strategies for the funding or practice of nature conservation, so that conflicting decisions on new reserves or widespread loss of habitat continue, if not in the specific study areas covered by the initiatives then in surrounding areas.

Some Biological Implications of Conservation on the Cheap

An exhaustive discussion of the implications of cheap conservation would require several book chapters based on extensive multidisciplinary discussion. Instead, this section offers a brief summary of some of the main biological implications, both positive and negative. The remainder of the chapter is then concerned with the reasons for, and some necessary responses to, cheap conservation with a view to addressing its biological disadvantages.

A desirable, and sometimes incidental, outcome of cheap conservation can be the likely long-term persistence of some species in large reserves drawn from land with few competing uses. In some cases, as in areas too steep, too arid, or too cold for commercial activities, the "protection" offered by formal reservation is questionable. The establishment of reserves in such areas could be seen as an empty gesture and, in the experience of this author, that view is often correct. But it could also be argued that such areas are at least secured against the advent of technology, infrastructure or market forces that would make them exploitable in the future for timber, grazing, mining or other uses. In other cases, cheap reservation does preclude existing or impending commercial uses. By the nature of the land so protected, the competing uses are usually extensive and based on native vegetation rather than intensive transformation (e.g., logging of native forests and grazing of native rangelands).

Many of the species inhabiting the unexploitable or agriculturally marginal areas can thereby benefit from cheap conservation. This is particularly so for organisms that are small or demand little space for the maintenance of viable populations. Even in large reserves drawn from unproductive country, the long-term viability of some species is uncertain. Sometimes this is because even large reserves are simply not large enough (e.g., Newmark 1987; Grumbine 1992). The viability of some species in large reserves can also be undermined by continued, illegal exploitation (e.g., Barzetti 1993; Parr et al. 1993; MacKinnon et al. 1994).

An undesirable outcome of cheap conservation is that species and assemblages typical of flatter, more fertile, commercially productive, expensive (mostly private) land, and those most at risk from outright loss of habitat, continue to languish with little or no effective protection (Maehr 1990; Pressey et al. 1996; Knight 1999) This operates at all scales. In New South Wales, at the scale of kilometres, valley bottoms and footslopes are more likely to be cleared, where soils are suitable, than steeper slopes. In the east of the State, generally over tens of kilometres, extensive clearing has affected the vegetation types of the flatter and more fertile parts of the coastal lowlands and tablelands (e.g., Adam 1987; Benson and Howell 1990; Benson 1991; Keith 1995; Pressey et al. 1996; Keith and Bedward 1999). Across hundreds of kilometres, the broad swathe of clearing and fragmentation on the western slopes and plains has greatly reduced once widespread vegetation communities (Benson 1991; Prober and Thiele 1993; Sivertsen 1993, 1994; Prober 1996).

If there are difficulties in maintaining species in reserves drawn from cheap land, these are much greater in landscapes subject to ongoing loss and fragmentation of native vegetation. Many species become extinct as a direct result of habitat loss (Hughes et al. 1997; Nee and May 1997). For many more, regional declines signal impending extinctions as local populations blink out in increasingly small and isolated fragments of vegetation and are not replaced by re-colonisation or reproduction (Beissinger et al. 1996; Bennett and Ford 1997; Fahrig 1997). In this context, cheap conservation can be seen as a diversionary tactic on the part of governments and agencies, giving the appearance of conservation progress, measured in hectares of reserves, while failing to deal with the most pressing and concentrated threats. This is in contrast to a strategy that seeks to minimise the cost of providing adequate protection to all the species or assemblages in a region (e.g., Ando et al. 1998).

Increasingly, priority conservation areas at all scales are being defined in terms of both endemism (or, more generally, irreplaceability) and threat (e.g., Myers 1988a; Sisk et al. 1994; Cole and Landres 1996; Pressey et al. 1996; Pressey 1997; Mittermeier et al. 1998; Cowling et al. 1999; Lombard et al. 1999). These analyses focus attention for conservation action on the very places that cheap conservation avoids—those with a high risk of adverse impacts from land use and with species and assemblages for which there are few or no options for conservation elsewhere (either because of natural rarity or because few occurrences have survived the transformation of the landscapes they inhabit). This approach to defining priorities emphasises the importance of establishing effective conservation management in areas that are expensive and inconvenient to protect. Put another way, it shows that the most important landscapes for both ongoing commercial development and nature conservation overlap. In New South Wales, the bulk of the unreserved native vegetation with high priority for conservation is in private tenure (Figure 5.2).

In contrast to vegetation with low priority for conservation, the high-priority vegetation is also concentrated on flat terrain and has a larger component on land with high capability for cropping or intensive grazing (Table 5.1). These are the hard options for nature conservation that have been avoided by successive State Governments for decades. The delay has meant continued loss of high-priority native vegetation and pre-emption by clearing of conservation targets now accepted as reasonable (Glowka et al. 1994; Anon. 1995; JANIS 1997; Soulé and Sanjayan 1998). Further delay will increase this loss and further compromise the achievement of targets.

Table 5.1: Areas of Remaining Native Vegetation in LP (low-priority) and HP (high-priority) Landscapes, Eastern 60% of New South Wales[a]

Biogeographic Region	Native vegetation in LP landscapes	Native vegetation in HP landscapes
Brigalow Belt South		
km² native vegetation	1097	1859
% private tenure	75.0	79.7
% low ruggedness [b]	15.5	99.9
% high land capability [c]	10.9	56.8
Nandewar		
km² native vegetation	1251	901
% private tenure	85.5	79.8
% low ruggedness [b]	2.6	99.7
% high land capability [c]	1.9	35.7
New England Tableland		
km² native vegetation	3937	1019
% private tenure	59.6	82.8
% low ruggedness [b]	2.5	100.0
% high land capability [c]	0.1	10.4
North Coast		
km² native vegetation	15453	432
% private tenure	54.8	80.6
% low ruggedness [b]	8.3	99.8
% high land capability [c]	1.4	14.7
South East Corner		
km² native vegetation	5626	87
% private tenure	27.6	85.1
% low ruggedness [b]	47.9	100.0
% high land capability [c]	1.9	0.0
South Western Slopes		
km² native vegetation	189	7309
% private tenure	67.7	83.7
% low ruggedness [b]	1.6	97.5
% high land capability [c]	12.9	49.9
Sydney Basin		
km² native vegetation	8388	310
% private tenure	53.8	75.8
% low ruggedness [b]	39.4	100.0
% high land capability [c]	3.0	43.4

Table Notes:
[a] Also shown are percentages of remaining vegetation in categories of tenure, ruggedness and land capability. These regions were selected for analysis because

they occur wholly outside the Western Division of the State and have a relatively uniform history of tenure and regulation of land use. In particular, the seven regions in the table historically had extensive areas of public land from which large reserves have been drawn over the last few decades.

[b] Original ruggedness values refer to the standard deviation of elevations in a radius of 1.75 km around each grid cell, initially at the nominal resolution of the digital elevation model available across NSW (250m), and then re-sampled to 1 km^2 resolution. Cutoffs between low, moderate and high ruggedness chosen at values of about 30 and 105 (maximum value was 272) to reflect strong differences in land use and tenure.

[c] Land capability refers to the suitability of landscapes for cultivation and grazing. Digital data from original 1:100,000 mapping were provided by NSW Department of Land and Water Conservation. High land capability includes map classes I-III described by Emery (1985), covering landscapes most suitable for intensive agriculture and grazing. Land capability mapping excludes some areas in public and private tenure (see Emery 1985 for details).

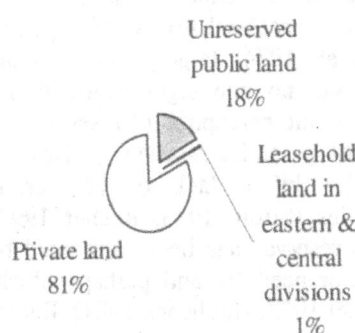

Figure 5.2: Distribution across Major Tenures of Remaining Native Vegetation with High Priority for Conservation in New South Wales

Some Reasons for Conservation on the Cheap

Responsibility for conservation on the cheap and its adverse implications for biodiversity can most easily be laid at the door of pragmatic politicians and bureaucrats, and not without justification. But other factors are involved. Scientists, including conservation planners, must also take some of the blame. The examples in this section are drawn mainly from New South Wales but most are likely to apply more generally.

Political and Bureaucratic Factors

Political and Bureaucratic Pragmatism. When it comes to decisions on land use and the allocation of funds for land management, money and power are often in the hands of people who are not committed to the cause of nature conservation. The interests of conservation, therefore, are often overridden by the imperatives of political survival and bureaucratic expediency. Thirty years after the New South Wales Fauna Protection Panel set out to systematically establish a system of representative reserves, based on the data on natural environments available at the time, Strom (1979b) described its achievements as "...a scramble for whatever was offering." Even a national review of gaps in the Australian reserve system (Specht et al. 1974) largely failed to arrest the trend toward reservation of land with no other significant uses. The main reason was the political and bureaucratic perception of reservation as a residual land use. The investigation of potential reserves in New South Wales has been impeded historically by a lack of co-operation from other land management agencies (Strom 1983; Recher 1990; Strom 1990), and a residual attitude to reserves has been reinforced by the need for reserve proposals to be referenced to, and perhaps blocked by, other resource agencies (McMichael 1973; Hitchcock 1981). Recent negotiations between agencies and interest groups in the State's eastern forests have promoted a more strategic approach to reservation (RACAC 1996; Pressey 1998), but the process has been restricted so far to public lands (the cheap option) where its ultimate effectiveness has been questioned by some stakeholders (Finkel 1998a, b).

Undiscerning Electorates. Related to the previous point, most voters are undiscerning about nature conservation and can be suitably impressed by announcements of new reserves, regardless of whether these new areas actually address regional, state or national priorities. This is not surprising. Even the concept of representativeness is arcane for most people, so there are few public and media debates about the achievement of conservation targets for species or vegetation types or about planning concepts such as irreplaceability, vulnerability, and the quantitative assessment of conservation priorities. Much of the public debate over the expansion, in late 1998, of the reserve system in north-eastern New South Wales was preoccupied with the wrong numbers—85 new reserves covering a total area of about 360,000 ha (e.g., Doherty 1998a,b). As impressive as these figures appear at first sight, neither is necessarily related to progress in protecting species or environments that actually need protection, a fact that was doubtless recognised by the Government but not acknowledged in its press releases. In the end, the wrong numbers won the day. Letters to the editor in the Sydney *Morning Herald* condemned conservationists for criticising the Government's reserve announcements, wondering how they could complain about such extensive additions to the reserve system. The leader of the State National Party has since been on television referring to the "endless avarice" of the conservationists.

Broad or Ineffectual Policy Frameworks. In principle, good policy frameworks for conservation planning can constrain the decision-space of politicians and bureaucrats to focus resources on the areas that most urgently need attention for conservation. The recent development of a potentially effective framework is evident in the evolution of forest policy in Australia. The National Forest Policy Statement (Anon. 1992) established three broad principles for forest reservation which were later made more specific (Anon. 1995; JANIS 1997) and, eventually, made fully operational in New South Wales by setting quantitative targets for individual species and forest types (RACAC 1996). These targets (and subsequent ones in later planning exercises) were very effective in framing the negotiations between key stakeholders in New South Wales (Pressey 1998) and probably pushed reservation further out into valuable production forest than it would otherwise have gone. In the end, though, the effectiveness of the new reserves established from this process, especially in the north-east, was not judged on how well targets were achieved, and neither the Government nor the responsible agencies have called for a rigorous review of target achievement, although the outcomes have been lauded politically in terms of numbers of parks and hectares (above).

In the end, the operational rules for implementing the national forest policy could therefore be seen as only marginally influential and the reasons for this are still being debated. One likely reason is that the full achievement of all targets would have left no room for a viable timber industry to which the New South Wales Government remains committed. The targets for some species and forest types were always going to be grossly under-achieved, and the debate over which features most needed reservation was not advanced enough at the time to influence the outcome. Another reason is that the biological requirements for an effective system of conservation areas (representation targets, size, connectivity, effective boundaries) are sufficiently numerous and open to interpretation that success on one or more fronts can always be claimed despite failure on others. This issue is probably much more generally applicable. For example, virtually any decision on a new conservation area could be promoted as addressing at least one of the many broad guidelines in the New South Wales Biodiversity Strategy (NPWS 1999).

Limited Capability of Responsible Agencies. The agencies charged with responsibility for protecting biodiversity are not always up to the task. Within the New South Wales National Parks and Wildlife Service, in the absence of explicit conservation goals, consistent data, and clear State and regional priorities, there are many pressures for *ad hoc* decisions on the location of new reserves. These include (Recher 1990; Whitehouse 1990; Dick 1997): external lobbying for the protection of well-known and charismatic places, including thematic campaigns (e.g., wilderness, rainforest) concentrated in the State's east; dispersal, without co-ordination, of responsibilities for reserve proposals within the Service; enhancements of acquisition funds from Treasury specific to particular environments; the continuing influence of political priorities; and the ongoing need for the Service to recommend protection through its statutory planning responsibilities and in response to land offers, tenure conversions, and development applications.

The agency will not be capable of making informed, strategic decisions about new conservation areas until a framework is in place for rationalising these competing demands against specific conservation goals and priorities. The development of such a framework is only just beginning. Similarly, the New South Wales Department of Land and Water Conservation is still grappling with its responsibilities in the preparation of community-based regional vegetation management plans, required by the

Native Vegetation Conservation Bill (1997), with no broad agreement yet on appropriate conservation targets or methods for establishing priorities. Day-to-day decisions about applications to clear native vegetation have nonetheless continued since the introduction of the Bill.

Conservation Planning Issues

Poor Criteria for Holding Decision Makers Accountable. Criteria for measuring progress in the development of reserve systems are generally not well developed. In Australia, one recommended indicator for national reporting on the establishment of a comprehensive, adequate and representative reserve system (see Anon. 1992; Anon. 1995; JANIS 1997 for definitions) is the "extent of each vegetation type and marine habitat type within protected areas" (Saunders et al. 1998), with the added requirements of percentage targets for each vegetation type and measurement of the protection given to within-type variation. Another national set of indicators (ANZECC 1998) adds, for terrestrial protected areas, the "percentage of the pre-1750 area" of each vegetation type reserved but, for marine areas, requires only the percentage of each marine region (Thackway and Cresswell 1996) in reserves. For New South Wales, the indicator for reporting on protected areas is the "area and percentage of the state ... and bioregions in protected areas" (EPA 1997). For three reasons, these indicators are necessary but insufficient:

- Percentages of administrative jurisdictions or natural regions in reserves are very difficult to interpret meaningfully because such large areas: (i) are heterogeneous with respect to threatening processes; and (ii) can have their conservation targets met by reserving areas within them that have least potential for land use and least need for protection, as shown in many other parts of the world (e.g., Beardsley and Stoms 1993; Aiken 1994; Pressey et al. 1996; Rebelo 1997; Barnard et al. 1998). Broad regional assessments must therefore be complemented by protocols for focusing attention on conservation priorities at finer scales (TNC 1997; Mittermeier et al. 1998).
- Even at a scale much finer than regions, the number of vegetation types or other land classes with reservation targets achieved indicates nothing about their relative need for protection or their respective fates if left unreserved. This problem is reduced, but still applies, if targets are set in terms of pre-European areas (ANZECC 1998) which will automatically adjust upwards, in terms of extant areas, for vegetation

types that have been largely cleared. Although assessments of gaps in reserve systems (e.g., Awimbo et al. 1996; Woinarski et al. 1996; Khan et al. 1997; Stoms et al. 1998) often include comments on conservation priorities, they rarely include explicit measures of reservation bias that can be tracked through time. Bias measures, especially those that relate to vulnerability to habitat loss, can encourage effective scheduling of conservation action among under-reserved species or land classes. They are particularly valuable for revealing the extent to which conservation has been done on the cheap (Pressey et al. 1996, submitted a).

- The principle of adequacy (Anon. 1992; Anon. 1995; JANIS 1997) is only partly addressed by targets for representation in protected areas. It also requires consideration of many other factors that influence the persistence of species within established reserves (e.g., size, connectivity, shape, the nature of reserve boundaries, adjacent land uses, disturbance regimes, resilience to climate change). These factors are necessary for a comprehensive assessment of the effectiveness of reserves and other conservation areas. Further work is needed to develop appropriate criteria and to understand their application in different contexts. For example, to what extent are factors such as connectivity and compactness inversely related? When is one preferred over the other? How can factors such as size and connectivity be applied without becoming disincentives to effective conservation in the fragmented, privately-owned environments that have languished because of conservation on the cheap?

Diverse, Uncoordinated Conservation Goals. One brake on the effectiveness of conservation planning is that different groups have different, and sometimes conflicting, ideas about what nature conservation means on the ground. Within New South Wales, different views are held within the National Parks and Wildlife Service, and the Service's approaches are often at odds with those of various influential lobby groups, who disagree among themselves. So wilderness, old-growth forest, representative examples of secondary forest, semi-arid rangelands, wetlands, and fragments of vegetation in privately-owned agricultural land are all competing for attention and resources. The priorities identified recently across New South Wales (Pressey et al. 1999 a) focus attention on areas of vegetation types with few or no options for conservation elsewhere (high irreplaceability) and most risk of loss if left unprotected (high vulnerability). The pattern of priority is almost the reverse of one based on wilderness or old growth. Similarly, the biodiversity hotspots of Mittermeier et al. (1998) based on endemism and threat do not overlap substantially with their major tropical wilderness areas. In Venezuela, protection of imminently threatened endemic animals would focus conservation efforts in the north, but the protection of non-endemics at risk would focus on the south (Rodriguez and Rojas-Saurez 1996). None of this is surprising—conservation priorities will naturally be different if conservation goals are different. What is needed is some coordination of approaches, and further investigation of the extent to which they conflict or can be achieved simultaneously, blended into an overall strategy for jurisdictions or natural regions. Without this coordination, alternative views of conservation priorities compete for political influence, and those offering the most hectares at the least cost are likely to win most often.

Immaturity of Conservation Planning as a Science. Whereas the field of ecology has been refined and made robust through the application of many thousands of minds over many decades, conservation planning has had the benefit of less time and fewer people. Accordingly, it is a much less rigorous field of investigation. This is not to say that all conservation decisions can be made objectively on the basis of agreed data. There will always be room and need for expert judgement about the best ways to protect areas and species, and always uncertainties about data and threats. It is to say that specific goals, analytical methods, and assumptions about the constraints on and opportunities for conservation should be spelt out before priority areas for conservation are identified. Aspects of this process are still poorly understood and one result is ongoing confusion about the appropriate use of various conservation criteria and planning procedures (Pressey 1997; Reid 1998). For example, an accepted way of comparing alternative approaches to selecting areas that will achieve representation targets for all the species or other features in a region is by measuring efficiency—how well can the targets be packed into a set of areas (Pressey and Nicholls 1989)? A smaller total area (a more efficient result) means less competition with other uses and more chance of the targets being achieved. This all makes sense. But there is an implicit assumption involved in this measure—that it is possible to construct a whole network of conservation areas that will collectively achieve the representation targets.

A more realistic scenario is that a system of conservation areas will develop incrementally in parallel with ongoing loss of native vegetation (Cowling et al. 1999). To deal with this scenario, effectiveness must be judged not in terms of efficiency but in terms of how well a conservation strategy is able to intercede in ongoing loss of vegetation to maximise "retention" (or to minimise the extent to which conservation targets are compromised by clearing over some time frame). This requires a modelling approach that simulates the gradual expansion of conservation areas while native vegetation is reduced in parallel. It could be that the best approaches in terms of efficiency are not the best for retention, that is, that different assumptions about the constraints on and opportunities for conservation require different approaches to planning. This issue currently underlies debate about how to identify biodiversity hotspots and remains unresolved. With such fundamental issues in conservation planning outstanding, science does not present consistent or effective advice to policy makers or a strong alternative to *ad hoc* decisions.

Data Issues

Lack of Data on Biodiversity. Lack of sufficient data can always be invoked as a reason for ineffective conservation decisions but, as indicated above, conservation on the cheap has usually proceeded in the presence of sufficient data to indicate that the real conservation priorities were not being addressed by pragmatic decisions. Even so, few parts of the world have high-quality, consistent data on biodiversity across extensive areas, the availability of which is essential for really effective conservation decisions. Although parts of New South Wales have among the best biophysical data sets in the world (RACAC 1996; Ferrier 1997), data on biodiversity across the State are inconsistent and patchy. Records of plant and animal species are biased geographically and taxonomically (e.g., Margules and Austin 1994; Ferrier 1997), and reliable statistical modelling of species' distributions is limited mainly to the north-east and south-east. Land classifications are necessary for conservation planning as surrogates for biodiversity, but there is no consistent map of vegetation or biophysical variation across the State at a scale useful for identifying the relative conservation priorities of specific areas (say 1:250,000, or preferably finer). For the maps of biodiversity surrogates (e.g., vegetation types) that do exist for parts of the State, there has been little testing of how well the map units account for species patterns and whether different classifications at different scales might be more informative (but see Ferrier and Watson 1997). What does all this mean? First, it means that even the most deliberate attempts to place conservation action in areas that appear to have high priority will be wrong to some extent because the best available picture of biodiversity is more or less (usually more) approximate. This approximation is something that conservation planners learn to live with, usually tempered by the assumption that planning with an approximate picture of biodiversity is better than planning at random. Second, when data on biodiversity are limited, and especially where the available picture of biodiversity consists only of broad land classes (e.g., vegetation types or land systems), reviews of existing conservation areas can fail to expose the limitations of conservation on the cheap. Specifically, the identities of assemblages and species left to fend for themselves in expensive, risky environments will remain unknown.

Lack of Data on Threatening Processes. An accurate picture of the biodiversity of a state or country, although difficult enough to complete, is only half the information needed for effective conservation planning. Conservation action is only necessary because of threatening processes, and a better understanding of these is urgently needed in New South Wales (NPWS 1999) and elsewhere so that conservation measures can be properly located and scheduled. Conservation on the cheap is about placing reserves in areas with least current threat, an approach that could be reversed with substantial benefits for nature conservation (e.g., Myers 1988a; Sisk et al. 1994; Cole and Landres 1996; Pressey et al. 1996; Pressey 1997; Mittermeier et al. 1998; Cowling et al. 1999; Lombard et al. 1999).

Effective conservation planning also concerns scheduling of conservation action to pre-empt the loss or degradation of areas considered valuable. Data on current or impending threats is therefore essential if the spatial and temporal options for nature conservation are to be properly resolved. The best available assessment of vulnerability to clearing across New South Wales has serious limitations (Pressey et al. 1999 a), and this is probably the easiest threatening process to understand because its distribution can be estimated with reasonable accuracy from remote sources. Grazing by stock is another very widespread threatening process in New South Wales (Graetz et al. 1995; Landsberg et al. 1997), and the major one in the semi-arid western rangelands. But an accurate assessment of vulnerability to grazing across the State is presently precluded by: (i) lack of data on the spectrum of grazing intensity; and (ii) limited information on the different responses to grazing of particular species, landscapes or vegetation types (Pressey and Taffs 1999).

Other extensive threatening processes, including alteration of river flows (Kingsford 1995), are difficult to map quantitatively for similar reasons. Conservation planning is fundamentally about risk management—understanding the implications of *not* applying limited conservation resources to a particular area in favour of some other area that appears more important and/or more imminently threatened. To the extent that the spatial distribution of threatening processes and their rates or imminence are poorly known, risk management is unlikely to be sound. Moreover, an effective alternative to conservation on the cheap is difficult to present.

Conclusions

Conservation on the cheap is a widespread phenomenon with important implications for the persistence of biodiversity. It results in assemblages and species that inhabit the more productive, commercially valuable parts of the world languishing without adequate protection and continuing to decline. The necessary responses to expedient, ineffective conservation decisions are numerous and suggested by the list of problems discussed in the previous section. Leaving aside changes to democratic political systems and the personal priorities of politicians and senior bureaucrats, practical responses to conservation on the cheap include:

- more specific policy frameworks that specify the types of natural features most urgently in need of conservation action;
- the development of decision-making frameworks that (i) require conservation agencies to deal transparently with explicit and, where possible, quantitative conservation goals, and (ii) involve testing of the effectiveness of decisions and, where necessary, adaptation of previous approaches;
- improved criteria for ensuring the accountability of people who make decisions about new conservation areas;
- improvements in conservation planning, particularly, (i) methods for reconciling divergent conservation goals, and (ii) methods for setting conservation priorities under conditions of incremental expansion of systems of conservation areas in parallel with ongoing loss of native vegetation; and

- better data on biodiversity and, in particular, on rates and patterns of threatening processes.

Perhaps one of the most important and widely relevant responses to conservation on the cheap is to focus conservation efforts more specifically on private lands—those areas that are generally the most productive parts of jurisdictions or natural regions, subject to the most alteration, and historically the most difficult to conserve. The picture of high-priority native vegetation occurring mainly on private tenure in New South Wales (Figure 5.2) is an unusual example of the importance of private land being quantified, but does not convey a fundamental new message. The importance of private land for nature conservation has been widely recognised, as have the difficulties of implementing effective action on private tenure (Moore 1987; Edwards and Sharp 1990; Maehr 1990; Farrier 1995; Tibbetts et al. 1995; Miller 1996; Bean and Wilcove 1997; Knight 1999). Money is a substantial impediment. The sheer expense of acquiring private land has been a major cause of conservation on the cheap, but substantial funds are required for effective conservation by other means as well. The extent and effectiveness of voluntary conservation agreements in New South Wales are limited by available funds for negotiation, planning, implementation and maintenance (Adam 1992; Keith 1995). Other approaches to cooperative management will involve the same types of costs. The situation becomes more complicated when protection is imposed on private landholders, diminishing the actual or potential commercial value of their land and opening debates about ethics, legalities and compensation (e.g., Farrier 1995; Tibbetts et al. 1995).

Notwithstanding these unresolved problems, efforts to protect the remaining pieces of natural or semi-natural habitat on private land are underway. Ideally, these efforts will combine local action with regional perspectives on conservation priorities. In New South Wales, as elsewhere, an explicit, consistent protocol is needed to identify priorities for conservation action across all tenures. This should be based primarily on: (i) the extent to which quantitative conservation targets for vegetation types or ecosystems are currently met in reserves and other conservation areas; and (ii) information on the vulnerability of those vegetation types or ecosystems to major threatening processes. Secondary or qualifying information should include data that are not part of the consistent jurisdictional or regional layers (e.g., localities and conservation status of species, distribution of land types mapped only for part of the planning area, cultural heritage values); and information on condition, configuration, connectivity and adjacent land uses for individual pieces of vegetation.

For at least two reasons, strategic conservation decisions on private land in New South Wales are more feasible than when Adam (1992) discussed the need for nature conservation on private tenure as an alternative to conservation on the cheap. First, the Native Vegetation Conservation Bill (1997) now provides a legislative basis for strategic regional assessments across tenures. Second, the National Parks and Wildlife Service now has considerable experience in developing extensive data sets and applying decision-support software for strategic planning in the public forests in eastern New South Wales (RACAC 1996; Finkel 1998a,b; Pressey 1998). This experience is an adequate basis to develop, in collaboration with other organisations, a protocol for identifying priority conservation areas across all tenures. The protocol can then evolve as new ideas are contributed and the need for adaptation to particular planning situations becomes apparent.

Once priority areas are identified, guidelines will be needed to apply specific types of conservation management. Reservation is only one of a wide variety of conservation measures applicable to natural or semi-natural areas (e.g., Farrier 1995; EPA 1997). These measures vary in their security (ease of removal) and effectiveness (level of protection for the range of biodiversity and cultural values). Application of the "right" measure to an area will rest on judgements about several issues, including constraints and opportunities determined by tenure, current use, adjacent land uses, and individual landholders; the threatening processes applying to specific areas and the effectiveness of different protection measures in preventing these; and the need for ongoing management of natural or anthropogenic processes.

Due to previous clearing, only a small fraction of the current conservation targets for some vegetation types or ecosystems in New South Wales are achievable. This problem is likely to be more serious with a refined set of conservation targets for Statewide land types and probably applies to many other parts of the world. Some targets can now only be achieved fully through re-establishment of vegetation. Priorities for this expensive and long-term enterprise are needed and will be guided by, among other considerations, (i) targets for vegetation types applied to areas where they once occurred, and (ii) the benefits of enlarging and connecting existing remnants.

Note

1. The data are for the end of 1994. The vertical axis in (a) is the percentage of the total area of each broad environmental unit in reserves. The vertical axis in (b) is the percentage reservation of that part of each broad environmental unit in public tenure. S1—flat slopes ($<3^0$); S2—moderate slopes (3-10^0); S3—steep slopes ($>10^0$). F1—low fertility geologies; F2—moderate fertility; F3—high fertility. See Pressey et al. (1996) for derivation of slope and fertility categories.

6 Threat to Biodiversity: The Invasion of Exotic Species
EMINA KRCMAR-NOZIC, G. CORNELIS VAN KOOTEN, BILL WILSON[1]

For some time, scientists have sought recognition of the threat that exotic pests pose for biodiversity (Liebhold *et al.* 1995; Niemela and Mattson 1996), and North American governments may now be starting to pay attention to this complex issue. Early this year, the US President committed $29 million in incremental annual funding to combat exotic pests. The announcement followed the removal of hundreds of trees in Chicago that were infested with the Asian long-horned beetle (Hagenbaugh 1999). This exotic timber pest spread to at least eight American states and is estimated to have killed more than a thousand trees in New York City alone.

In this chapter, we summarise available information on exotic pest invasions and provide economic insights that serve as input into policy and management of this problem. We begin in the next section by defining and classifying exotic pests, and discussing means by which they are introduced. We then examine the role of globalisation and international trade, followed by a consideration of the economic aspects. Most of our examples focus on forestry and forest management because introduced forest pests are among the most devastating exotics in economic and ecological terms, causing potential losses of species thus threatening biodiversity. We conclude by considering some ways to manage exotic pest invasions.

Background to Exotic Invasions

Exotic species can arrive in their new locations naturally and/or assisted by human activities. Plant seeds, fungus spores and insect eggs, cocoons or larvae can be transported via storms or other anomalous weather. Animal, plant or human vectors can carry pathogens. Humans in particular provide opportunities for many species to overcome geographic and climatic barriers to arrive in new areas as hitchhikers in and on imported plants and animals, plane and ship compartments, in shipping containers and wood packaging, and in bilge water (Wilson and Graham 1983). Importation of any living or untreated material constitutes a potential source of exotic pests.

Different terms are used in the literature to describe this movement of species—invasive, alien, exotic, foreign, immigrant, introduced, non-indigenous and non-native. These terms all refer to a species that is "...beyond its natural range of potential dispersal" (USA Office of Technology Assessment, hereafter OTA, 1993). This definition is based on species ecology and recognises the importance of human activities in species movement. The term "biological invasion" or "bio-invasion" has a similar connotation, referring to "... the expansion of a species' geographic range into a new area" (Liebhold et al. 1995). *Exotic* refers to introduced organisms that can be both beneficial (crops, ornamentals, game animals, domestic livestock) or harmful (e.g., tree diseases), while *invasion* connotes mainly the expansion of a species. We use the terms interchangeably.

Three processes are common to all bio-invasions: introduction, establishment and spread (Mooney and Drake 1986; Drake et al. 1989; Liebhold et al. 1995). An introduced organism becomes established once it is able to reproduce and maintain a minimum viable population. Successful establishment in non-native habitat depends upon a complex of factors, including primarily the size of introduction, the level of competition (predation, diseases, etc.), and habitat suitability. However, these conditions are not always necessary for successful exotic establishment. Past invasions of exotic insects illustrate the ability of exotics to change feeding habits in response to available sources and hosts. For example, in British Columbia a wood-boring beetle from the subtropics has adapted to feeding on local tree species (Humble et al. 1998).

Spread refers to the expansion of an established exotic into adjacent areas. The majority of introduced species never become established and, among those that do establish, only a few become pests with significant impacts (OTA 1993).

Williamson (1996) discusses a "rule of ten" for the introduction, establishment and spread of exotic plant arrivals—one in 10 imported plants "escapes" and becomes introduced in the wild, one in 10 of those establishes, and one in 10 of those spreads and becomes a pest. Thus, an estimated one in a thousand exotic plant arrivals becomes a pest. However, the data for plants supports using a range between one in 5 and one in 20, depending on the type of plant (Williamson and Filler 1996). It appears, however, that the probability of other (i.e., non-plant) species becoming pests may deviate significantly from the rule of ten (Williamson 1996). The task in the study of bio-invasions is to estimate potential introductions and the chance of development into a pest.

Pests are usually classified into insects, pathogens and plants. Examples of introduced organisms can be found in every sector of human activity from agriculture and forestry to human health. Not all introductions are pests: about 90 percent of North American food and feed production is based on introduced species. Those exotics that cause the most damage are accidentally introduced insects and pathogens, but introduced plants can also be destructive, competing with native vegetation for space, nutrients and water. We provide examples of forest pests that have had devastating impacts on the regions they invaded.

The gypsy moth (*Lymantria dispar*) is an example of an intentionally introduced insect that escaped to became one of North America's major pests. At the peak of its outbreak in 1981, the gypsy moth defoliated more than 6 million hectares of forestland in the eastern USA.

A forest disease, chestnut blight, changed the species mix in North American forests. Chestnut blight is caused by the fungus *Cryphonectria parasitica*, which is of Asian origin, and was first detected in New York City in 1904. By 1950, nearly all American chestnuts over a region of about 81 million ha had been destroyed by chestnut blight (Liebhold *et al.* 1995). Dutch elm disease is caused by the fungus *Ophiostoma ulmi* and was introduced into North America in 1930; it is rapidly altering the urban forest.

Invasions of exotic plants are a major problem in subtropical North America. The tree species *Melaleuca quinquenervia*, native to Australia, was introduced into North America in 1906 as an ornamental plant. Since its establishment, *Malaleuca* has invaded the Florida Everglades, seriously altering the fresh water hydrology of South Florida, increasing the fire hazard, and impacting tourism and outdoor recreation values (Liebhold *et al.* 1995). The ecological impact of the *Melaleuca* invasion includes the replacement of saw grass marshes, sloughs, and forests with maleluca monocultures (Bright 1998; OTA 1993).

Scotch Broom (*Cytisus scoparius*), native to southern Europe and northern Africa, arrived in the USA as an ornamental. Broom is now widespread in the US Pacific Northwest, invading and displacing native grasslands, pastures and parklands. The competitive advantage of broom has produced considerable additional stress on the Garry Oak-Arbutus ecosystem of south coastal British Columbia.

While most bio-invasions are the result of accidental introductions, many non-indigenous species were intentionally moved from their native habitat. Of 235 invasive woody plants in North America, 85% were introduced for ornamental and landscape purposes (White 1997). Other introductions were to reduce soil erosion or support wildlife populations (Wallner 1997). Kudzu (*Pueraria lobata*), for example, was introduced into the USA in 1876 as a forage crop and an ornamental plant. Subsequently, it was classified as a weed and removed from the list of USDA permissible plants in 1953.

Deliberate introduction of exotics is not restricted to plants. Many animals and fish have been introduced as pets or to fight native pests, only later to become significant pests themselves. European rabbits introduced with settlers into Australia became a plague until another exotic, a Brazilian rabbit virus, stopped their spread in the 1950s (Bright 1998).

Understanding and predicting pathways for exotic organism introductions is necessary in order to reduce the rate of potential invasions. One proven pathway for the entry of exotics is through (increased) trade in animal and plant material for agriculture. Trade in such products includes the potential introduction of both exotic plant species and their associated insect and pathogenic pests. Imports of logs and unprocessed wood products also constitute a major pathway for the entry of forest pests (USDA 1991; 1998a).

Pathways for the introduction of exotics are facilitated by new modes of transportation. The survival rate of exotic hitchhikers is much higher than previously because of the speed by which organisms arrive at new locations and find a suitable host. The cargo compartments of airplanes are highly susceptible to invasion by moths and beetles, and these are not always controllable by routine spraying. The rise in container shipments has increased the risk of bio-invasions because many containers provide an excellent pathway for soil borne pathogens, insect larvae and even snakes.

International Trade and Bio-invasions

Increased world trade is a significant factor in the current acceleration in bio-invasions. Trade patterns help explain trends in the introduction of exotic organisms. The emergence of new trading entrants has served to produce a relatively new array of possible exotic bio-invaders. Although movement of organisms between the Euro-Asian and American continents occurs in both directions, higher rates of establishment of Euro-Asian species in North America than in the opposite direction have been observed (Niemela and Mattson 1996).

Major factors contributing to increased global trade include large reductions in transportation and communication costs, trade liberalisation and globalisation of trade institutions. New regional and global trade agreements have been a catalyst for increased trade. Societal changes in the countries of Eastern and Central Europe, along with the opening of China in the late 1970s, have created new markets around the world. The record economic expansion in the world's largest importer (the USA) and booming trade in high-tech products have reinforced the growth in global trade. The trend in world trade is depicted in Figure 6.1 (World Trade Organisation 1998).

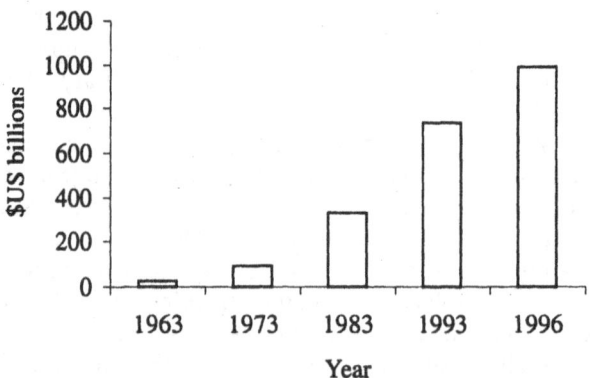

Figure 6.1: Growing World Trade, 1963-1996

Unlike accurate data on world trade, total numbers of both native and exotic species are unknown and estimates vary substantially across studies. The OTA (1993) estimates that the total number of introduced species in the USA exceeds 4,542 (Table 6.1), but this does not distinguish between beneficial and harmful species. The OTA (1993) estimates that 15% of all exotics in the USA cause significant harm to human health or industry, or to agriculture, forestry and protection of natural areas.

Table 6.1: Estimated Numbers of Exotic Species in the United States

Category	Number	Percentage of total species in the USA in category
Plants	>2000	–
Terrestrial vertebrates	142	6%
Insects and arachnids	>2000	2%
Fish	70	8%
Mollusks (non-marine)	91	4%
Plant pathogens	239	–
Total	**>4,542**	

Pimentel et al. (1999) estimate that as many as 50,000 exotics may have invaded the USA. The range in estimates about exotics results from at least three factors. First, there is a difference in the terminology employed by various researchers. Second, the high costs of resources involved in gathering information on bio-invasions makes it impossible to obtain reliable estimates. Finally, the entry of new organisms and the prolonged dormancy of some exotics makes information updating difficult.

Because of the high uncertainty associated with every stage of potential invasion by non-native organisms, making a distinction between introduced and established species is crucial. Further, in accounting for the number of exotics, one needs to consider the sectors that are impacted. Analysis of the impacts of exotics has traditionally focussed on agriculture and forestry, but many introduced pathogens have had great impacts on human health (e.g., AIDS, influenza) and have led to high costs in health care, prevention and research. While the focus of measurement and monitoring is generally on exotics related to the primary sectors, inclusion of all exotics would lead to significant differences in estimates. A meaningful response is to improve international cooperation in the study and monitoring of the movement of exotic organisms, and the development of an international database, similar to that available for trade.

Even more important than accurate numbers of introductions are the rising rates of introduction, especially in the last decades. Data on introductions can be found for specific categories in a particular region; for example, Sailer (1983) reports introductions of insects into the USA over the period 1640-1980, while Bright (1998, p.144) provides information on imports of woody plant species into Central Europe for 1500-1916. Though many authors point to a relation between increasing trade and bio-invasions, comparing these trends and establishing cause and effect is not easy. Factors that make it difficult to establish a relationship between trade and bio-invasions include: 1) estimates of introductions are species and region specific, and often do not include bigger animal species, plants and pathogens; 2) different time horizons; and 3) missing and non-accurate data on introduced species.

Insights from imports and introductions of exotic forest pests into Canada are illustrative. Twenty-nine forest insect species are known to have entered Canada between 1882 and 1989 (Montreal Process Liaison Office, hereafter MPLO, 1997). In addition, pine shoot beetle (*Tomicus piniperda*) was introduced in 1993 on Christmas trees imported from Ohio. About ten forest diseases were introduced in the same period, most after first establishing in the USA (MPLO 1997).

Recent introductions and establishment of exotic bark and wood-boring beetles in British Columbia are particularly alarming because of changing patterns and rates of arrival. Nineteen species of bark and wood boring beetles are known to have been introduced in western Canada after 1992, with six now established and attacking BC's forests (Humble et al. 1998). Approximately 87% of all ambrosia beetles (*Scolytidae*) known to occur in BC are non-indigenous.

One of the known sources of entry of exotic wood boring beetles is through wood package material used for shipment of heavy commodities, such as granite and wires from China and granite from Europe and South America (Allen 1999). Pests introduced in untreated shipping packaging and dunnage find their way to forests close to the port of entry or in-land where the transport containers are opened.

Canada ranks eighth in the world with US$201.0 billion of imports in 1998. The growing trend of imports into Canada is depicted in Figure 6.2—the USA, Asia and Europe are the largest sources of Canadian imports. Akin to other regional trading agreements, the North American Free Trade Agreement (NAFTA) promotes trade flows among Canada, the USA and Mexico. The volume of Canada-US trade, the nature of this trade and the openness of the border for business and tourist travel provide ample opportunities for the transmission of exotics that establish in one of the trading partners. The integration of many North American ecosystems makes the trading partners particularly vulnerable to exotic establishment in either jurisdiction.

More detailed research is needed to establish a definitive link between trade growth and exotic introductions. It is likely that it is not the sheer volume of trade that accounts for increases in bio-invasions, but rather such things as the region of origin, packaging material, and effort devoted to monitoring and prevention.

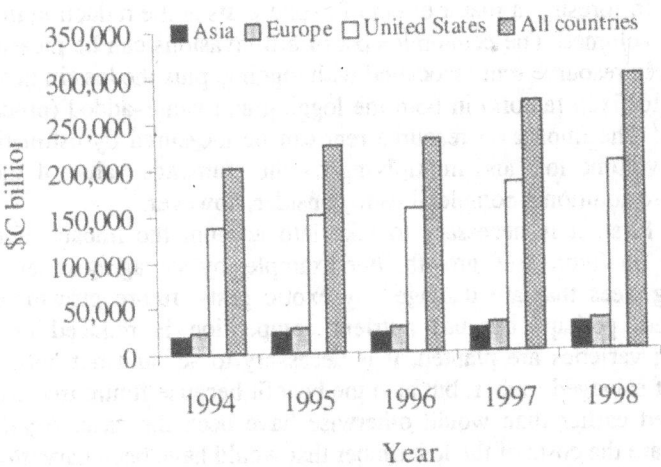

Figure 6.2: Value of Canadian Imports, 1994-1998

Economic Costs of Bio-invasions

There is a growing need among policy makers, regulatory agencies and the scientific community for estimates of the economic losses associated with exotic invasions. This need has motivated a number of studies on economic impacts of bio-invasions. Recent studies include OTA (1993) and Pimentel et al. (1999), although these studies come up with disparate estimates of economic costs. Some estimates of economic costs are not based on economic theory and, as a result, may double count costs or inadequately balance costs against benefits. In this section, we provide some guidance as to the appropriate measurement of the economic costs of bio-invasions. We first discuss economic aspects more generally and then provide some estimates of the costs of bio-invasions, focusing particularly on forestry.

Theoretical Aspects

Exotic pests affect economic rents in forestry, agriculture and the fishery, and have an adverse impact on human health and ecosystems more generally. Each sector has its own specific points of vulnerability to attacks from exotics, and we consider each sector in turn.

In forestry, a major effect of exotic pests is the reduction in timber harvest volumes. The economic cost of bio-invasions can be measured by the loss in resource rent associated with logging, plus the loss in quasi–rent (return to fixed factors) in both the logging and value–added (processing) sectors.[2] The impact on resource rent can be measured by estimating the timber volume lost and multiplying by the stumpage value of the logs. There are additional complexities to consider, however.

First, it is necessary to take into account the impact of current damage on future tree growth. For example, by salvaging older, slower growing trees that are damaged by exotic pests, future growth is often enhanced, perhaps because nutrient competition is reduced or faster-growing varieties are planted. It is necessary to account not only for the value of salvaged timber, but also the benefit because future tree crops are harvested earlier than would otherwise have been the case. Against this benefit are the costs of the lost timber that would have been harvested at its "usual" time, including the benefits from "normal" future harvests.

Second, as noted in the preceding paragraph, estimating timber losses due to pests is difficult. The problem is even more complicated because of variations in survey methods, the need to measure the intensity of damage caused by individual pests, sorting out interaction effects among different pests (including between exotic and indigenous pests), and so on.

Finally, if timber harvest levels are regulated, as is the case in many jurisdictions including Canada, it is necessary to determine whether damage from pests has a real effect harvest volume. In the absence of any impact on harvest volume the economic costs may be small and confined to the costs of salvaging and regenerating the site, if necessary.

Impacts on jobs and community stability are often cited as potential "economic" costs of exotic pest damage, but this is misleading. Employment as such does not constitute an economic benefit or cost, but is rather an impact. Suppose forestry sector wages are strengthened as a result of the ability of organised labour to capture a larger share of the resource rents. Any displaced labour due to a reduced harvest would, allowing that the economy was operating at full employment, obtain employment in other sectors, albeit at a lower wage. While the costs of seeking new employment are an appropriate economic cost, the reduction in earnings is an income transfer and not an economic loss.

The costs of preventing and monitoring pest outbreaks in forestry, including inspection and quarantine, can also be considered a cost associated with bio-invasions. Efficient funding allocation requires that expenditures on monitoring and prevention be balanced against expected benefits. In an optimal allocation, society would spend at the margin an amount on monitoring and prevention that equals the expected marginal value of the timber loss prevented.

Agriculture is quite consistent with forestry, except that in agriculture the cropping cycle is annual rather than 20 or more years.[3] However, the potential damage from an exotic pest in a given year can be much greater than in agriculture, while spill-overs into subsequent years are less likely. Agriculture does illustrate the care required in estimating the costs of exotic pests. Pimentel *et al.* (1999), for example, estimate the damage to crops caused by exotic pests that were introduced along with the exotic crops for which the damage is calculated. The calculation could be improved by considering the introduction of the crop and its associated pest as a single event rather than as separate events.

Suppose exotic crop X is introduced to replace indigenous crop Z, but with X comes pest y; assume the pest does not affect any other crops or any other sector. If the benefits from growing X, net of any y damage, exceed the benefits from growing Z, then society is better off by introducing exotic crop X.

Economic effects on human health can be calculated once the relationship between the exotic pest and health has been established. For example, various strains of influenza have affected people's health and directly contributed to the death of some victims. The economic damage is determined as the sum of the days of work lost multiplied by the average daily wage (value of the lost work), plus the number of deaths multiplied by the value of a (statistical) life. In addition, expenditures on cures and the dis-utility associated with being ill (perhaps measured using a contingent valuation device) should be included on the cost side. Again, the marginal cost to prevent outbreaks (including monitoring and flu shots) should equal the expected benefits of these actions. Economic factors to allocation are often tempered with the reality of humanity and public institutions.

The economic damages of bio-invasions on ecosystems more generally are measured not only by lost values associated with commodities traded in markets (wood products, agricultural output), but also by the nonmarket damages associated with loss of environmental amenities. Bio-invasions may reduce populations of wildlife, hunting or fishing success, viewing opportunities and biodiversity more generally. Exotic pests cause defoliation of trees that reduces scenic amenities; they change ecosystems so that they function less effectively. All of these changes can be valued, albeit with methodological limitations, using a variety of nonmarket techniques, such as hedonic pricing, the travel cost method and contingent valuation method (see van Kooten and Bulte 2000).

Lost tourism revenues are frequently cited as a major cost of bio-invasions that affect ecosystems and, to the degree that the reduced revenues exceed the costs of providing the tourism services these reductions constitute an economic cost (see van Kooten 1995, 1999). The actual loss in economic surplus (lost benefit) to the economy from changes in tourism caused by exotics may be small, but tourism can generate substantial employment and economic impacts (particularly at a regional level). The consumer surplus accruing to tourists may be substantial, although these may accrue to non-residents. Such surpluses consist of nonmarket benefits associated with outdoor recreation, scenic amenities, option value, and so on. The loss and distribution of these surpluses need to be considered in estimating the cost of bio-invasions.

Currently there is no study that systematically includes the nonmarket impacts of exotic pests. Measurement of these costs poses a challenge for economists and likely requires significant input from biological scientists.

Some Estimates of the Economic Damages from Forest Pests

Here we present the results of some analyses of the economic consequences of different forest pests that have invaded the USA and Canada. As noted above, not all studies distinguish between economic costs (and benefits) as surpluses and other economic, social and ecological impacts. In the forest sector, information is generally available on timber or forest product losses, and/or the costs of control measures. Thus, the available data might understate the total economic cost of bio-invasions.

Estimates of timber losses are usually done for each pest individually and then added up to obtain the total loss due to pest attacks. This approach may result in serious estimation errors. For example, timber losses are the results of tree mortality and/or growth loss. Some insects and diseases cause tree mortality, while others cause defoliation that does not kill trees immediately, but does decrease productivity. A strict comparison of economic losses between areas affected by major defoliators is not possible. The extent of growth loss varies with damage intensity, weather and site conditions, tree age and general forest health. Tree mortality due to defoliation depends on the number of successive years of defoliation, as well as on the type of pest, the tree species, site quality and environmental disturbances (including from logging) in the region. If estimated losses are summed over each pest group, it may overstate total timber losses and associated economic costs since the impacts of simultaneous attacks of different pests on the tree may overlap. On the other hand, simultaneous or sequential attacks by various pests may weaken the tree and increase the rate of growth loss and mortality, resulting in an underestimate of the total losses due to a particular pest (USDA 1991; Hall and Moody 1994; NFDP 1999).

We present case studies of a few exotic forest pests for which data on economic damages are available. Each pest is presented separately in order to provide a flavour for the significance of the problem and the order of magnitude of economic costs.

Because of available historical information, the gypsy moth is often used in literature as a template for estimating economic consequences of forest pest invasions (Wallner 1996, 1999). An amateur entomologist imported the gypsy moth to Massachusetts from France. In 1869, a number of the imported gypsy moths escaped and started slowly building up numbers. Twenty years later, its population boomed and gypsy moth now occurs in most hardwoods of eastern North America with isolated infestations on the west and south of the United States. Gypsy moth prefers all types of oak, but as caterpillar numbers increase it attacks many other hardwood species as well (Nealis and Erb 1993). Its first outbreak in Canada occurred in 1969, a 100-year lag after its introduction to North America. In 1991, the gypsy moth defoliated 347,415 hectares of hardwood forests in Ontario. Within less than twenty years of its establishment in Canada, it became one of the most widespread among native and non-native pests of Canada's forests.

Timber losses reported in Table 6.2 are due to the European strain of the insect. The Asian strain, despite numerous introductions, has not established in North America, so only control costs are incurred at this time.

Table 6.2: Costs of the Gypsy Moth Invasion, United States and Canada

REGION	Period	Area infested (mil ha)	Timber losses[a] ($ mil)	Control costs[a] ($ mil)	Source
European Gypsy Moth (*Lymantria dispar*)					
Pennsylvania	1981	>6	>72	>9	Wallner 1996
Pennsylvania	1969-88	–	219	–	Gottschalk 1990
USA	1980-94			11[b]	Pimentel 1999
				30[b]	Wallner 1996
USA	1995			8[c]	Wallner 1996
Canada	1982-92	0.553[d]	–	–	Hall &Moody 1994
Asian Gypsy Moth (*Lymantria dispar*)					
Pacific NW	1993			25	Wallner 1996
N & S Carolina	1994-95			9	Wallner 1996

[a] Losses and costs in $US. Control costs include research, eradication and suppression costs.
[b] Average annual costs of eradication, suppression and research in the USA. Wallner's (1996) estimate is expressed in 1995 dollars.
[c] This number refers to the costs for traps at an estimate of US$20 per trap (for both European and Asian gypsy moths).
[d] Quebec and Ontario are the only provinces where gypsy moth established, with some isolated spots in the Maritimes. Value refers to cumulative area infested.

As a defoliator the gypsy moth mainly slows timber growth, although successive defoliation does result in tree mortality. Its major impacts are in the area of recreation, aesthetic values, human health (allergies) and nuisance effects, but the costs of these impacts have not been considered in the studies cited. Thus, the numbers reported in Table 6.2 underestimate the true costs.

Dutch elm disease is another forest pest whose impacts are well known. Dutch elm disease, caused by the fungus *Ophiostoma ulmi*, also known as *Ceratocystis ulmi*, was introduced into the USA in 1930 from Europe, presumably from Holland. Its vector, the European elm bark beetle, spread the disease rapidly across the country. About 46 million out of 70 million elm trees have been killed since the introduction of the disease (Wallner 1996) with an estimated value of US$430 per tree (USDA 1991), or total losses of more than US$20 billion (in 1991 dollars). Additional millions were spent removing dead trees (US$215 per tree), replacing them ($40-100) and protecting surviving elms.[4] In 1945 Dutch elm disease was introduced into Quebec from the USA. In one year, it killed 600,000 elms in Quebec, and has killed about 80% of the 35,000 elm trees in Toronto (Hubbes 1999).

There are now about 700,000 elm trees in Canada and their value exceeds $C2.5 billion (Hubbes 1999). The losses of elms in Winnipeg due to Dutch elm disease went from 2.5% per year in 1975 to near 5% in 1996 despite mitigation efforts (Westwood 1991; Hubbes 1999). It costs $200 per tree to save elms in Winnipeg, with a success rate of some 70%. Results are summarised in Table 6.3.

Table 6.3: Impacts of the Dutch Elm Disease in the USA and Canada

REGION	Period	Trees killed ('000s)	Timber losses ($US bil)	Control costs[a] (billions)	Source
USA	1930-76	46,000	20.20	$US 11.73 – 14.49	Wallner 1996
Quebec	1945	600			Hubbes 1999
Toronto	–	28			
Manitoba	1975-96	2.5–5%[b]	–	$C 0.015[b]	Westwood 1991

[a] Control costs include research, eradication, suppression cost and replacement cost of lost trees.
[b] Annual

A new form of Dutch elm disease hit Southern England in the late 1960s and killed about 17 million out of 23 million elms by the 1980s (Hubbes 1999). This new form, caused by a different fungus, is believed to have been introduced into England on logs imported from Canada.

The pine wood nematode (*Bursaphelenchus xylophilus*), which is a native of North America, has resulted in dramatic forest losses in Japan's red pine forests. This organism has been a subject of great interest and controversy. By a complex and not completely explained mechanism, it causes pine wilt disease. The pine wood nematode was introduced into Japan on logs from North America in the early 1900s. Until 1984, it infested some 25% of Japan's forested area of 26 million ha, with timber losses as high as 2.4 million m³ in the worst years. After suppression efforts in recent years, the disease still causes annual timber losses of over one million cubic meters (McNamara and Smith 1993).

After 1984 when pine wood nematodes were found in wood shipments from North America, European countries introduced various import restrictions. In 1988, the European and Mediterranean Plan Protection Organisation (EPPO) designated the pine wood nematode and its vectors as a high-risk quarantine pest. This decision constituted a non-tariff barrier to international trade and contributed to reduced coniferous wood exports from North America to Europe (Berghdal 1988), causing exporters to use drying kilns to kill the pest. The trade restriction also led to international disputes within the General Agreement on Tariffs and Trade (GATT) (McNamara and Smith 1993).

Estimates of the economic losses presented above are based on historic data. They likely underestimate true economic costs, because data are missing and not all sources of costs are included. There is a fear that the economic losses due to potential future bio-invasions might be more severe than those of the past. These concerns initiated several recent risk analysis studies on exotic species introductions.

The US Department of Agriculture (USDA 1991, 1998a) undertook several risk analyses of imports into the USA of raw wood from several sources—Russian Far East, New Zealand, Chile and Mexico. The results of these analyses suggest the substantial potential impacts of exotic species that inhabit raw logs unless they are further treated to eliminate unwanted visitors. For example, estimates of the potential financial effects on commercial timber stands in the western USA of imports of larch from Siberia over the period 1990-2040 are provided in Table 6.4. Not included in these estimates are the control costs associated with local eradication of pest introductions or establishments and general suppression. Economic costs related to loss of recreational and tourism benefits, and other nonmarket amenity values, are also not included (see USDA 1991 for details).

Table 6.4: Projected Timber Losses from Forest Pests due to Imported Logs from Siberia and Russian Far East, 1990-2040

Pest	Affected Area (mil ha)	Total economic costs ($US mil 1990)	
		Best case	Worst Case
Nematodes	10.8	33.35	1,670.00
Larch canker	0.3	24.90	240.60
Annosus root disease	3.9	84.20	343.90
Defoliators	31.2	35,049.00	58,410.00
Spruce bark beetle	3.3	201.00	1,500.00

Environmental and Ecological Impacts

Forests continually adapt to natural disturbances and pests are a major natural disturbance of forests. Concerns arise about the ability of forest ecosystems to adapt to the rate, character and magnitude of disturbances caused by human activities, and how such disturbance impacts on the ability of forest ecosystems to adapt to exotic bio-invasions. Along with their large economic effects, some exotic pests have had dramatic ecological effects in forest ecosystems in terms of species mix, habitat, hydology, ecosystem dynamics, loss of biodiversity and, in the most extreme cases, complete loss of particular species (Filip and Morrell 1996).

Insects and pathogens are a normal part of a forest ecosystem including when their population numbers increase during outbreaks or remain high over a prolonged period. In such cases, insects and pathogens are destructive to current ecosystems. Exotics can significantly disrupt the ecosystem balance. There are several explanations why exotics are relatively more disruptive than native species and why this gap is increasing (Haack and Byler 1993; Liebhold et al. 1995; Niemela and Mattson 1996). First, exotic species operate in new ecological conditions where there are no natural enemies and indigenous tree species lack established defences. Consequently, there are no natural mechanisms to limit the spread of the exotic pest. Second, environmental stress associated with human activities has made many forest ecosystems more vulnerable to both native and exotic pests, although successful invasions of undisturbed systems are also common. Anthropogenic stresses include human population growth, air pollution, climate change, habitat modification, and ecosystem fragmentation due to land management. Ecosystems with low diversity are more susceptible to bio-invasions. For instance, exotic (and native) insects and disease often successfully attack monoculture plantations.[5] This risk holds true for both agricultural crops (Ireland's potato blight, USA's cotton weevil) and forest plantations (e.g., Bright 1998 concerning Monterey pine). Finally, increasing rates of international travel and trade make the incidence of accidental and/or purposeful introductions of non-native organisms more likely.

The environmental and ecological impacts of potential pest introductions are difficult to assess because of the variety and complexity of ecosystems they attack. Potential ecological impacts also vary with the introduced pest. However, a selection of general concepts can be applied (USDA 1991) to forest ecosystems based on (a) the proportion of the total host cover in the ecosystem; (b) the role of the host in the ecosystem; (c) adaptability, aggressiveness and spread of potentially introduced pests; and (d) the effects of introduced species on biodiversity. The potential effects on biodiversity include (i) suppression of native species and replacement by introduced species; (ii) local elimination of native species; and (iii) a threat to rare and endangered species in direct and indirect ways (Perrings 1995). The concepts can be applied to agriculture, aquaculture and other sectors.

If the risk of the exotic pest spreading is high, then large-scale infestation and tree mortality are more likely to occur. Ecological impacts of large-scale infestations include short- and long-term impacts. Long-term impacts are more important from an ecological perspective and depend on how quickly and completely the system recovers. Depletion of forests may influence changes in food and habitat supply for wildlife species, flora and fauna diversity, ecosystem hydrology, forest fire regimes and nutrient cycles.

Managing Bio-invasions

Potential devastating impacts of exotic pest invasions call for systematic and careful decision making and policy (Norton and Mumford 1993). The common feature of a bio-invasion is uncertainty, whose magnitude varies with the three stages of introduction, establishment and spread. While the introduction and establishment of exotics have not usually been observed (except for rare cases), the spread of many exotics is well documented. Mathematical models of spread have been developed and have produced some success in predicting rates for the spread of exotics (Hengeveld 1989; Liebhold et al. 1995).

Clearly, it is necessary to study in greater detail the links among the introduction, establishment and spread of non-indigenous species. Unfortunately, it is generally not possible to determine the probability that an exotic pest invasion will lead to harmful effects. Likewise, it is difficult to predict the *ex ante* costs of damage from an exotic pest. This implies a need for careful study of the pathways of introductions. It is these pathways which have changed so greatly in the last few decades as a result of globalisation of trade and travel and developments in the field of transportation.

Given the inherent limitations to assessing the risks of introduction, establishment and spread, the realities of globalisation, and the increasing limitations on available options to control/eradicate exotic pests, the focus must be on reducing or preventing exotic pest introductions. We classify measures against exotic pests according to their relationship to the three stages of bio-invasion. The purpose of risk assessment is to identify all potential sources of risk and uncertainty (i.e., known as well as unknown "risks"), to identify all potential impacts, not only those previously identified, and to evaluate these impacts. Highlighting the risks and their impacts allows for the development of measures to prevent losses or actions to reduce the losses. The value of pest risk assessment lies in the quality and comprehensiveness of the biological and ecological information on target pest species and their economic significance. Obtaining necessary data is expensive and time-consuming.[6]

Summary information about potential policy measures, and their accompanying possible success and costs, is provided in Table 6.5. Qualitative estimates of uncertainty/risk associated with each stage of bio-invasion are typical for pest risk analysis (Orr et al. 1993).

Table 6.5: Classification of Measures to Prevent Bio-invasions

Stage	Level of uncertainty or risk	Measure against bio-invasion	Success	Costs
Introduction	VH uncertainty	Prevention	relatively H	relatively L
Establishment	H uncertainty	Eradication	M	M
Spread	H risk	Suppression, control	L	H

VH–Very High, H–High, M–Moderate, L–Low

Policy for dealing with bio-invasions must be general in order to be applicable to different sectors. International agreements that regulate the movement of species are one approach to addressing bio-invasions. Bright (1998), for example, lists 23 global or regional agreements that refer to exotics, but they are limited in scope when it comes to practical application. The most applicable international agreement is the International Plant Protection Convention (IPPC), which is focused on phytosanitary conditions to protect against agriculture pests. The IPPC has serious limitations as a template, including a lack of implementation funds, disparate national commitment, and an application limited to commercial crops. There is no similar international effort to protect fauna or non-commercial plants. Another potential template is the 1973 Convention on International Trade in Endangered Species of Wild Fauna and Flora (CITES) which focuses on the international movement of rare plants and animals. However, CITES focuses on specified species and with bio-invasions one problem is identifying which species to target. CITES has also proven vulnerable to strategic behaviour in exporting countries and lacking in enforcement options.

In addition to treaties, there are other international vehicles that attempt to regulate the movement of organisms. These consist of various sector-specific codes that regulate activity in, for example, fishing, forestry and agriculture.

At one time, bio-invasions were rare but they have become frequent due to trade liberalisation and global movement of people. Globalisation has introduced new trading players and reduced border controls, thus both broadening the supply of exotics but also increasing the chance that exotic pests cross international and biogeoclimatic boundaries. Bio-invasions are an inherent risk of the increased benefits of trade and globalisation. Promising courses of action include international agreements, perhaps within the World Trade Organisation. Efforts to restrict the untreated movement of goods and people from high risk zones through border controls and inspections, standard prescriptions on packaging materials (e.g., treated wooden crates and dunnage), and preventative spraying of containers and aircraft can all serve to reduce the transmission of exotic pests. While some of these measures are acceptable, others are likely to be resisted because of the costs they could impose. There is a need for public education about exotic invaders and international information on exotics that is regularly updated and readily accessible. In the end, the most effective and efficient option is likely going to be prevention at the point of introduction.

Notes

1. This chapter was drawn from a larger project on exotic species supported by the Science Branch and Socio-economic Research Network of the Canadian Forest Service.
2. See van Kooten (1999) and van Kooten and Bulte (2000) for a discussion and application of these concepts in the context of forestry.
3. The same comments apply to the fishery, except that dynamic considerations again come into play.
4. These costs ($255–315 per tree) are an alternative estimate of the costs of lost elms and cannot be added to the (essentially) nonmarket values lost due to destroyed elms. Rather, these costs are an alternative measure, constituting an estimate of averting expenditures.
5. For a discussion of the major softwood plantation jurisdictions see Wilson et al. (1998) and for a review on recent trends in plantation management see Hogan and Wilson (1999).
6. Wallner (1999) reports recent USDA pest assessment studies on raw wood imports into the USA ranged from US$28,000 (New Zealand logs) to US$500,000 (Siberian logs). The latter study invested in developing a methodology for pest risk assessment (USDA 1991).

7 Economic Perspectives on Preservation of Biodiversity
R. DAVID SIMPSON

There is an old saying that "economists know the price of everything and the value of nothing." While I can understand how people from other disciplines could reach this conclusion, I think it's generally inaccurate. Economists typically do not care how many dollars and cents we are willing to part with for something, except inasmuch as dollars and cents provide us with a useful shorthand for discussing more meaningful tradeoffs. In fact, a point often emphasised in introductory economics courses is that monetary amounts are simply units of account, with no absolute significance. Monetary amounts reflected in prices are meaningful only to the extent that they reflect the relative importance attached to one thing compared to another.

This is the most important thing to understand about economic analysis: all decisions are made in relative terms. I may prefer preserving natural habitat to clearing more land for crops, I may have the opposite preferences, or I may be indifferent between the two. Inasmuch as these possibilities are exhaustive, this may not seem an objectionable statement. Its implication is important, however. There is no room for competing absolutes. One cannot say, "it is imperative both to save biodiversity and to feed the world's poor" if these objectives are in conflict. We could argue long and hard about whether or not these objectives are in conflict, or if both objectives could not be achieved if only some other (presumably less deserving) group could be compelled to make greater sacrifices. While this issue is not considered further here, it should be noted that it would be disingenuous to suppose that biodiversity can be preserved without creating some "losers."

Two issues are important in determining who should be made "winners" and who "losers" by decisions to preserve or destroy biodiversity. These issues arise in most economic decisions, and are referred to as matters of equity and efficiency.

(1) The first important issue with respect to equity is that we should be concerned if we feel the "losers" to be more morally deserving than the "winners," or saying almost the same thing, if equally deserving groups receive very different treatment. There are two ways in which decisions regarding biodiversity preservation threaten equity, and these considerations go in opposite directions. The first is that the costs of biodiversity preservation are borne disproportionately by the poor, and some, at least, of the benefits would appear to accrue disproportionately to the rich. A great deal of natural habitat has already been destroyed in the developed industrial countries. Denying poor countries the opportunity to destroy their biodiversity is seen in some quarters as denying them the opportunity to enhance their standard of living. In addition, biological diversity (as measured by numbers of species, at least) tends to be greater in low- than in high-latitude countries, and the former tend to be poorer than the latter. Thus, preserving biodiversity will call for greater sacrifices in terms of foregone development in poorer countries.

A further equity concern involves obligations to posterity. Fundamental notions of fairness suggest that one generation should not be denied opportunities available to another. Thus, while we do not know whether or not our great-grandchildren will appreciate whales and pandas as much as we do, we may feel duty bound to preserve these species for them (and they may feel duty bound to do the same, *ad infinitum*).

(2) The second important issue in thinking about the "winners" and "losers" from biodiversity preservation involves efficiency. Economists use the word efficiency in a very specific way: an outcome is efficient if no one can be made better off without making someone else worse off. Note that this formulation is neutral with respect to the attributes of winners and losers, in contrast to what was said about equity. A situation may be economically "efficient" even though a small sacrifice made by the wealthiest would result in tremendous benefits to the poor. Despite this shortcoming of "efficiency" as a guide to policy, it still seems reasonable to require that final outcomes, in contrast, perhaps, to initial allocations, be efficient. We would not want to settle for an outcome in which someone can be made better off without hurting anyone else.

Efficiency is an important concept in economics largely because one can rigorously establish sufficient conditions for its achievement. Without going into great detail, a market economy is efficient if property rights are well defined, transactions are voluntary, and no participant in a market is powerful enough to dominate it. Consider on the first of these conditions in thinking about what economics has to say about biodiversity. To say that property rights are well defined simply means that it is clear who owns what. This is typically not the case with biodiversity. We may think that each and every one of us has the right to enjoy, for example, the continued existence of endangered species such as spotted owls or giant pandas. In other words, we may feel that we all "own" these species, in the sense that they should not be eradicated without our consent. Yet the legal ownership of the habitat that supports these and other endangered species is often held by private parties. These owners of the habitat can impose an *externality* on the rest of us by managing their lands for their own benefit while reducing our benefits from biodiversity.

A great deal of emphasis is put on the internalisation of these externalities in the literature on the economics of biodiversity. The idea is that, if the landowner is required to compensate the rest of us for the costs she imposes on us by degrading the habitat she controls and consequently reducing biodiversity, she will then have an incentive not to degrade the habitat. A couple of things are worth noting here. The first is that economists do not typically recommend that "bad" activities be curtailed altogether. Virtually any reasonable person would agree that the extinction of species is a bad thing. Yet most people would also say that there are limits to the steps they would take to save endangered species (see Pezzey 1997). Few of us are saintly or fanatical enough to starve ourselves in order to save endangered species. Yet an extreme commitment to biodiversity preservation would necessarily require a much lower human population. Thus, internalising externalities typically involves a balance between the "bad" associated with biodiversity loss and the "bad" associated with reduced production of food, fibre, housing, industry, recreation and so on.

The second thing to note is that it can be extraordinarily difficult to define this balance. Consider my decision to spend $1.49 on a loaf of bread. I know how much money I have, what other things I need or want to buy, and I have a pretty good idea as to how much enjoyment I will get from the peanut butter and jelly sandwiches I make from the bread. The grocer who sells the bread, the baker who produces it, and the farmers who provide its ingredients all have pretty clear ideas as to their costs of providing their goods, and what they can do with the revenues their products generate.

I do not experience any deep philosophical turmoil as I wrestle with the decision of whether to buy bread, but perhaps I should. Maybe the grocer, the baker and the farmers should be searching their souls as well. The farmer may have cleared land, destroying natural habitat in the process, in order to plant more wheat. He may have used toxic chemicals that run off into the local water supply, poisoning fish, or fertiliser that may cause eutrophication. Unlike the private satisfactions I get from eating bread, or its producers and sellers get from their profits, we have very little idea as to how we might quantify the regrettable side effects of bread production. Theory tells us we should "internalise the externalities" in order to preserve biodiversity, but the theory we have reviewed thus far gives us few clues as to exactly how much we should change the price of a loaf of bread to accomplish this objective.

Economic Valuation

What is biodiversity worth? What is its value? Recall that economic value is determined by relative considerations. It is important to be clear about vocabulary here. The term "value" is used in a very different sense in economics than in philosophy or psychology. In those disciplines, or in common usage, one might think of a person's "values" as the bedrock moral absolutes underlying behavior (interestingly, economists group such concepts under the rubric of "preferences," a term that may seem inappropriately casual for deeply held feelings). To an economist, value can only be expressed in relative terms. The value of one thing is always phrased in terms of how many units of another a person would be willing to give up for it. Now it's true that economists often discuss values in terms of monetary units (prices), but to say that the value of an apple is fifty cents and that of an orange a dollar is just another way of saying that one orange is worth two apples.

The notion of relative values applies more broadly than to just questions of how-much-is-this-worth-relative-to-that. The context might be more appropriately phrased as how-much-is-this-worth-relative-to-that-under-these-circumstances.

These circumstances might include a number of temporal and spatial factors, but the most important consideration is how much of the various goods and services in question we already have. One of the most important, and perhaps least appreciated, principles of economic valuation is that values are determined "on the margin." This means that the value of something is determined not by the total contribution it makes to our wellbeing, but, rather, by the incremental contribution that a little more of it would make.

The classic example of this principle is the so-called diamonds-and-water paradox. Why is it that diamonds, which have so few practical uses, are worth so much more than water, which is absolutely essential for life? The answer can be illustrated by thinking about whether this would continue to be true if the relative abundance of the two substances were reversed. If water were rare and diamonds plentiful, water would be much more valuable. As it is, however, having another litre of water available would, for most of us, make virtually no difference, whereas diamonds are so rare as to be of great symbolic, if not necessarily practical, value. This notion is summarised in the principle of diminishing returns: the more you have of something, the less is an incremental increase in the amount of that thing worth to you. A more pertinent example in the context of biodiversity pertains to the value of ecosystems (and this is discussed below).

Economic Values of Diverse Natural Ecosystems

Now consider some potential economic values of diverse natural ecosystems and how we might try to estimate them. For this purpose, values might be categorised as follows:
- the contribution of diverse natural ecosystems in the production of other commodities;
- diverse natural ecosystems as sources of new products; and
- the esthetic, ethical or even spiritual values associated with diverse natural ecosystems.

Before discussing these values in more detail, it is necessary, first off, to admit that the phrase "diverse natural ecosystem" is vague. What does each of these three words mean? There appears little consensus on what it means for one ecosystem, or collection of organisms (or collection of organisms and certain elements of their abiotic environment), to be more diverse than another. While economists have little to contribute to this issue, it is important to note that it is difficult to value something that is not well defined.

The second word is also problematic. What, if anything, is "natural" (see Budiansky 1995)? Many areas have been inhabited by humans for millennia. At what point in our physical, cultural or technological development did people stop being "natural"? In fact, one might argue that "natural" areas are an increasingly unnatural phenomenon. Relatively untouched natural areas remain so as a result of what one might regard as highly "artificial" restrictions on incursion and development. Moreover, with nuclear fallout, greenhouse warming, ozone depletion and other global changes, there no longer are any truly pristine areas. Perhaps, by natural areas we have in mind areas that have been kept more or less in the state in which they existed before the human population began its dramatic rise as a result of falling birth rates and longer life expectancy.

Finally, the notion of an "ecosystem" is imprecise. Perhaps the problem of defining an ecosystem is akin to that which economists encounter in talking about "markets." It is a convenient abbreviation for a useful concept, but we are hard-pressed to say exactly what is included and excluded in any particular instance. In any event, without an adequate description of what constitutes "diverse natural ecosystems," valuation is difficult.

Value as a "Production Facility"

Let me now take the categories of value I've outlined above in turn. The first are values associated with the production of other things. Examples abound: hunting and gathering are still important in some ecosystems; wild species emerge from their natural habitats to provide pollination and pest control in adjoining agricultural areas; wetlands filter water for drinking and fishing; hillside vegetation prevents erosion, mudslides, and flooding; diverse communities of primary producers, predators, and scavengers cycle nutrients. Without these services of nature, agriculture would be less productive, homes less secure, and water sources less reliable. However, it is important to distinguish between total benefits and value on the margin.

Costanza et al. (1996) estimate that the world's ecosystems have a value of some $US33\times10^{12}$, compared to a global output of $US18\times10^{12}$. This value is too low. The value of the earth's ecosystems to humans is certainly higher since a catastrophic loss of all ecosystems would result in the demise of human life. Knowing this is not very useful, however, because we never face a decision about whether or not all of the earth's ecosystems should be obliterated. Rather, we face what are, on a global scale, relatively minor or marginal changes: to fell a stand of trees, convert an existing habitat for a threatened or endangered species to some other land use, to flood a river valley, or to fill-in a wetland. In this sense, ecosystems are much like water in the above example.

There are several reasons to wonder whether the consequences of such actions will be severe. First, on a global scale, there are still a lot of places that can serve as farms and homes. Perhaps the most tragic thing about environmental catastrophes resulting from unwise land use is that they affect the poor, who tend to be stuck where they are, much more than they do the mobile rich. A second consideration has to do not so much with the consequences of degrading natural ecosystems as with the constraints on doing so. To the extent that many of the effects of such degradation are local, local economic, political and social institutions may evolve so as to prevent degradation.

A third reason for scepticism concerning the effects of ecosystem degradation on the production of other goods is that measured economic activity does not appear to be declining as a result of such degradation. One needs to be careful in thinking about this, however. What are the effects of ecosystem degradation on the production of things that are bought and sold in markets? Here there is potential for confusion. It was noted above that "externalities" arise when one person does not take into account the effects of her actions on others. Person A may not take into account the flooding that persons B, C and D, who live downstream, experience when A fells a hillside forest. This is not to say that the effects on persons B, C and D will not be reflected elsewhere in the measured performance of the economy. B's and C's farm production, for example, may be lower, and D's residential property may decline in value. This is the essence of "green accounting" efforts: to determine what the economy-wide effects of environmental and resource degradation may be. That many such green accounting exercises reveal little effect of environmental degradation on measured output suggests that these impacts are, in fact, negligible.

Some caveats are in order. First, a basic principle of accounting is that one should include in an assessment of current performance any improvement or deterioration in future capabilities. One often encounters the concern that past and current activities are setting into motion an impending unravelling of basic ecological processes with potentially catastrophic consequences. I have no expertise that would allow me to comment on such claims, but I admit to some scepticism. A second caveat is that the relevant issue may not concern whether we are likely to experience declines from the *status quo* so much as whether we could improve upon the *status quo* by better preserving our biological resources. Undoubtedly we could, but there seems to be little way of knowing by how much. Finally, there are some technical issues in the aggregation of economic data that might lead one to question the conclusion that economic production is not being compromised by ecological decline. This is the matter of what are known in the green accounting economics jargon as "defensive expenditures." Suppose that a wetland that had been purifying water for a city's water supply is drained in order to build a housing development. The city, if it is to maintain its water quality, may need to build an expensive water filtration plant. If one looks at aggregate economic statistics, the construction of the water filtration plant would appear as an increase in economic production, whereas its construction just balances the loss of the diverse natural ecosystem.

Biodiversity as a Source of New Products

The second category of values concerns the role of diverse natural ecosystems as sources of new products. This differs from the first category, which includes actual physical products and services provided by particular natural communities as a result of their ongoing biological functioning. The second category includes what are known as *nonrival* goods. Nonrival goods are ones where one person's ownership does not physically preclude another's use (the term *physical* is used as things like patent and trademark law may *legally* preclude another person's use).

Consider as an example one of the reasons most often given for preserving biodiversity, namely, that it can serve as the source of new products. The cure for cancer, a better breed of corn or a super-strong adhesive might all be found by searching among natural organisms. In each case, the resulting commercial product is unlikely to depend on the continuing existence of the ecosystem from which it was first isolated. Products derived from natural sources are modelled from a genetic blueprint that can be used to make essentially limitless replicas. While we cannot all eat of the same apple, we can plant seeds from which we can grow virtually identical apple trees. Things like blueprints and genetic sequences are examples of nonrival goods.

The value of biodiversity as a source of new products is extremely low (see Simpson et al. 1996). The reason is that, if there is a lot of biological material over which a search for useful new products can be conducted, the value of an individual piece of such material is not worth very much. There are literally millions of species that could potentially be the sources of new medicines, foods and other products. It may not be apparent that millions of *different* species are, in fact, substitutes for each other as leads in new product research. After all, one species is distinguished from another by its unique genetic constitution, but even different genetic packages can contain instructions for the synthesis of substitutable chemical entities. Think, for example, of the different species of plants that produce caffeine.

In thinking about the value of biodiversity as a source of new products, some have asked, "What is the probability that a collection of species will yield a chemical compound of commercial value?" Multiplying this probability by the money generated from such a find, they arrive at an estimate of the value of biodiversity for this purpose. But this is the wrong question because different species could potentially be the source of the same product. The right question is, "By how much does the continuing existence of a collection of species increase the probability that a compound of commercial value will be found?" This is typically a much smaller number.

As a simple example, suppose that there is a one in ten thousand chance that any species, tested at random, will yield a commercially successful product. Suppose further that a commercial success is worth a billion dollars. If there were only one species that could be tested for the new product, its value would be

$$\frac{1}{10,000} \times \$1,000,000,000 = \$100,000$$

Now suppose that there are two species, each of which is equally likely to yield a commercially successful product. How much is the second worth, given the existence of the first? Well, the first yields a product with a probability of 0.0001, so the probability that the second is not needed is 0.9999 (=1 − 0.0001), so the incremental value of having the second is:

$$\frac{1}{10,000} \times (1 - \frac{1}{10,000}) \times \$1,000,000,000 = \$99,990$$

This is not much lower than the value associated with a single species. However, now think of how much extra-expected income is generated by the one millionth and first species under these circumstances. The millionth-and-first species will only be the source of a new product if the first million species that could be tested do not yield the product. Thus, the expected value of the millionth-and-first species is:

$$\frac{1}{10,000} \times (1 - \frac{1}{10,000})^{1,000,000} \times \$1,000,000,000 = \$3.7 \times 10^{-39}$$

There are thirty-eight zeroes before one encounters the first significant digit to the right of the decimal point!

This is a classic example of the principle of diminishing returns. The more we have of something, the less valuable is a little more of it. More details about what happens when one models the situation more realistically are provided in Simpson and Sedjo (1996a, 1996b) and Simpson et al. (1996), but the principle remains the same. One thing we can be pretty sure of is that the potential for new product development does not provide a compelling motive for the conservation of biodiversity.

Esthetic, Ethical and Spiritual Values

It is the third source of value that might be most important. It may surprise non-economists that economists would even consider esthetic, ethical and spiritual values, let alone find them compelling. After all, economics is often briefly, and accurately, described as the study of how people allocate *material* resources between competing needs and wants. But people regularly consult their tastes, their ethical precepts, and their spiritual beliefs in making these decisions. We determine how many tangible goods to produce, to consume and to preserve in accordance with our intangible beliefs and desires. Thus, these beliefs and desires are very relevant in economic analysis.

Regrettably, there is a substantial gap between recognising the conceptual importance of these intangibles and being able to measure them in practice. It is easy enough to measure relative worth when we see the price for which one thing is traded relative to another, but it is considerably more difficult when, as in the case of biodiversity, ownership is not well defined and transactions and prices cannot be observed. The usual procedure for getting around this problem is simply to ask people what unpriced things, like the continued existence of endangered species, are worth to them relative to the other things on which they spend their money. This survey procedure is referred to as the *contingent valuation* (CV) method.

The CV method is subject to a multitude of criticisms that are beyond the scope of the discussion in this chapter. Nonetheless, consider two aspects. The first is that CV was designed to elicit values that could not be inferred from any other data source. These values are variously referred to as "passive-use," "nonuse" or "existence" values. Existence values are ethical, aesthetic or spiritual values that are posited to be entirely independent of any human use. Even if I never see or otherwise benefit from biodiversity, can I realise some satisfaction from knowing that it is there—that is exists? Since, by definition, these benefits are wholly independent of any purchases made in markets, we cannot infer their magnitude from data on any actual purchases. Unless transactions are made in markets, the magnitude of such values necessarily remains hypothetical.

The second criticism is known as the *embedding* problem, but one might think of it as the $25 problem. I say this because "about $25" seems to be a common answer to a great variety of questions of the form: "What would you be willing to pay to prevent the extinction of the spotted owl?" "To save starving children in Rwanda?" "To protect the *palazzi* of Venice from flooding?" When asked such questions, a lot of people scratch their heads for a moment and answer, "About $25." Incidentally, the problem is referred to as "embedding," since when a subset is "embedded" in a greater set, the CV answers do not seem to change as much as might be expected. That is, people may give roughly the same answer when asked how much they would pay to save the spotted owl as they would when asked how much they would pay to save all endangered species.

Considerable refinement in CV survey methods has led to what seem to be more plausible, or at least internally consistent, responses. These developments beg some troubling questions, however. Why bother surveying people at all if we already know what the "plausible" answer is? Are the costs of doing a survey that is sufficiently careful as to be reliable prohibitive? Moreover, how do we decide when to conduct expensive surveys? Here there is at work something akin to Heisenberg's uncertainty principle (that we can never measure both the size and position of a particle because the act of measurement itself displaces the particle). We can only determine the value of something by devoting resources that could well prove to be worth more than the thing we are measuring. To put it another way, we should only go to the considerable expense of attempting to measure the value of things we think are worth measuring. The fact that we only measure the value of some small subset of things whose value we might try to measure may mean that respondents only express values for things that are mentioned in surveys.

The answer to the question of when to conduct an expensive survey has all too often been when there is a lawsuit with astronomical amounts at stake. As emphasised above, however, value is always relative to circumstances. Prince William Sound (site of the infamous *Exxon Valdez* oil spill) was felt to be important precisely because it was considered one of a dwindling number of relatively pristine areas in the world. Exxon may be culpable for having fouled that area, but can it reasonably be held accountable for the demise of the other habitats that made Prince William Sound that much more valuable?

Put it another way: How much might we be willing to sacrifice to save each of the things in the set of things about whose continuing existence we care? This depends crucially on our prediction concerning the continuing existence of every item in the set. We have only limited resources. What would we be willing to pay to save both the spotted owl in the Pacific Northwest and the Giant Panda in China? What about species as yet undiscovered in the rainforests of the Amazon and the highlands of New Guinea? For that matter, what would we be willing to contribute to all of the causes about which we care, including not only the preservation of biodiversity, but the Venetian *palazzi*, the Rwandan children, and all other worthwhile causes to which we may or may not be asked to contribute? Even if we could elicit honest and thoughtful responses to hypothetical questions, we would have to aggregate what *everyone* in the world would be willing to pay for *each* thing they care about, bearing in mind the contributions they have already pledged or will pledge for every *other* thing.

In the final analysis, the estimation of ethical, aesthetic and spiritual values amounts to multiplying very small numbers (what individuals would be willing to pay to maintain any particular element of biodiversity) by very large numbers (the number of individuals who value the item). One cannot know what the results of such an exercise might be, but this is probably the most compelling reason for being concerned about biodiversity preservation.

Some Loose Ends

Before considering some practical issues related to the economics of biodiversity conservation, there are some additional concerns to be examined. The first concerns the philosophical foundations of economic analysis. Economists typically assume that "preferences are primitive." You may recall that that "preferences" are what economists call the deep-seated tastes, ethics and other "values" (in the psychological-philosophical-vernacular sense, now) on which people base their economic decisions. By "primitive," we mean that they are givens, and thus outside the scope of economic analysis. This assumption allows us to make normative judgments about when one situation is better than another. People know what they want, the argument goes, and better situations are those in which people are better able to get what they want.

This formulation has its problems, of course. We all know that getting what we want does not always make us happy. Moreover, we do not always know what we want.

Finally, there are situations in which you would be happier if I wanted different things. If I bought the last chocolate bar in the store, you would be happier if I would have liked chocolate bars less. If I am less willing than you are to make financial contributions for the preservation of biodiversity, you would be happier if I cared more about biodiversity than I do. By declining to specify why it is people like what they like, however, economists by and large ignore an important real-world phenomenon: advertising. Certainly, an important element of the strategy of many conservation organisations is an attempt to convince other people to change what they care about. This is a problem that limits economic analysis, at least as practised by most resource economists.

Another important assumption underlying much of foregoing discussion is that things are generally continuous. This means that small actions have small effects. Reducing habitat by a small amount, for example, results in a small reduction in the biodiversity supported in that habitat. This assumption is not innocuous, because many biologists are concerned with radical discontinuities (see Chapters 2, 3 and 4). The state of a system may change suddenly when a threshold is exceeded, or a little additional degradation may result in an irreversible unravelling. At the risk of sounding cavalier about such an important issue, let me just say that natural scientists have failed to convince this reasonably inquisitive layperson of the likelihood and imminence of such threats.

Intergenerational equity is an issue of great importance to ethicists (see Chapter 11 in this volume). At one level, issues of our obligations to the unborn involve deep philosophical questions. These are the sorts of things that economists often regard as "primitive preferences," and leave at that. There's another way to look at things that can be helpful, though. Economists often presume that intertemporal decisions are made on the basis of a positive discount rate. If, for example, I apply a discount rate of five percent, then I value the promise of a dollar one-year from now as being worth ninety-five cents today. When we apply such reasoning to the more distant future (say 100 years from now), we get into questions of ethical obligations to posterity. It may seem to be ethically indefensible to suppose that benefits received by our descendants should be discounted—after all, should not everyone be treated equally?

A response to this concern might be that historically it is earlier rather than later generations that have been short-changed. Few of us would be willing to trade places with ancestors who constantly struggled to forestall death from famine, disease or predation. The historical pattern has, by and large, been one in which earlier generations pass on to their successors ever greater reserves of technology and knowledge. No one will deny that the services of nature are and will always be necessary to support human life and wellbeing. Alarmists have not convinced me either that technological advance necessarily threatens the continuing existence of our natural life support system, or that that life support system is in any imminent peril from any source.

Finally, although the list of excluded considerations is longer, there is the issue of uncertainty. Contrary, perhaps, to the impressions of many non-economists, questions of how best to make decisions under uncertainty receive a great deal of attention in economics. There are basically two principles. First, if one is *risk averse*, one should insure against unfavourable outcomes. By risk averse is meant the asymmetry in the perception of good and bad outcomes. To put it another way, many are reluctant to gamble large amounts even when the odds are fair. In fact, most are willing to pay something to avoid exposure to uncertainty: we buy car, home and health insurance. This might also apply to biodiversity. We may be willing to "pay a little extra" to preserve diverse natural ecosystems because we are uncertain as to what the consequences of their degradation will be.

The second fundamental principle in the analysis of uncertainty is what is known in the economics and finance jargon as *option value*. Even if one is not risk averse—if one does not perceive an asymmetry between "good" and "bad" outcomes—one may still assign positive value to the option of deferring irreversible decisions. An example arises in the value of biodiversity for creating new products. Even if we maintain enough biodiversity to meet our current new product research needs, it may still be wise to maintain some extra biodiversity capacity in the event that our future new product needs are greater than those we face at present. If, for example, an epidemic of a terrible new disease were to break out, we might want to have more species over which to search.

These principles are well known in economics, and it's possible in many instances to calculate the insurance premium a person would be willing to pay or the value of an option to him. People too often jump to the conclusion that, because insurance is important and options are valuable, we should greatly inflate our estimates of the value of biodiversity to reflect these considerations. Many writers have, for example, advocated the establishment of safe minimum standards for ecological resources (see Chapter 10). These are proposed limits beyond which no further degradation would be allowed. These safe minimum standards are problematic for a couple of reasons, however. We do not know where to set them, and an absolute standard can be seen as a limiting case of an option and/or insurance pricing problem. Since optimal option or insurance pricing problems involve such absolute standards only under extreme assumptions on uncertainty and risks, setting safe minimum standards begs the question of whether the risks involved are really so extreme, or whether we might be better served by a more flexible approach.

Policies for Biodiversity Preservation

Notwithstanding the forgoing discussion, society should undertake some efforts to preserve and protect diverse natural ecosystems. On the one hand, I do not believe that preservation of biodiversity at or near current levels (if we can define them) is a critical issue for humanity. But for some of the same reasons, I also believe that society need not make great sacrifices in order to preserve extensive, diverse natural ecosystems. Biodiversity is relatively plentiful, so the value associated with marginal changes is not large. At the same time, however, there are abundant locations where farming, manufacturing and construction can occur. Thus, it is often not very expensive to plan farming, manufacturing and construction in those areas where the impact on biodiversity will not be great.

There are two types of contributions economists can make to the study of biodiversity. The first is the one outlined above: valuation. This is probably putting things a bit too optimistically. We cannot accurately estimate values, but we can, by considering things like relative abundance, get some notion of what things are and are not important. Even though, or perhaps especially because, they are poorly understood, intangible considerations may constitute good reasons for preserving biodiversity.

That brings me to the second contribution economists can make. Given a decision to save some amount of biodiversity, economists can give useful advice on how to accomplish this objective most cost-effectively. Some clarification may be helpful before going into more detail. Non-economists often confuse economics with marketing. Just for the record, economists typically do not have any special expertise on the subject of getting people to do things they do not want to do—such as contribute large amounts of money to the preservation of biodiversity. In fact, many economists believe that you cannot get people to do things they do not want to do without compensating them enough to make it worthwhile for them to do so.

The conservation and environmental policy prescriptions of many advocacy groups confirm the old adage that "a little knowledge is a dangerous thing." I often feel that the greatest contribution economists can make is to tell well-meaning people gently but firmly how *not* to conduct efforts to save biodiversity. A misconception frequently encountered in discussing conservation strategies is the belief that establishing *some* commercial activity involving biodiversity is going to generate substantial revenues for conservation. It is often hastily concluded that activities are commercially viable simply because there is *some* potential value, but costs of investment and production are ignored. Organisations at work in the developing tropics, for example, often seek to establish *integrated conservation and development projects* (ICDPs), under which commercial activities are undertaken in, for example, ecotourism, non-timber forest product collection or biodiversity prospecting. The basic idea is that greater revenues will be generated from these purportedly benign activities than would come from alternative, more destructive activities.

ICDPs beg two questions, however. First, if they are commercially viable, why does an outside organisation need to come in to establish them? That is, why does the private sector not undertake them? The second question is, if ICDPs are not commercially viable, would it not make more sense to use the money for conservation more directly? That is, if an ICDP does not generate enough money to justify the investment made in it, why not take the money invested and apply it to conservation directly?

Biodiversity preservation in the nations of the developing tropics is an extremely difficult proposition, complicated by a lack of both physical and institutional infrastructures. Things should be easier in wealthier countries, where one can be reasonably certain that land ownership will be respected. The conservation problem in the wealthier nations is, then, really one of which habitats to protect. While specific applications can be very difficult, a basic economic principle should guide choices. The costs of habitat protection are minimised when the incremental cost of protecting additional biodiversity is equalised across all protected habitats.

Application of this principle is difficult, because we are often unsure as to what it means to protect additional biodiversity. A number of attempts have been made to define consistent indices of diversity, so as to facilitate this sort of rational conservation planning. These attempts have been plagued by several difficulties. One is simply complexity. In order to implement a genetics-based index, for example, we would have to have considerably more information than is available about most species (as evidenced by the fact that many biologists believe that most species are as yet unidentified). Another problem is that there remains considerable disagreement about what are the criteria for preserving diversity. The construction of diversity indices is in a sense a circular exercise. We define diversity in such a way as to put the greater emphasis on preserving the things we care about the most. But if we knew precisely what it was we cared about, defining and calculating the indices would be trivial.

Having said all this, however, there is some considerable progress being made in analysing conservation priorities. If we are willing to take as our measure of diversity numbers of species, there is useful guidance being offered. Researchers have developed algorithms for maximising the number of species preserved for any given expenditure of money, and rapid progress is being made in this area (e.g., Csuti et al. 1997; Pressey et al. 1993; Chapter 5).

Conclusions: Four Suggestions for Research

Let me conclude with my four suggestions for further research.

Predicting Catastrophe. While I expressed scepticism above about the likelihood or imminence of catastrophic ecological breakdown, this remains the most important question. If better modelling were to reveal that we are in imminent danger of an ecological meltdown, there would be important implications for valuation and policy.

Measuring Economically Relevant Ecological Production. Perhaps aggregate statistics do not yet reflect the economic effects of ecological degradation, but this could be due to problems in measurement. Better studies of the contributions of healthy ecosystems to things that most people care about are needed.

Defining Plausible Ranges on Intangible Values. Many economists feel that estimates reported for intangible values are just too high. There has been considerable work on the decision-theoretic foundations of nonmarket (existence) values, but more is in order, as are greater efforts to relate these values to observable economic phenomena.

What is Biodiversity? Definitional issues have largely been ignored, but some huge problems facing those who want to "save biodiversity" concern finding a proper measure for what biodiversity is. What is it that is to be saved, and when we can conclude that we have lost or saved it. Given the apparent fact that we cannot save it all, we need some better guidance as to how biodiversity can be quantified.

8 Biodiversity: Forests, Property Rights and Economic Value
ROGER A. SEDJO

If biodiversity is so valuable in the development of valuable drugs and pharmaceuticals and improved agricultural germplasm, why isn't it being better preserved? Even more critically, if biodiversity is an essential ingredient to life on the planet, how come it isn't being treated as "infinitely important?" Two possible answers are examined in this chapter.

First, the values may be substantial but the absence of clear, well-defined property rights may make the resource rents difficult to capture. A "tragedy of the commons" may prevail in which the open access nature of the resource results in an overexploitation. Being owned by everyone, biodiversity becomes the responsibility of no one.

Second, biodiversity may, in fact, have only a limited value *at the margin*. For example, there may be so much wild genetic resources available that any particular piece has a very low expected value. In the real world the issue is not an "all or nothing" issue—either maintaining all biodiversity or losing it all. Rather, the issue is whether we should protect this one species, or whether this one area should be protected from conversion or development.

Loss of Biodiversity and Land Conversion

It is widely recognised that most losses of biological resources are the "unintended consequence" of human land conversion activities. Since there are not clear property rights to the "essence" of wild genetic resources, the potential benefits from these resources are external to the land developer and thus the resource is treated as valueless, since no one, including the land developer, can benefit by capturing the resource rents of wild genetic resources.[1]

In this context, one can view this as an example of the tragedy of the commons. Since the essence or "blueprint" of wild genetic resources are not owned, the chances of capturing any benefits to future developments utilising these resources is viewed as negligible and therefore their values are ignored. But before considering the value of biodiversity and the role of property rights, it is worth examining the role of forests and deforestation in biodiversity.

Evidence of the Role of Land Conversion: The World's Forests

Forest ecosystems are often viewed as important sources of biodiversity or, alternatively, as indicators of the condition of the world's biodiversity. One concern is that the loss of tropical forest will result in losses of important biodiversity. Thus, to the extent that island biogeography is operative, deforestation increases the pressure on some species, so that some species are probably being driven into local and global extinction (see van Kooten, et al. 1999 for an overview). Consider the following idea: If the concern about deforestation is warranted on the basis of the loss of important biodiversity, then reductions in the rate of deforestation should be a positive signal. Furthermore, forest expansion should generally be seen as a signal of decreased pressure on biodiversity.

Data exist that allow us to say something fairly definitive about forest area and how it has changed in recent years and decades (FAO 1993; 1997). Also, we can make observations on the condition of forests, although these will necessarily be somewhat subjective and thus less definitive. Consider first the issue of global deforestation. Here we find both "good news" and "bad news." Deforestation is proceeding at very different rates in different parts of the world.

The Good News. Data from the UN Food and Agricultural Organisation (FAO 1997) show that no net deforestation is occurring in the temperate forests of the Northern Hemisphere. In fact, most of the Northern Hemisphere, including Europe, North America and much of the former USSR, and developed Asia and Oceania, experienced modest increases in forest area in the 1990s (Table 8.1). The Russian Federation was excluded since reliable data for the period 1990-95 are unavailable.

Table 8.1: Forest area change in developed countries, 1990-1995[a]

Regions	Forest area change 1990-95 (million ha)	Annual (million ha)	Annual (%)
Europe	+ 1.94	+ 0.39	+ 0.27
Former USSR without the Russian Federation	+ 2.78	+ 0.56	+ 1.12
Temperate/boreal North America	+ 3.82	+ 0.76	+ 0.17
Developed Asia-Oceania	+ 0.24	+ 0.05	+ 0.06
All developed countries (without the Russian Federation)	+ 8.78	+ 1.76	+ 0.12
All developed countries (without former USSR)	+ 6.00	+ 1.20	+ 0.18

[a] Russian Federation is excluded since reliable data for 1990-95 is unavailable.
Source: FAO (1997)

In Europe, for example, reforested areas abound. The forest area of France, for example, increased by 50% between 1790 and 1890, and again increased by 50% between 1890 and 1990 (France Ministry of Agricultural and Fisheries 1995). More generally, European forests have expanded as agricultural lands were abandoned and have reforested naturally.

What about forest condition? There is evidence that in many places in the temperate world forest volume has been increasing. Although this is not an unequivocal indicator of improving forest condition, in many cases it is probably a good proxy for improving condition. In the USA, for example, forest inventories have shown an increasing forest stock between 1950 and 1990, indicating the recovery of many forested areas, especially in the east and south. The evidence for increased stocking in Europe and Japan is the same. Much of this increase is due, not to tree planting activities, but through the process of natural regeneration, thereby restoring many of the native species that had been displaced by the original clearing. Even where tree planting is involved, it often replaces agricultural activities that are far less hospitable for biodiversity than a planted forest. Also, some data show that natural reforestation is occurring in Russia as well (Economic Commission for Europe/FAO 1989; Wilson et al. 1998).

More generally, Table 8.2 shows that Europe, North America, Australia, Japan and New Zealand have all experienced significant expansion in forest area over the last decade, and one-half of the developed world has experienced an expansion of 2.7% in its forested area. All of this evidence suggests that the outputs of the forest, including environmental and ecological services, are stable or probably on the rise in temperate regions.

Table 8.2: Comparison of 1980 and 1995 Forest Cover

Region	Percent change from 1980 forest cover
Developing World	+2.7%
Europe	+4.1%
Temperate/boreal North America	+2.6%
Australia, Japan and New Zealand	+1.0%
Developing World	-9.1%
Asia/Oceania	-6.4%
Africa	-10.5%
Latin America and Caribbean	-9.7%

Source: FAO (1997)

The Bad News. Table 8.2 also presents the "bad news," which is that deforestation in the tropics and developing world continues at a fairly rapid rate. To be sure, it is not at such a rate that most "tropical forests will be gone by the year 2000," an assertion that was commonly made by many "experts" when tropical deforestation first became an issue in the early 1980s. Nevertheless, the reality is that tropical deforestation continues almost unabated as tropical forestland continues to be converted to other uses.

In the 15 years from 1980 to 1995 the total area of tropical forest has been reduced by 9.1% (Table 8.2). Additionally, there is evidence that the "condition" of tropical forests has deteriorated. Forest disturbances are frequent, both from shifting cultivators and from selective logging, and the forest stock is down in many tropical forests.

Of course, not all forests "are created equal." Some forests have superior timber; others have more abundant wildlife or provide superior biodiversity and genetic resource habitats. Old forests provide different habitats from young forests, and so forth. Furthermore, humans have demonstrated that, with a concerted effort, serious damage can be done to biodiversity, forest or no forest. For example, the human directed extermination of predators, such as the wolf, occurred even as the forests were beginning to expand. But, other things being equal, an intact forest is probably necessary to provide the host of outputs and services that would be lost, in whole or in part, if the forest area were converted to other uses.

The Value of Biodiversity

Now examine in greater detail (a) the nature of biodiversity as a good and (b) the question of why wild genetic resources and biodiversity have economic value. Possible sources for a value for biodiversity can be found in the following forms. First, biodiversity has value as part of the life support system of the planet. In the absence of some amount of biodiversity, life on the planet would not be possible. Second, biodiversity provides a host of ecosystem services in the form of hydrological control services, climate moderation, wildlife and genetic resource habitat, and so forth. Third, biodiversity in the form of wild genetic resources may have value as an input into the production of other desired goods such as pharmaceuticals and increased vitality of agricultural seed. In this context, certain wild plants may be used to produce natural products or chemicals and molecules from wild plants, animal, anthropoids, or microbes may be used as a "blueprint" in the development of synthetic products (see Sedjo 1992 for more detail).

For all of the above uses, the demand for biodiversity is a "derived demand," derived directly from its value as an intermediate input for the production of other desired services, such as a livable planet, ecosystem services, new drugs and improved seeds.

Finally, biodiversity may have value in itself—spiritual, intrinsic or whatever—and in this case the demand is no longer a derived demand, but demand for biodiversity is a final demand as a consumption good. It has value as a final consumption good in the same sense that a scenic view, an inspiring sight (e.g., the Grand Canyon or the Golden Gate Bridge) or great art has intrinsic value. In the same mode, there may be an "existence value" to knowing that biodiversity, or certain biodiversity, exists.[2]

The remainder of this chapter focuses on biodiversity as an input, leaving aside for the moment consumption and existence values. Notice, however, that the critical issue of biodiversity and human survival is treated as a question of biodiversity as an input into human survival and not a question of biodiversity for its existence value or final consumption.

Property Rights: Capturing Returns to Biodiversity

How can the rents associated with wild genetic resources be captured? Although the expected value of individual wild genetic resources may be small, not all wild genetic resources have small value.[3] Additionally, it has been argued that the development of some degree of property rights is a necessary condition for an economic agent, be it an individual or country, to be able to capture any economic rents associated with valuable wild genetic resources (Sedjo 1992).

Typically, property rights in society are associated with phenotypes, but not genotypes. For example, one can have property rights or ownership to an individual plant or animal, e.g., a person may own a dog or a sheep, a phenotype, but typically property rights are not given to the genetic "blueprint" for sheep, that is, the genotype. However, where there are "genetically engineered" animals, as in recent cases, property rights for the genotype or "genetic blueprint" do exist in the form of intellectual property. Wild genetic resources, which are the result of natural processes, typically resist ownership. However, just as the ownership of land, which generally bestows the ability to limit access, creates a quasi-ownership status over wildlife on the land by virtue of landowner's ability to limit hunting access, so quasi-ownership of wild genetic resources can be achieved through the ownership or control of land with wild genetic resources.

In that context, the literature discusses two ways whereby these types of externalities, created by lack of property rights, might be internalised (Sedjo 1992). Demsetz (1967) argues that, where property rights do not exist, institutions may evolve to provide property rights, *if the values are substantial*. Also, Coase (1960) has suggested that contracts among the effected parties may occur to internalise the externality, *if transactions costs are not prohibitive*.

Thus, ownership or sovereignty over land can provide a vehicle for controlling access to important genetic resources. The control of the land and access, coming from sovereignty, can provide the basis for contracting arrangements, in the spirit of Coase, between genetically rich countries and firms that seek wild genetic resources. The firms have the ability, directly or indirectly, to utilise these genetic resources in the development of a product, which is then tested, marketed and commercially distributed.

Additionally, in the spirit of Demsetz, the recent Biodiversity Treaty coming out of the 1992 UNCED meeting in Rio moved in the direction of providing sovereign countries with property rights to wild genetic resources. However, not all countries have signed the Treaty and the degree of "ownership" provided by the treaty is still clouded. Nevertheless, quasi-biodiversity rights have emerged using sovereignty control of access and contracting as the bases for these "rights."

Biodiversity as an Input into Pharmaceuticals

Species may be valuable as sources of unique genetic resources such as molecules or naturally-generated chemical compounds. These can be used as natural products, which have valuable pharmaceutical and drug properties. Alternatively, wild genetic resources may provide a "blueprint" from which scientists can develop synthetic genes, which can be used for the development of useful drugs. In the case of crops, these wild or semi-wild genetic resources may provide the input necessary to improve crop seed (e.g., wheat or maize) to insure vitality or provide desired traits (e.g., resistance to disease or drought).

Biodiversity as a Lottery

Biodiversity in the form of the various wild genetic resources found in nature, most of which will never have development uses for natural or synthetic products, can be viewed as a natural lottery. As with a lottery there are lots of tickets. There is a high payoff jackpot, but a very low probability of winning the jackpot and thus a very low expected value of any given ticket. In lotteries in the USA, the prize or jackpot is often several millions of dollars, but the expected value of any ticket is only $0.50.[4]

Biodiversity as input into the development of new pharmaceuticals can be viewed essentially as a lottery. A lottery involves the random selection of a winning ticket from a very large group of tickets, most of which are ultimately valueless. There are only a few winners. Since the expected value equals the probability of a successful draw time the value of the successful draw (e.g., Expected Value = probably of success × value if successful), the expected value may be very small even if the prize is large. For example, if there are 10 million tickets and a prize of $5 million, the expected value equals only $0.50. So, even with a large payoff, the expected value of each ticket will be small. Alternatively, if there are relatively few tickets, the expected value will be considerably larger. For example, if there are only 1,000 tickets, the expected value of each ticket, given a prize of $5 million, would be $5,000.

Similarly, we can view wild genetic resources as a lottery—the prizes awarded in the form of income to firms that develop important drugs using inputs from wild genetic resources. In economic terms, the market for wild genetic resources as inputs into drugs and pharmaceuticals is illustrated in Figure 8.1. Although the demand may be substantial, the relatively large supply generates a low equilibrium price. Thus, even though the firm that successfully develops and commercialises the "cure for cancer" will reap large revenues, the market value of the marginal species as an input into drug production can be very small. As with a lottery, even though there is a jackpot wild genetic resource, namely, the genetic resource that provides the critical input for the drug that "cures" cancer, the market value of the marginal species is small. Since there are millions of wild species on the globe, the expected value of any specific species, or genetic constituent from a wild species, is likely to be very small (Simpson et al. 1996).[5]

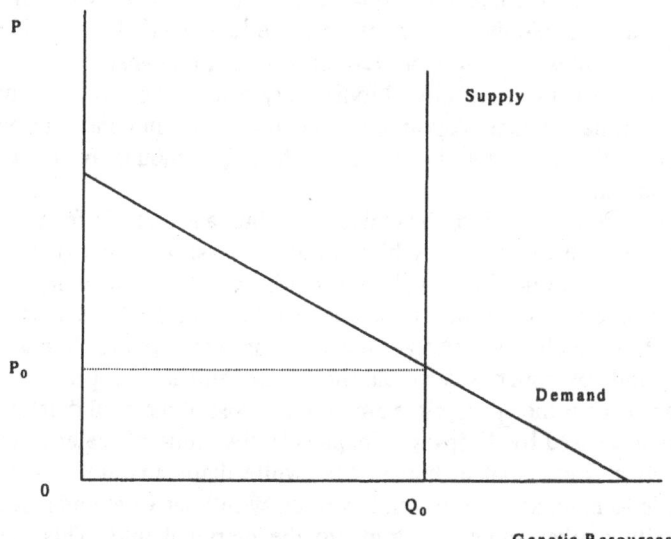

Figure 8.1: Demand and Supply of Wild Genetic Resources for Pharmaceutical Use

Of course, in the global system there is more than a single disease for which a cure would be socially and financially valuable. However, due to the well-known redundancy in the natural wild genetic resource system, there is more than a single jackpot ticket. Thus, suppose that there are ten species that contain the natural compound that is the critical component to developing the cure for cancer. The value of these ten species as a cure is not independent. After the compound is recognised in one of them, the value of "discovering" the other nine would be expected to fall substantially.

An implication is that the loss of any one of these species is less critical since there still exist nine other similar species yet to be discovered that can provide essentially the same genetic material.

Biodiversity as an Input into Human Existence

Although biodiversity has been treated as input into the production of pharmaceuticals, it is clear that inputs into drugs, and other genetically-dependent products, perhaps constitute only a minor reason why humans are concerned about biodiversity. A much more fundamental reason is that biodiversity provides a life support system in which humans, and all other life on earth, exist. In this context biodiversity can be viewed as a public good, like national defence. A public good is nonrivalry in consumption so that one person's consumption does not affect the amount available for others to consume.

As a critical input into the existence of humans and of life on earth, biodiversity obviously has a very high value (at least to humans). But, as with other resource questions, including public goods, biodiversity is not an either/or question, but rather a question of "how much." Thus we may argue as to how much biodiversity is desirable or is required for human life (threshold) and how much is desirable (insurance) and at what price, just as societies argue over the appropriate amount and cost of national defence.

As discussed by Simpson (Chapter 7), the value of water is small even though it is essential to human life, while diamonds are inessential but valuable to humans. The reason has to do with relative abundance and scarcity, with market value pertaining to the marginal unit. This water-diamond paradox can be applied to biodiversity.

Although biological diversity is essential, a single species has only limited value, since the global system will continue to function without that species. Similarly, the value of a "piece" of biodiversity (e.g., 10 ha of tropical forest) is small to negligible since its contribution to the functioning of the global biodiversity is negligible. The global ecosystem can function with "somewhat more" or "somewhat less" biodiversity, since there have been larger amounts in times past and some losses in recent times.[6] Therefore, in the absence of evidence to indicate that small habitat losses threaten the functioning of the global life support system, the value of these marginal habitats is negligible.

The "value question" is that of how valuable to the life support function are species at the margin. While this, in principle, is an empirical question, in practice it is probably unknowable.

However, thus far biodiversity losses appear to have had little or no effect on the functioning of earth's life support system, presumably due the resiliency of the system, which perhaps is due to the redundancy found in the system. Through most of its existence earth has had far less biological diversity. Thus, as in the water-diamond paradox, the value of the marginal unit of biodiversity appears to be very small.

The "market" for biodiversity as a life support system is presented in Figure 8.2. In the figure, demand does not intersect the price axis and, thus, total value can be viewed as infinite, or at least very large.[7] Nevertheless, the marginal value of biodiversity as a life support system (given by P_0) could be modest despite its large total value.

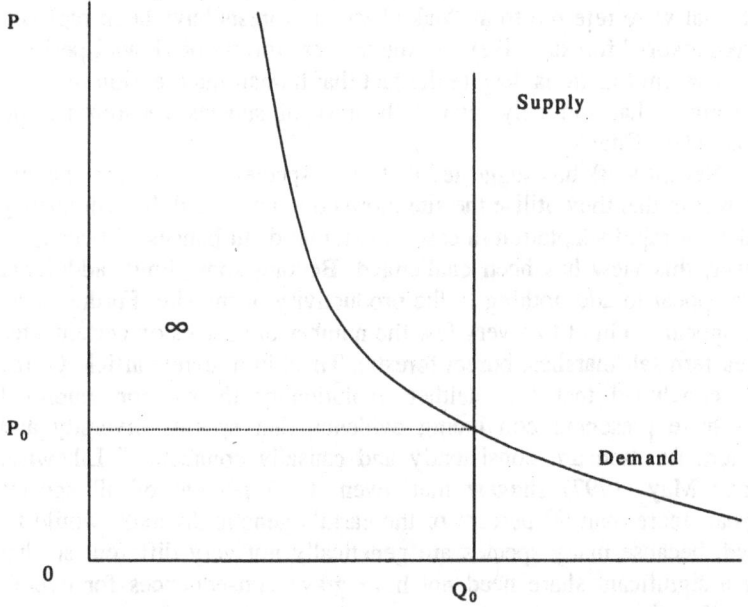

Figure 8.2: Demand and Supply of Biodiversity as a Life Support System

Some related ecological issues

It is maintained that there are important "keystone" species, namely, species that are essential to maintain a host of other species. The value of the keystone species would equal the value of the host of species dependent upon it. Empirically, however, there do not appear to be many "critical" keystone species. There are examples of specialised predators being threatened when its sole food source moves to extinction (e.g., the blackfooted ferret, the prairie dog), but these situations appear rare and the linkages to other species in the system limited (see also Budiansky 1995).

As noted, the global system appears to have a high amount of biological redundancy. Therefore, the system functions of any given species can be taken over by other species. An example is the horse chestnut tree in the eastern US hardwood forests. This tree was common until the end of the 19th century at which time it was eradicated by a disease. Nevertheless, the forest continued to perform its ecosystem functions unhindered as other tree species replaced the horse chestnut. Forests that were referred to as "oak-chestnut" forests have been replaced by "oak-hickory" forests. Likewise, the tropical forests of Hawaii perform their ecosystem functions despite the fact that human intervention over the past centuries has radically altered the mix of species constituting the ecosystem (see Chapter 6).

Recent work has suggested that more species on a site are "better" than fewer in that they utilise the site more completely and the redundancy provides for rapid adaptation in case of external disturbances and changes. However, this view has been challenged. Beyond some limit, additional species appear to add nothing to the productivity of the site. Furthermore, nature appears to limit to a very few the number of species on certain sites (e.g., eastern salt marshes, boreal forests). Thus, in a review article Grime (1997) concluded that "... neither evolutionary theory nor empirical studies have presented convincing evidence that species diversity and ecosystem function are consistently and causally connected." Likewise, Nee and May (1997) suggest that, even if 95 percent of all species disappear, more than 80 percent of the earth's genetic diversity would be retained, because many species are genetically not very different so that losing a significant share need not have grave consequences for overall genetic diversity.

More generally, much of this discussion involves the question of the inherent stability of the global ecosystem. At one extreme is a very fragile and unstable system that may be likened to a "house of cards." At the other extreme is the very stable system represented by a "bucket of billiard balls." The critical question is, "Which of these systems more accurately reflects the essence of the system of global biodiversity?" A "null hypothesis" approach would suggest viewing the system as inherently stable in the absence of strong empirical evidence to the contrary.

Issues in Genetic Contracting

A Case Study of Costa Rica

Utilising control of access, genetically rich countries can negotiate contracts that sell a collection of wild genetic resources in return for payments or other considerations. INBio, a quasi-governmental organisation, has been given the exclusive right to inventory and collect species samples by the Costa Rica government. It has the right to negotiate sales of the rights to collections of its wild genetic resources. The best known of these is a contract currently being implemented in Costa Rica between INBio and Merck, a major pharmaceutical company. One aspect of this arrangement called for INBio to collect a predetermined number of species, of a certain mix and with the location noted, so additional samples could be obtained if needed. In return, Merck makes a direct payment for the material received and agrees to pay INBio some predetermined portion of the gross receipts, say one percent, generated from any commercial product generated from these wild genetic materials, either as natural products or through further development of related synthetic products.

The arrangement with Merck does not preclude INBio making other collected samples available to firms other than Merck. However, Merck has exclusive rights to the development of the species in the collection it receives and INBio will not make these species available to other buyers unless Merck gives up its rights for development. For its part, Merck has a period of time in which to determine which species it wishes to develop. The remainder of the species are then "released" back to INBio. INBio can then make these species available to other firms. In essence, Merck receives the "right-of-first-refusal." In turn, should Merck develop a commercial product from one of these species, the contract calls for all the royalties to go to INBio.

Finally, since INBio has the right to negotiate to provide species to other firms besides Merck, on whatever terms it desires subject to its earlier exclusivity arrangements, INBio can be viewed as the exclusive agent for the sale of the rights of development of Costa Rica's wild genetic resources.[8]

Yellowstone National Park

A similar, but somewhat different contracting arrangement was made between the US National Park Service and Diversa Corp., a San Diego firm. Diversa purchased the right to commercialise the thermophile collections in the hot springs at Yellowstone National Park for $175,000 over 5 years and royalties of 5% on the profits of a commercial product (*Science*, 22 August 1997).

Some Limitations

Although INBio has exclusive rights to contract for the wild genetic resources of Costa Rica, such organisations and arrangements are possible for other countries as well. However, additional players create difficulties and complications. In many cases even rare wild genetic resources are found in a number of countries. Thus, for example, Colombia, Panama and Venezuela may all have many of the same wild genetic resources as Costa Rica while not being bound by the exclusivity agreement between INBio and Merck. Thus, exclusivity might be limited to individual countries and it might be advantageous to specify exclusivity in that the developer (company) would only draw a given species from one country and that it would make full payments to the country from which the initial wild genetic resource was obtained. A contract might require that the company exclusively draw a particular type of resource from one country while allowing the company to draw different genetic resources from a number of countries. Thus a company would have only one supplier for any given wild resource. Similarly, a company may wish that it be the exclusive recipient of the specific genetic materials it receives.

Who does the collecting? In the case of Costa Rica, the plant collecting was done by an indigenous organisation, which then delivered the collected species to the user, Merck. An alternative way of organising would be for the country to "sell" collection rights to user firms or collector intermediate firms.

Exclusivity. If widespread collection is allowed then it would be difficult to guarantee exclusivity, and it may be difficult to control the distribution of samples. In the INBio-Merck agreement, INBio controlled collection and there was also a degree of exclusivity in the distribution of species samples. The agreement called for Merck to receive a number of samples, say 1,000, to which it has exclusive rights for a limited period (e.g., one year). At the end of that period, Merck would indicate which species it wished to keep in an exclusivity relationship and for which species it no longer wanted exclusive rights. Commonly, Merck would release most (e.g., 980 of the 1,000), with INBio then free to provide these species to other firms. For the other 20 species of which Merck wished to continue exclusive use, Merck would make a further modest payment. In return, INBio guaranteed that these species would not be given to other firms. Obviously, the more countries with overlapping resources, the weaker each country's bargaining power. Also, however, to the extent that overlapping resources indicate availability, concerns about extinction diminish.

Price Determination and Auctions. In the INBio-Merck contract, the price and terms were negotiated. Another possibility is to have a competitive auction. In this case the country would state the terms of the arrangement and the highest bidder would get the contract. Of course, the amount that firms would be willing to bid depends upon the terms built into the contract. What services does the country provide? For example, does it collect the samples? Does the contract call for exclusive rights to the buyer, and if so, to what degree? Genetically rich countries also have to realise that there are other countries that can be sources of many (most) of the genetic resources.

Distribution of Genetic Resource Rents within a Country

There are two separate issues regarding property rights and wild genetic resources. The first deals with economic efficiency and the desire to create property rights so that incentives are in place for protecting wild genetic resources. The second is the question of income distribution and to whom the rights are allocated. In concept the rights could go to *a* country, to *an* owner, on whose lands the wild genetic resources reside, or to local peoples, such as tribes that held long-term communal control over these lands.

The focus of economists is on efficiency considerations on the assumption that owners, whether government, private or tribal, will respond to incentives to protect value. However, in many situations there may be major disagreement over who should be assigned the property rights. The international biodiversity treaty moved toward assigning those rights to the country government, but left the internal distribution of rights to the discretion of the sovereign nation.

Political Stability, Civil and Legal System

As with other investments, a country's political system and physical and social infrastructure are important. It is not a coincidence that Costa Rica has a well-developed and functioning civil service, legal and political system that promotes confidence among investors.

Risk Sharing

There are uncertainties in the development of products based on wild genetic resources. As noted, the vast majority of genetic resources have little if any commercial value, but costs must be incurred to make that determination. Finding valuable genetic resources is expensive and the full development, marketing and distribution of a product is very expensive. Perhaps one of the most effective ways of risk sharing is to set low prices for the provision of the samples and try to generate returns from the "royalties" from successful products.

From the country's point of view, it wants to make available to bona fide developers as much genetic material as possible to maximise the probability of successful products, from which it can collect royalty revenues. Thus, it has an interest in making the material available at a low price, thereby increasing the expected products that are developed.

Conclusions

Some biodiversity is necessary for human existence, so in some sense, some biodiversity is infinitely valuable. However, at the margin, biodiversity is less critical to human life and thus less valuable.

How valuable is biodiversity as an input into pharmaceutical products? There are two possible answers to this question. First, the values may be substantial, but the absence of clear, well-defined property rights may make the resource rent difficult to capture. The absence of property rights may result in the market and the social system substantially undervaluing these resources. Hence, the inadvertent losses of wild genetic resources may reflect not their low value, but the inability to capture that value due to the absence of adequate property rights.

Second, it may be that biodiversity, like a lottery, has only limited value *at the margin*. For example, there may be so much wild genetic resources available that any particular part of this stock has only a very low expected value.

Reviewing the evidence we find that there has been some emergence of property rights for valuable common property resources, as anticipated by Demsetz (1967). However, the evidence also finds relatively few natural product based drugs being developed by pharmaceuticals, and there is some evidence that developers are losing interest. Furthermore, a recent study with by Simpson et al. (1996) suggests that the marginal value of wild genetic resources as input into pharmaceuticals is at most modest and probably very small (see also Chapter 9 in this volume).

The conclusion, therefore, is that the contribution of biological diversity to the production of products and services (viz., ecosystem function) is small, mainly because such values are relevant only at the margin. Unless biodiversity has significant value as a final consumption "good," principally existence value, the economic case for incurring large costs to protect biodiversity at the margin is weak.

Notes

1. It is not a simply a matter of the state exercising its sovereign control, since historically the "blueprint" for these materials were treated as global common goods. This point is developed below.
2. The option value of knowing that the resource exists for further use is probably more an option to its future use as an input than as a final consumption good.
3. Other natural resources also may have low expected values. For example, until recently the probability of drilling and finding a commercial oil well was estimated at about one in ten. Nevertheless, it was economically sensible to search for oil, despite these odds.

4. Typically, the expected value of the lottery ticket is about one-half the ticket price, indicating that about one-half of the proceeds of the lottery are returned in the winnings with the other half covering costs and being given to the local authority as a supplement to tax revenues.
5. In fact, the situation examined by Simpson et al. (1996) was somewhat more complicated in that it included redundancy in wild genetic resources. Specially, there was more than one plant species that contained the critical "cure for cancer" natural compound, thereby recognising the inter-dependence between the order and value of the "find" of these useful species.
6. The current rate of lose of biodiversity is usually estimated by "species losses." However, current rates of loss are difficult to estimate.
7. It might be argued that the total market derived value is constrained by income and cannot exceed the $16 trillion global GDP.
8. This arrangement is similar in many respects to contracts negotiated between small biotech companies, which have developed valuable artificial genes, and large drug companies, which then further develop and commercialise these into marketed products.

9 Economics, Endangered Species and Biodiversity Loss: The Dismal Science in Practice

ERWIN H. BULTE, DAAN P. VAN SOEST,
G. CORNELIS VAN KOOTEN

Economists have developed a lucid and consistent framework to analyse biodiversity and loss of species. Conservation of species is considered an investment. It can take the form of refraining from current consumption in order, for example, to allocate space (habitat) and management services to enhance survival of species, thereby enhancing possibilities for future consumption. Such investments should only be undertaken if the *rate of return*, broadly interpreted as a social pay off that includes market and nonmarket values, is competitive with other social investments. Few economists have put it more succinctly and lucidly than Swanson (1994):

> "The fundamental force driving species' decline is always the relative rate of investment by the human species. It is the human choice of another asset, over a biological asset, that results in the inevitable decline of that species. Extinctions, whether of specific breeds or of general diversity, are the result of their non-inclusion in the human asset portfolio" (p.805).

In other words, every species has to "earn" its place in the sun. Economists do not shy away from the next step either, arguing that nature conservation can only be successful when "utilisation" of resources is based on proper economic valuation and allocation rules (e.g., Swanson and Barbier 1992). Economics is the ultimate exercise in anthropocentric analysis (see Chapter 10).

The economic position is increasingly recognised by ecologists who, among other things, attempt to apply it as an argument for halting ongoing loss of biological diversity. Implicitly, conservation can be promoted by demonstrating that "saving" species and ecosystems promises higher monetary value than their conversion into other assets (Costanza et al. 1997). Thus, for example, Ehrlich and Wilson (1991) argue that we should care about biodiversity because "... humanity has already obtained enormous direct economic benefits from biodiversity in the form of foods, medicines and industrial products, and has the potential for gaining many more." In addition, there is the "... array of essential services provided by natural ecosystems, of which diverse species are the working parts" (p.760). Ehrlich and Wilson also mention that preserving biodiversity is a moral responsibility, an important issue to which we return later in this chapter.

Some conservationists are sceptical about entering the economic arena to improve the prospects of nature conservation. Some may feel that the act of valuing nature implies a sell out to commercial interests.

> "Unfortunately, the political effectiveness of narrowly utilitarian arguments for large protected areas ... is weak, in part because the promise of long-term economic and health benefits to society as a whole appears to be abstract to individuals and corporations more concerned with survival and short-term economic gains" (Soulé 1991, p.746).

It is argued, in other words, that although nature conservation may be worthwhile from the perspective of society certain influential groups in society prevent it from happening. Others have more practical objections to economic valuation (Sagoff 1988, 1994).

Provision of nature (conservation) is inadequate from a social perspective, because private agents cannot capture all of its benefits—this constitutes a market failure (which is discussed in more detail below). Yet, even if this market failure can be corrected, two problems remain. First, public provision (the usual solution to this form of market failure) is unlikely to result in the success that many wish, as discussed by Sinclair (Chapter 4) and van Kooten (Chapter 10). In some cases, policy failure can lead to greater deterioration of nature than market failure, as Shleifer and Vishny (1998), among others, point out.

Second, as we show in this chapter and much to the disappointment of conservationists, economic arguments are generally *not* sufficient to halt further deterioration of nature. Even if we correct for market and policy failures, and strive to maximise the overall well-being of society, measuring the economic benefits and costs of conservation in accordance with economic principles, we may still find that conservation of nature and biodiversity is *not* a competitive investment. Although the total economic value (the sum of market and nonmarket values) of biodiversity conservation may be enormous, the marginal value is often small—the value of protecting an additional species or hectare of habitat is sometimes insignificant (see Simpson et al. 1996). Thus, Costanza et al.'s (1997) estimate that the globe's ecosystem services are worth some $33 trillion annually, or nearly double the value of the world's annual output, is not very helpful. As a (global) society, we never have to decide whether to eliminate or retain all of the globe's ecosystems. Investment decisions are made at the margin—whether to harvest another hectare of rainforest, another elephant, or the next ton of fish.

We present our argument by summarising the key results from three studies—conservation of the high-profile rainforests of Costa Rica, the benefits of conserving biodiversity, and protection of elephants in Africa. The Costa Rica example highlights the importance of market failure, while stressing the role of international cooperation to compensate that country for benefits that accrue to those living in other (mainly rich) countries—that is, the international spillovers. The second example relies on an abstract model that considers the value of preserving species at the margin (see also Chapter 8). Finally, we consider the economically optimal number of elephants for African range states to support, given that their habitat could also be used for other purposes (such as growing crops). The three cases illustrate a more general principle—that conservation efforts should not necessarily be based on human preferences solicited on (hypothetical) markets. If the "economic case" for conserving rainforests in Costa Rica and elephants in Africa is weak, what are the prospects for millions of species whose forms and functions are, as yet, unknown to humans? What about species, such as worms and beetles, or habitats that do not "excite" in the same way that elephants and rainforest do? We return to this issue in the concluding section.

Conserving Rainforests in Costa Rica

Forest conservation is an investment in natural capital that yields a return in the form of biodiversity, carbon sink and tourism benefits, as well as benefits from the sustainable harvests of wood and non-timber forest products. Often the opportunity costs of forest conservation are the foregone agricultural net returns. The objective of land-use policy should be to maximise social welfare by balancing the marginal benefits of forest conservation against its marginal costs, which enables one to compute optimal forest stocks for different regions.

Two problems are apparent. First, many of the benefits of forest conservation are inherently uncertain. Given that deforestation is (to a certain extent) an irreversible event, a deterministic approach to cost-benefit analysis will underestimate the true value of standing forests as it ignores the benefits of being "flexible" and able to take advantage of new information that comes available as time passes. The benefits of remaining flexible are referred to as (quasi) option value. While it is always possible to convert a forest to agricultural land in the future, it is not possible (quickly) to restore a forest that has been cleared. This asymmetry is an argument for cautionary management. Second, many of the benefits of tropical forest conservation accrue to citizens in other countries, such as the forest's carbon sink benefits and its preservation value.

Here we ignore uncertainty and quasi-option value (see Bulte et al. 2000), focusing on the second problem by distinguishing between optimal forest stocks that take transboundary benefits (spillovers) into account and those that ignore them. It is against these two benchmarks that the current forest stock is to be compared.

Detailed data on 307,000 hectares in humid Costa Rica are available, enabling us to compute the agricultural value of land. The value of forestland in agriculture (which we denote by P_A) is a shadow price determined from a large linear programming model (Schipper et al. 1999). While the first few hectares are extremely valuable and useful for growing high-value crops such as banana, it is clear that bringing extra land into production results in a reduction in net agricultural returns. This is true because expanding the agricultural area implies encroaching upon land of lower quality (it is assumed that the landowner brings the best soils into production first, and then moves onto increasingly inferior land). This implies that the productivity of land in growing a given crop falls as more forestland is converted to agriculture, but more importantly that farmers are required to switch to less profitable crops as well. Bananas just don't grow on all soils. In addition, increasing transport costs brings about declining profitability at the margin.

While our data suggest that a non-linear relationship exists between the value of land in agriculture (P_A) and the amount of land converted from forest to agriculture, we also consider a linear relationship for illustrative purposes. The functions are described in Appendix A to this chapter.

The benefits of forest conversion need to be compared, at the margin, to the benefits of forest conservation. Denote by B the annual per-hectare benefits of sustainable forestry, which equal the sum of carbon sink/uptake benefits, biodiversity preservation benefits (including nonuse values), tourism benefits, and the benefits of sustainable harvesting of timber and non-timber forest products. We assume that B is constant across the forest (which assumes that the study area is small compared to overall tropical forest area in the region). Estimates of the monetary values of these forest services are available in general (e.g., van Kooten and Bulte 2000), while Bulte et al. (2000) indicate that these benefits may be considerable for the study region. Erring on the positive side, it is estimated that the annual benefits of natural forest conservation amount to about $200 per hectare (Table 9.1), with carbon sequestration making up the majority of these benefits.

Table 9.1: Annual Benefits of Primary Forests, Atlantic Zone, Costa Rica

Item	$ ha^{-1} year^{-1}
Production Function	**$75**
- Sustainable timber harvests	50
- Sustainable extraction of NTFP	20
- Sustainable ecotourism	5
Regulatory Function	**$105**
- Carbon uptake and storage [a]	105
Habitat Function	**$20**
- Existence value	10
- Biological prospecting (incl. pharmaceutical value)	10

Source: Bulte et al. (2000)
[a] Assumes 100 tonnes of C stored per ha, $15 per tonne C and a 7% discount rate.

The model for finding the optimal forest stock to preserve is discussed in Appendix A. The marginal agricultural value functions for the linear and non-linear specifications are displayed in Figure 9.1. For the linear specification, agricultural benefits become negative after about 270,000 ha of primary forestland (of 307,000 ha) have been converted. Thus, even if the benefits of retaining forests are zero, no less than 37,000 ha would be kept with the linear specification. Regardless, agricultural benefits will fall below forest benefits (since $B > 0$) at a certain point and the landowner will simply choose to retain the forest.

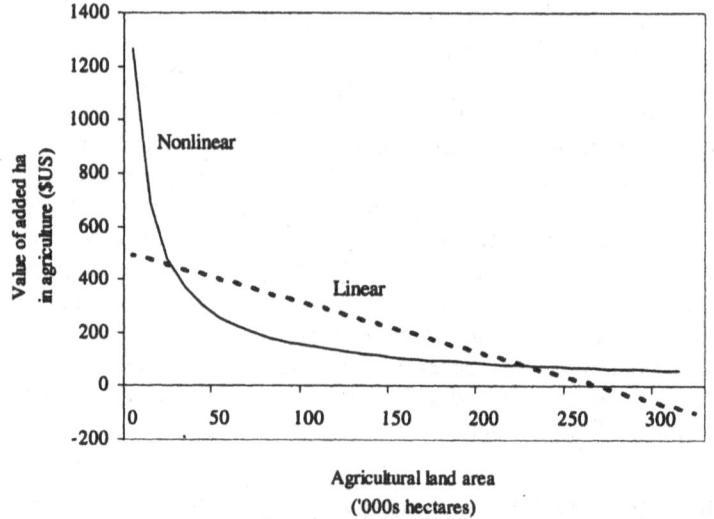

Figure 9.1: Marginal Value of Land in Agriculture, Two Valuation Functions

Assume first that the Costa Rican government is concerned only with domestic benefits of forest conservation, ignoring spillovers, perhaps because there are no international transfers for carbon uptake or species conservation. Specifically, assume that the government takes the production function of natural forests (timber, non-timber forest products and ecotourism) into account, but that it does not care about regulatory and habitat functions that accrue to those outside its borders. This implies that the government (or landowner) sets forest benefits at $75 per ha (substitute $B = 75$ in equation 9.2 of Appendix A), and compares these to the benefits from having that land in agriculture, as spelled out by either the linear or non-linear functions in Figure 9.1. As a sensitivity analysis, we also calculate optimal forest stocks for half and double this benchmark value of the forest benefits (Table 9.2). Optimal forest stocks for the case where only domestic forest benefits are taken into account are found in the first two columns of Table 9.2. Optimal stocks range from none (for the non-linear marginal agricultural value function) to 126,000 ha.

Table 9.2: Optimal Forest Stocks to Hold in Humid Costa Rica (hectares)

	Domestic forest benefits ($B = 75$)		Global forest benefits ($B = 200$)	
	Non-linear	Linear	Non-linear	Linear
Benchmark	0	68,000	176,000	111,000
½ × benchmark	0	55,000	21,000	76,000
2 × benchmark	126,000	94,000	247,000	180,000

Source: Calculation

Next assume that Costa Rica takes transboundary spillovers into account, perhaps because the international community provides compensation for these benefits. For example, Costa Rica might be provided subsidies based on the carbon-sink and biodiversity functions of its protected primary forests. The subsidy would amount to $125 per ha, or total benefit of protecting forest of $200 per ha (substitute $B = 200$ in equation 9.2 of Appendix A). Optimal forest stocks to protect are displayed (for the linear and non-linear functional forms for marginal agricultural benefits) in the final two columns of Table 9.2. Optimal forest stocks in the case of foreign compensation range from 21,000 ha to 247,000 ha, nearly double those when there is no compensation.

The optimal stocks in Table 9.2 should be compared to current forest stocks in the study region of about 80,000-100,000 hectares. The remainder of the land has already been converted to agriculture. In the absence of compensation and for the benchmark case, there is currently too much forest and further deforestation can be expected. Future deforestation depends on the specification of the marginal agricultural value function. If this function is non-linear, which we believe is the more likely from inspection of the underlying data, all of the remaining forest should be cut (the optimal stock is 0 hectares). No more than 10,000-30,000 additional ha should be harvested if the linear specification is "true," but this amount represents a substantial disinvestment in natural capital. Only if the benefits of forest conservation are severely underestimated can the current stock be considered optimal or even sub-optimal (see the 2 × benchmark scenario).

For the case of compensation, benchmark optimal stocks are consistently larger than the extant stock, suggesting that too much forestland have already been converted to agriculture. Indeed, in this situation investments in forest regeneration should be considered, although it is likely that secondary and plantation forests are imperfect substitutes for primary forests. If forest clearing were reversible, the stock should be increased by about 90,000 and 10,000 ha for the non-linear and the linear specification, respectively. Our conclusion that the current stock is too small is true, unless the benefits of forest conservation are significantly overestimated (see the ½ × benchmark scenario in the last two columns of Table 9.2).

Based on these findings, we conclude that there are real opportunity costs involved in forest conservation, namely agricultural revenues foregone, and that, if benefits of forest conservation are modest, further deforestation may be economically optimal. Further, compensatory payments from countries experiencing spillover benefits from Costa Rica's efforts to protect its primary tropical forests are important determinants of the optimal forest stock. If compensatory payments are provided (say for carbon sink functions), the optimal level of forest stocks is likely higher than current stocks. This insight suggests that international compensation for spillover benefits from conservation of natural capital need to be taken seriously, and institutions and incentives need to be developed to bring them about. Finally, the specification of the agricultural benefits function matters a great deal: there are large differences in the optimal forest stock for the linear and non-linear specifications of the marginal agricultural benefits function. Unfortunately, gathering the data to determine which specification is most apt is cumbersome. This suggests that much uncertainty will surround most estimates of the optimal forest stock, giving rise to, among other things, the issue of quasi-option value discussed above.

Does Species Richness Matter?

The world's species richness is not known with any accuracy, nor is there reliable information about biodiversity decline over time (Mann 1991). Nevertheless, biodiversity decline is considered one of the most prominent contemporary ecological issues, and extinction of species is typically assumed to involve economic costs (e.g., Soulé 1991). One asserted major cost of biodiversity decline is the pharmaceutical value of the genetic information that is lost (see Chapters 7 and 8; Randall 1991a).

Documented extinctions since 1600 have been fairly modest and roughly consistent with the background rate of extinction (or normal evolutionary turnover) as predicted by the fossil record (Edwards 1995). Yet, it is often argued that undocumented extinctions are orders of magnitude greater than the geological average (Smith et al. 1995). Most extinction estimates are based on the species-area curve, an empirically derived relationship between habitat size (H) and the number of species (S). In any time period t, this relation is given by $S_t = \alpha H_t^\gamma$, where α and γ are parameters that can be estimated. Consider the loss of species between periods 0 and 1 as predicted by the species-area relation:

(SL) $$\Delta S = S_0 - S_1 = S_0 \left[1 - \left(\frac{H_1}{H_0}\right)^\gamma\right].$$

It is clear from relation SL that a very important determinant of species loss between two periods, ΔS, is the initial 'stock' of biodiversity S_0. Assume that the total number of species amounts to 10 million, and that 3/4 of these are found in tropical forests (S_0 = 7.5 million species). Furthermore, let $\gamma = \frac{1}{4}$ and assume an annual rate of tropical deforestation of 0.6%, which is likely the current rate (van Kooten et al. 1999). Then, S_1 = 7.5 million $(1 - 0.006)^{1/4}$ = 7.489 million species. Thus, SL projects that some 11,275 species will go extinct each year as a result of tropical deforestation. If the total number of species is nearer 100 million, as has been argued by some (e.g., Chapter 2 in this volume), the same rate of deforestation (0.6%) is projected to result in an annual loss of 112,750 species.

One is inclined to assume that "high estimates" of biodiversity and loss of species promote conservation. For a given rate of habitat conversion, higher estimates of S_0 translate into more extinct species, which, *ceteris paribus*, is consistent with higher costs. This is one reason why ecological uncertainty about the number of species is potentially relevant for policy. We consider the viability of the economic approach to conservation, and analyse whether biodiversity loss is likely to pose an important economic problem. We also question whether ecological uncertainty about species richness has economic implications.

In an influential paper, Simpson et al. (1996) estimated the pharmaceutical value of biodiversity. Their main assumptions and outcomes are discussed in Chapters 7 and 8. Here we extend their model somewhat to explore the impact of uncertainty about species richness on the loss of biological prospecting (pharmaceutical) value associated with species decline. The mathematical details of the analysis are provided in Appendix B.

Assuming that habitat conversion (tropical deforestation) proceeds at a rate of 0.8% per year, which is the latest FAO (1997) rate, but may be slightly higher than the current actual rate. Using this rate in SL implies a higher rate of species loss than indicated above. Then, from equation (9.6) in Appendix B, it is possible to compute the associated economic cost in terms of pharmaceutical value foregone.

In the base case, we use the parameter values provided by Simpson et al. (1996), but vary the total number of species. In Figure 9.2, the economic cost of biodiversity decline is plotted against various estimates of the extant number of species (S) for a tropical deforestation rate of 0.8%. The base case results indicate that economic costs are negligible for both low and high estimates of the number of species, and significant for somewhat average values. For few species, costs are low because the species-area curve predicts that deforestation will drive very few species to extinction. Costs are also low for high S because then the pharmaceutical value of the extinct species is negligible due to redundancy. Essentially, pharmaceutical costs of species extinction fall to zero for biodiversity levels of more than, say, 700,000 species.

This implies that uncertainty about the number of species, an important topic for ecologists, is irrelevant from an economic perspective. The economic cost of biodiversity decline for both modest estimates (say 4 million species) and high estimates (100 million species) are virtually zero. In Figure 9.2, we do not consider cases where species exceed one million, or about 50% of the current species count. Additional species have almost no pharmaceutical value and their extinction results in negligible economic costs from this perspective. The economic cost of biodiversity decline is only significant when the total number of species in tropical forest ecosystems is low, between 20,000 and 500,000 species, or a fraction of current biodiversity. For example, when the number of species is reduced to 100,000, the economic cost of biodiversity decline as a result of 0.8% deforestation amounts to $12 million in the base case.

In Figure 9.2, we also demonstrate the effect of doubling the revenues per successful product and the probability that sampling a species yields a successful commercial product. The former increases the economic costs of biodiversity decline, but does not qualitatively affect the main result of the base case. The latter increases the marginal value of species when there are few left, but decreases their value when biodiversity is higher. The marginal value will fall relatively faster because increasing the probability of a success increases redundancy.

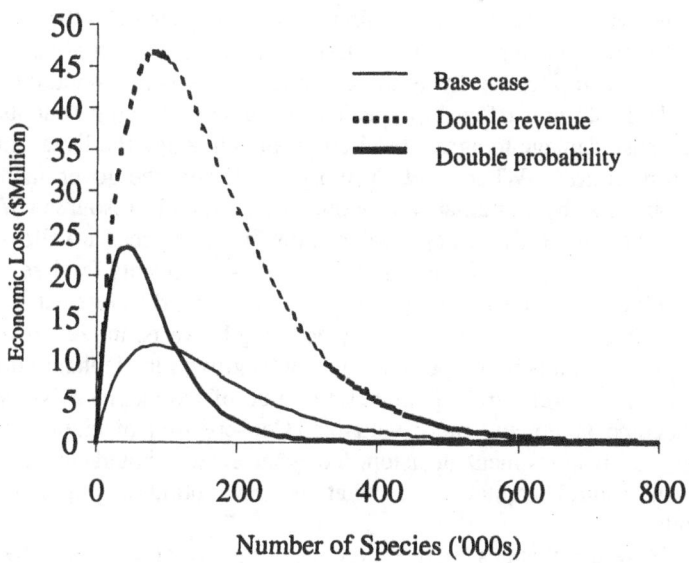

Figure 9.2: Economic Losses and Number of Species

Conserving Elephants in Africa

Populations of the African elephant (*Loxodonta africana*) have declined by more than half since the mid 1970s (Said et al. 1995). Since 1989, both the African and Asian elephant (*Elephas maximus*) have been listed under Appendix I of the CITES agreement, effectively banning international trade in ivory and other elephant products. There has been debate about whether such a ban contributes to conservation of elephants, or instead reduces the incentive for African range states to invest in maintaining elephant herds (Bulte and van Kooten 1996, 1999a). Here we present some evidence on optimal elephant populations in Kenya and Zambia. The focus is not so much on determining whether countries would "hold" larger elephant stocks when a ban on ivory trade is in place versus the trade case, but rather on comparing potentially optimal stocks to the current population.

Bulte and van Kooten (1999a) analysed models with poaching, and models without poaching, assuming full enforcement at zero cost (1996). Since the main results are rather similar, we consider only the simplest case and ignore poaching. We use a model in which African governments maximise social income from three sources—tourism, agriculture and ivory. Elephants are a flagship species that attracts foreign tourists, but they do cause damage to agricultural crops and endanger the lives of those living in rural areas. Where trade in ivory is allowed, the government can earn an income by sustainably cropping this valuable resource. With a trade ban on ivory, only domestic sales at much lower prices are allowed.

Governments have the option to harvest elephants (and sell their ivory) today, investing the proceeds at a certain market interest rate, or delay their harvest to a future date. By delaying harvests, interest revenues are foregone, but this is compensated for by (i) growth in elephant numbers (new calves are born) and (ii) increased value of the elephants' ivory, as tusks become larger and more valuable. Conservation of elephants thus amounts to an investment decision. To what extent should governments invest in natural capital (i.e., what is the optimum population of elephants)?

How do changes in the three key sources of income affect the incentive to invest in elephant conservation? Clearly, a government chooses to hold more elephants if tourism benefits are relatively more important, as is the case for Kenya compared to, say, Ivory Coast. Kenya will also choose to hold elephants in inverse proportion to foregone agricultural revenues, suggesting that more elephants will be conserved in extensively managed grazing areas relative to areas of more intensive agriculture. Finally, consider ivory prices. High prices have an ambiguous effect on the decision to retain elephants. On the one hand, higher prices increase the incentive to keep many elephants as it makes "growing elephants" more competitive compared to growing crops. On the other hand, high prices imply that there is a large sum of money "up for grabs," which can be realised by drastically culling the stock. The proceeds can then be invested elsewhere at the prevailing interest rate. Therefore, if interest rates are high, governments have an incentive to liquidate (or "mine") elephants in the short run, living off interest income into the future. High interest rates are therefore consistent with low elephant stocks, while, if interest rates are sufficiently low, elephants are treated as a valuable source of ivory over extended periods and countries would tend to have relatively large elephant populations.

Two important conclusions emerge from our research and are summarised below. First, our numerical findings indicate that, for interest rates below about 5%, the effect of an ivory trade ban is to lower elephant numbers below what would be optimal in the absence of a trade ban. Conversely, for interest rates higher than 5%, elephant populations are expected to be greater under the trade ban. Given that interest rates in developing countries tend to be much higher than in developed countries, elephant populations are best protected by a trade ban. For the case of Kenya and assuming a relatively high price of ivory, for example, we find that the economically-optimal elephant stock varies from 10,000 (for an interest rate of 12%) to about 23,000 elephants (for an interest rate of 0%).

Our second major conclusion is that current elephant numbers exceed those that are economically optimal under both the trade and no-trade scenario. For realistic discount rates, say between 5% and 15%, the optimal stock is smaller than current stock estimates. This is evident from Table 9.3, where the results for Zambia and Kenya are summarised.

The current (1994) elephant herd in Kenya is about 24,000 animals, while it is about 23,000 elephants in Zambia. Our calculation of optimal Kenyan stocks is for a simple model that ignores poaching, while Zambian stocks are calculated from a more elaborate model that captures poaching and anti-poaching enforcement. By ignoring anti-poaching enforcement costs in the Kenyan model, we underestimate the cost of supporting an elephant herd, and therefore overestimate the "true" optimal level of elephant stocks. This strengthens our qualitative result that, from an economic perspective, elephant stocks are currently too large.

Table 9.3: Protecting Elephants in Zambia and Kenya: Optimal Stocks

Interest rate	Ivory Trade Ban		Trade	
	Kenya	Zambia	Kenya	Zambia
0%	15,700	16,240	22,900	18,080
4%	15,700	15,960	14,800	16,220
6%	15,700	15,820	13,200	15,430
8%	15,700	15,690	11,700	14,720
12%	15,700	15,430	10,000	13,490
16%	15,700	15,190	8,000	12,460

Source: Bulte and van Kooten (1996, 1999a)

That elephants attract tourists is not sufficient to warrant conservation of current stocks. Further "disinvestment" in this form of natural capital is likely called for and we expect to see continued reductions in elephant populations in the future, regardless of whether a trade ban is in place or not. One caveat exists. If there are important spillover benefits associated with elephant conservation in the form of nonuse values (elephants in particular are capable of arousing warm sentiments), and if African range states are compensated for these benefits, the "true" economic stock may be larger than the current stock. Then it may be wise to allocate additional habitat and management services (protection from poachers) to their conservation.

How Competitive are Investments in Nature?

Economic decisions are made at the margin, and it is only at the margin that society is indifferent between conserving and depleting natural capital. Depleting natural capital (say liquidating ivory or valuable trees) implies generating immediate revenues that can be invested elsewhere in the economy. If society decides to conserve natural capital, its return should equal the return on alternative investments that are foregone. As is obvious from Table 9.3, high interest rates (i.e., profitable investment opportunities elsewhere) are consistent with small forest reserves and few elephants. As most of the globe's biodiversity is located in developing countries where capital is scarce (and thus, in theory, capable of generating high rates of return at the margin), the prospects for conserving biodiversity and endangered species look bleak.

This conclusion might be overturned if international spillovers, and compensation for these spillovers, are taken into account, as shown for Costa Rican rainforests. Countries that invest in natural capital could be compensated for carbon sinks, protection of biodiversity or nonuse values that accrue to global society. Bulte and van Kooten (1999b) demonstrate that such nonuse values are an important determinant of the optimal stock of minke whales in the Atlantic Ocean. Minkes are a source of meat and oil and a useful resource for that reason, but they compete with humans for herring and capelin because they prey on these species. The optimal minke whale stock is heavily influenced by assumptions with respect to their nonuse value. While knowledge of actual nonuse values and associated levels of compensation is not required in the case of minke whales, since these are made known through the International Whaling Commission, this is not the case for other species competing for scarce land resources in developing countries.

Even knowledge about nonuse (preservation) values, as determined by willingness to pay (WTP) surveys, for example, is inadequate, however. What is needed is information about marginal nonuse values, about marginal WTP. Bulte and van Kooten (1999b) show that both extinction and strict preservation (consistent with the current moratorium on commercial whaling) can be advocated, depending on what we assume about WTP at the margin; WTP at the margin can be constant, so that the first whale is as valuable as number 85,001, or it may be a declining function in stock size. The latter assumption seems most sensible since it says that people are willing to pay substantial amounts to increase the numbers of a rare species, but not much to increase the numbers of an already abundant species. Indeed, if people only care about the survival of a species, WTP may be positive for populations near the minimum viable population, and zero for protecting additional animals. A similar conclusion is reached with respect to pharmaceutical value and species richness.

Information about marginal preservation values (marginal WTP) is clearly needed for policy analysis, and has heretofore been an area of neglected research. If natural capital is subject to the conventional economic law of decreasing marginal utility, and there is some evidence that this is indeed the case, then marginal nonuse value is declining. This could impact incentives to invest in natural capital.

Inclusion of international and/or domestic nonuse values in the evaluation of biodiversity's worth to society is certainly not a panacea to ensure that conservation and economic efficiency go hand in hand. Even if we include nonuse values in an economic analysis of forest conservation or endangered species protection, it is possible that economics prescribes disinvestment in the natural capital stock. While total preservation value for many high-profile species may be large, at the margin it is likely to be small as long as such species are not threatened or endangered. For other species, total nonuse value may be insignificant because humans may simply not care much about them (as is likely the case for many life forms). It is clear such species need a special plea for their survival if there are opportunity costs involved and that it may only be possible to protect them as part of a larger ecosystem (protected area).

A corollary to these results is that, if the stock of a natural asset is drawn down (whether rainforests or elephants), its marginal value increases. Eventually, species or habitat conservation becomes a competitive social investment. If the number of species declines over time, and redundancy in genetic information is reduced, the value of species conservation at the margin increases. Eventually, conservation of natural habitats may become a profitable investment. But this may not be the case until current (rainforest, elephant, or other natural) stocks are severely depleted. For example, as we showed, the number of species should be decimated before their pharmaceutical value is sufficient to make biological prospecting a viable economic reason for retaining species richness. We also showed that proper economic reasoning leads to the preservation of some stock of tropical rainforest (level of biodiversity), but there is no guarantee that ecologists will be satisfied that it is adequate.

The opportunity costs of conserving some habitats are greater than others. Habitats located on fertile soils in easily accessed areas near human populations will be converted first, and conserving sizeable shares of such areas may be ruled out on economic grounds. Land for which few competing uses exist (deserts, marginal agricultural lands, etc.) may well be allocated as natural habitat, but even these may not be safe in the long run (as argued by Sinclair in Chapter 4; see also Chapter 4). Swanson (1994) argues that, in addition to space, policy makers should allocate management effort to the resource or habitat in question. The probability that an allocation of effort will be economically efficient, however, declines as the quality of the natural asset (or its uniqueness) worsens. This implies that long-run viability of marginal lands is also by no means assured.

Some ecologists and economists may oppose this pessimistic picture and counter by arguing that we have underestimated the true economic value of natural habitats and biodiversity by omitting crucial functions (hence values) of nature. For example, it is often argued that biodiversity is linked to "productivity" and "stability" and that certain "life support functions" can only be provided by natural capital (e.g., Common 1995). However, we argue that (many of) these functions can just as well be served by "managed ecosystems," such as some production forests and agricultural systems. Recent ecological insights indicate that, although diversity may contribute to productivity and stability, it only does so at a decreasing rate. Baskin (1994), for example, notes that

> "... beyond a certain level of diversity, these effects reach a point of saturation. ... [T]he biggest gain in stability came with the first 10 species in [the] system; beyond 10, additional species didn't seem to add much stability ... [and] although biodiversity is valuable up to a certain point, most ecosystems contain more diversity than is needed to reach peak productivity" (p.203).

Discussion

Economists specialise in issues related to efficiency, but many environmental problems are of an ethical nature (Johansson-Stenman 1998). Although it is often useful to make explicit tradeoffs between economic loss and biodiversity protection, it is by no means obvious that efficiency should dominate decision making in nature conservation. Ultimately, deciding how much natural capital to retain cannot be determined exclusively by economic reasoning, but will require moral discourse. Howarth and Norgaard (1993, 1995) demonstrate this point with overlapping generation models. When rights to natural resources and environmental services are redistributed to future generations, a new efficient path of resource use arises, wherein discount rates are lower and resource and environmental values are higher. Clearly, there are difficulties redistributing rights to as yet unborn generations, but the main lesson is that economic efficiency (i.e., cost-benefit analysis) is determined by the distribution of rights, and that such distribution decisions are ethical.

Denying the primacy of rights and responsibilities to human beings can itself challenge the utilitarian framework of cost-benefit analysis.

Advocates of alternative moral philosophies appeal to a nonanthropogenic value system, perhaps arguing that other creatures are part of God's creation and that destroying them is sinful. Others believe that we have a moral obligation to conserve products of natural evolution, the process that produced us, while still others accept the concept of species egalitarianism. Some of these issues are discussed further in Chapters 10 and 11.

Where does this leave us? First, we would like to argue that economic reasoning is clearly important in developing instruments to achieve nature preservation objectives in cost-effective fashion. Innovative instruments like conservation banking (or tradable development rights, see for example Shogren 1998) may promote nature conservation at lower cost than the command and control approach to setting aside habitat as prescribed, for example, by the US Endangered Species Act (see Brown and Shogren 1998). Second, it is an open question whether we need to follow economic efficiency rules to their conclusion and disinvest in natural capital when the rate of return of such capital is (temporarily?) deemed insufficient. As stated above, this may conflict with ethical considerations. Currently it is an open question whether injecting a new ethic will make the economic realities of the opportunity cost of conservation go away.

Appendix A: A Model of Rainforest Conversion in Costa Rica

Denote the total area of forestland plus agricultural land available in the study region by L. Land either remains forested or is converted to agriculture. The function describing the net benefits of forest conservation is given as $B[L - A(t)]$, where $A(t)$ denotes the amount of land in agriculture at time t. The region's annual flow of benefits is

$$(9.1) \quad \pi(A, B) = \int_0^A P_A \, da + B(L - A),$$

where the first term on the right-hand-side measures total benefits from agriculture (as the area under the marginal benefit curve) and the second term measures total forest benefits. If the landowner maximises the infinite discounted sum of annual benefits from the land, the optimal forest stock that should be held is given by:

(9.2) $$\frac{B}{r} = \frac{P_A}{r} - c,$$

where r is the discount rate and c is the one-time cost of agricultural conversion (Bulte et al. 1999). It could be that c is actually negative because clearing the forest yields timber revenues that exceed harvest costs plus the costs of preparing the land for agriculture.

Optimal forest stocks can be obtained by solving Equation (9.2) once we determine an expression for P_A—the marginal value of land in agriculture as a function of the agricultural land base. Linear and non-linear specifications are employed: $P_A = \delta - \gamma A$ and $P_A = \delta A^{-\gamma}$, where δ and γ are positive parameters to be estimated and A is the amount of forestland that has been converted to agriculture. The parameter δ measures the net return to the "best" hectare in the study region. The parameters are estimated using OLS regression analysis and are as follows (Bulte et al. 1999):

Parameter	Linear Specification	Non-linear Specification
δ	139.467	20.96
γ	0.525	0.89

Appendix B: A Model of Species Loss

Let p be the probability with which any randomly sampled species yields a successful commercial product, R is the associated (net) revenue of successfully developing such a new product, and C is the cost of research and development. Then the expected value of sampling a species is $pR - C$. Sampling is treated as an independent Bernouilli trial with each species having an equal probability of being a successful product (which is a simplification). Over time, society will demand new products, such as cures against new infectious diseases. This will increase the value of biodiversity prospecting. Define λ as the mean arrival rate of this "demand" for new products. The increase in (marginal) value from an additional species, or marginal value function, is

(9.3) $$V(S) = \left(\frac{\lambda}{r}\right)(pR - C)(1-p)^S > 0,$$

where r is the discount rate and S the number of species. Due to redundancy in genetic information (once a successful product is found, further discoveries add little for that particular application), marginal value is a declining function in the number of species; that is,

(9.4) $$\frac{\partial V}{\partial S} = \left(\frac{\lambda}{r}\right)(pR - C)(1-p)^S \ln(1-p) < 0.$$

Total economic cost as a result of losing ΔS species is measured as the relevant area under the marginal value curve, obtained by integrating equation (9.3):

(9.5) $$\int_S^{S+\Delta S} V(z)dz = \left(\frac{\lambda}{r}\right)\frac{pR-C}{\ln(1-C)}(1-p)^S[(1-p)^{\Delta S} - 1].$$

It is possible to calculate ΔS from the species-loss relation (SL) in the text. The cost of research, C, is known, and past experience gives some idea about the expected revenue of a success, R, and the probability p that a randomly chosen piece of genetic material (biodiversity) will yield success. Then, one can estimate the cost of losing species using (9.5), which is done in the text.

10 Biodiversity and Ethics: Religion, Science and Economics
G. CORNELIS VAN KOOTEN

"Religion without science is blind. Science without religion is lame." (Albert Enstein)

Introduction

Taking as a starting point the view that there is a growing international consensus in favour of protecting biodiversity, efforts are now aimed at developing a new "Earth Charter" that will provide a legal and political framework for guiding local, regional, national and international efforts to protect biological resources (Norton 1999). Such a Charter needs to balance two diametrically opposed views of "how to deal with" nature. The first is that associated with the "Deep Ecology" movement, although it is often subscribed to by a variety of others who would not think of themselves as deep ecologists. It attributes inherent (intrinsic) value to all forms of life, ranging from bacteria to the largest animal species. In its most radical form, value is attributed even to trees and wild rivers. This is the biocentric or nonanthropogenic view of nature and value. Its main tenant is that "… an irreversible human intervention in nature is wrong" (Solow and Polasky 1999, p.19).

In contrast, the anthropocentric view recognises that humans make decisions about nature, including whether nature should or should not be treated as having intrinsic value, and thus valuation is inherently an anthropogenic exercise. In this view, nature only has instrumental value, which is associated with the value it has for humans. Because it is essentially utilitarian, the anthropogenic view is generally associated with mainstream (neoclassical) economics (Norton 1999).

The advantage of economics over other ethical systems is that it provides an explicit means for valuing nature (in monetary terms), one that eludes many other fields including biology. This is not to say that the biocentric approach fails to provide values. Certainly, intrinsic values are exactly that, but what biocentricism lacks is a measure of value that can be used to make real-world decisions about nature. For example, in choosing where to locate a hospital in a tropical forest region, it may be necessary to trade off loss of one species or population against another. Choosing site A results in the loss of some population x of a species, while choice of B results in the loss of population y. Choosing cannot be avoided, regardless of any principle to the contrary. While the deep-ecology biocentric ethic leads to political and social gridlock (neither site can be developed), the economic approach provides a criterion for deciding on a course of action; economics has the ability to make tradeoffs, while biocentrism does not. Yet, there is no over-arching principle for deciding that the economic approach is somehow better than the deep ecology approach. Simply noting that the one provides a criterion for choosing is inappropriate justification for its preference as an ethical system. While economics chooses elements of nature on the basis of their instrumental value and deep ecology chooses on the basis of their intrinsic value, there is no means of choosing between the two valuation systems.

This dilemma and its practical resolution are seen in the US Endangered Species Act (1973). While the courts have interpreted the Act as bestowing rights on species that go beyond instrumental values (because species are to be preserved "whatever the cost"), a number of exceptions have been built in to take account of economic considerations. These include explicit waivers granted by the Endangered Species Committee (created by the Congress to get around the ESA if need be), or implicit ones granted to landowners with approved habitat protection plans. There also exist considerations that recognise budgets are limited and that costs and benefits of protecting species need to be traded off in deciding where scarce resources to protect species are to be concentrated (Solow and Polasky 1999). Further, the ESA does not protect insect pests or viruses dangerous to human health. In essence and from a practical standpoint, the ESA attempts to balance the different biocentric and anthropocentric ethical viewpoints.

The Earth Charter is more ambitious, however, attempting to develop a universal code of conduct, or ethic, that expresses the shared values of all people on earth, regardless of their cultural-religious background. As Norton (1999) points out, it needs to find a middle ground between the opposing ethical views expressed above. He suggests that this compromise can be found if both economists and deep ecologists are willing to abandon their monistic valuation approaches and the dichotomy between instrumental and intrinsic environmental values. He argues that humans value nature in many ways, along a continuum from entirely self-directed and consumptive uses to human spiritual values and aesthetic values, as well as other forms of noninstrumental valuation. Unfortunately, neither side is likely to accept this "continuum," with the economist responding that the economic method of valuation can be extended to include these "non-instrumental" values, and the deep ecologist crying foul because it is unacceptable in their ethical system to permit certain species (or populations) to go extinct (as might sometimes be required by such a compromise).

In this chapter, I examine ethical issues relating to biodiversity from several perspectives, including that of science versus religion. I also consider the role of recent developments in economics as they pertain to the debate about ethics generally and an ethics of biodiversity more specifically. I make a distinction between "low-level" ethical norms, which relate to whether one considers species to have intrinsic or instrumental value, and "top-level" ethical norms that relate to the more fundamental (religious) ground motives that govern people's lives (Dooyeweerd 1979, 1980). Low-level norms do not shed light on the higher norms. Yet, as I argue, attempts to develop a consensus universal earth ethic are based on low-level norms. Hence, even though an Earth Charter may well contain some statement that many might regard as a universal ethic, it may ring hollow.

I begin in the next section with a review of biocentric and anthropocentric valuation. Then I briefly consider whether science and religion are in conflict, because, if they are, then the prospects of achieving compromise on a universal earth ethic is in jeopardy. I conclude that they are in conflict because they are rooted in different religious ground motives. In particular, I argue that the norms of science are of the low-level type because they are endogenously determined, while top-level norms are external to the systems that science considers. I expand on this in section following the one on top-level ethical norms (science and religion), where I consider top-level norms in the context of a non-neoclassical view of "economic man."

If compromise on a universal earth ethic is improbable, or meaningless if accomplished, is there not an alternative? One approach to the protection of biodiversity that does not require a farcical process of constructing (artificial) consensus over an environmental ethic is to obtain only a consensus to protect biodiversity and a desire to construct appropriate social and economic institutions for doing so. (The ESA might be considered a first example of this approach.) The institutions constitute the legal and political framework for guiding local, regional, national and international efforts to protect biological resources, with a desire to protect species constituting the "moral grounds." Such agreement may be easier to achieve than agreement on a universal earth ethic, while the institutional framework can be developed by beginning with a view of human nature and human interactions that is more realistic than that used by neoclassical economists. It also requires that deep ecologists look to a defence of nature through political processes rather than confrontation. On the economics side, the place to begin thinking about an appropriate institutional framework is with a different view of economic man than that employed by neoclassical economics. Therefore, in the next to last section, I provide a link between the new economics and ethics, and I offer some thoughts about what this approach implies for the protection of biodiversity. I finish with some concluding observations.

Low-level Ethical Norms: Biocentric and Anthropocentric Valuation

In this section, I briefly review the main arguments concerning the biocentric (Deep Ecology) and anthropocentric (instrumental) approaches to the protection of nature and biodiversity. Biocentrism takes as its starting point that all species, human as well as non-human, have equal status; if humans are to continue to exist, then all species must be prevented from going extinct. Thus, if biodiversity is to be accorded either first-principle or pre-eminent status, anthropocentric valuation is clearly not acceptable (Ehrenfeld 1988). Biocentrism says that species have intrinsic value and humans are duty bound to preserve them, regardless of the costs.

The duty-based approach of biocentrism does not survive critical scrutiny. Assume that there are at least two moral goods—preserving biodiversity and enhancing the life prospects of the world's worst-off people. Which takes pre-eminent status—the life of a human or that of another life form? Randall (1991b) makes the case that "the claims of humans trump those of non-humans," and, in my view, any reasonable human would reach the same conclusion. Human life is more important than that of other life forms. Further, if biocentrism is "... carried to its logical conclusion, only a hunting and gathering society would be permitted" (Castle 1993, p.286).

Nonetheless, when the choice is not so stark (choosing to sacrifice human life for some other forms of life), it is reasonable to expect that humans should make some sacrifices for nature. The point is that such sacrifice cannot be unlimited. When, then, should preservation of species become an overriding constraint on human behaviour?

Christian writers also point out that species have value beyond an anthropocentric one, but such value is not intrinsic—the Christian ethic is neither biocentric nor anthropocentric. Species have value to the Creator and humans do not have the right to destroy species (or even individuals) wantonly (Schaeffer 1970). Rather, since humans are considered to be the pinnacle of creation (created in the image of God), they have a stewardship responsibility for the creation (Cobb 1988). However, that responsibility has been abrogated as a result of sin. While the Christian view points to sin as the root cause of irresponsible behaviour toward creation, this aspect of the Christian viewpoint is often forgotten (Beisner 1997).[1] Importantly, the Christian view asserts that sin prevents realisation of effective policies for achieving a harmonious relationship between humans and the environment. Along with humanity's fall into sin, the creation also became "polluted" or imperfect (Schaeffer 1972; Grizzle and Barrett 1998). Thus, while Christianity states that humans have an obligation to preserve the creation, it also points to an inability to achieve what is desired. (Other religions also stress the importance of human responsibility to the environment, but they have had no greater or lesser success in applying this ethic in practice.) This, then, provides a case for the imposition of constraints on human behaviour, constraints imposed by the authority, much like a safe minimum standard might constrain economic efficiency (see below).

Secular approaches to a biodiversity ethic are essentially limited to (1) utilitarianism, (2) libertarianism, and (3) contractarianism.[2] Utilitarians consider only instrumental values of biodiversity and maximisation of social utility to be the basic criterion of morality, with social utility defined either as the sum, or the arithmetic mean, of the utility levels of all individuals in the society. Although "...the recent environmental movement has witnessed an intensive search for an environmental ethic not based on utilitarianism," none has been found (Castle 1993, p.285).

Utilitarianism forms the foundation for cost-benefit analysis. The utilitarian social welfare function can be specified as:

(SWF) $W = W[U_1(m_1), U_2(m_2), ..., U_n(m_n)]$,

where W is total society welfare, U_i refers to the utility of the ith individual in society, m_i is the individual's income (representing the ability to purchase goods and services, including biological assets), and there are n individuals in society. Cost-benefit analysis assumes additive (strong) separability of the social welfare function, so that total social welfare is simply the (unweighted) sum of the welfares of the individuals in society. This assumes that all individuals count and they count equally. Further, if the marginal utility of income is constant and equal across individuals (a dollar contributes the same increase in utility for a poor person as a rich one), then welfare is simply the sum of everyone's income. The problem with utilitarianism is that it permits the large sacrifice of some (say landowners) to the benefit of the majority, as long as the gain exceeds the loss. The utilitarian ethic permits the suppression of individual rights for the good of the collective.

In principle, if social well-being is maximised, the gainers should be able to compensate the losers and still be better off. However, providing compensation may not only be costly (transaction costs could be high), but compensation will change the distribution of income, perhaps in a way that affects economic efficiency. In other words, the decision that maximises (SWF) under one income distribution may no longer be the optimal decision once the income distribution is changed (as a result of compensation paid). Compensation could change an efficient policy to protect a particular habitat into an inefficient policy. A review of some compensation issues in the context of the ESA is provided by Innis (1999).

One variant of utilitarianism suggests that species be included in the summation of well-being (welfare). This implies expanding the welfare function (SWF) to include the utility of (individual members of?) species. However, assignment of species' preferences, so that they can then be included in the universal "sum," is a human task, so the utilitarian cannot avoid anthropocentric valuation.

Libertarianism originates with classical liberal philosophy; central to libertarian ethics is the concept of individual rights and private property, even to the point that "... taxation of earnings from labour is on a par with forced labour" (Nozick 1974, p.169). Debates over rights and privileges with regard to use of natural resources (e.g., grazing or timber harvesting "rights"), and biodiversity, are ongoing. Most would reject libertarian philosophy because it places onerous limits on society's ability to control private land-use decisions that affect wildlife habitat, often requiring the public to provide compensation to landowners to protect species. However, libertarians are quite likely to be receptive to cost-benefit analysis, but with restrictions on what can be done to reduce the welfare of some in order to enhance the total welfare of all. Libertarians would clearly give pre-eminent status to humans.

A contractarian case for preserving biodiversity relies upon thought experiments (Rawls 1971). In some experiments, the possibility that one is "born" non-human is accepted. Preservation of species relies upon the notion that one has a chance of being "born" into a non-human species that might one day be forced to extinction by human action. Therefore, similar to the Rawlsian principle that gives priority to the least-off individuals in society (but subject to the principle of liberty), it is concluded that extirpation of any species is wrong. The argument falters on the same grounds as above—the claims of humans have priority over those of non-humans. While equality between humans and non-humans might be acceptable to deep ecologists, it cannot be the foundation upon which to base a society (Castle 1993). Another problem with this approach is that it is based on a presupposition (that differences between humans and non-humans are only biological) that has no more right to priority claim than an alternative presupposition (that only humans matter).

Randall and his colleagues (Randall 1988, 1991b; Randall and Farmer 1995; Farmer and Randall 1998) have used contract arguments to modify the utilitarian approach to valuation in the context of biodiversity. Although the focus is on human preferences, inclusion of a safe minimum standard (SMS) constraint is considered to be a component of a just constitution. The cost-benefit approach emerges as a second-best result: "... a plausible contractarian solution is to maximise net benefits (to satisfy preferences) subject to a SMS constraint (because participants in the "veil of ignorance" process would insist on it)" (Randall 1991b, p.17).

The most common theme in terms of a potential compromise in the ethical frameworks presented above is the possibility of including a constraint on human behaviour that takes into account biodiversity value outside of its instrumental value. However, such a compromise is antithetical to deep ecology because it still values humans higher than other life forms, but it agrees with many religious ethical systems and possibly the Darwinian notion of competition (i.e., survival of the fittest species, in this case humans). It is also antithetical to utilitarianism because it imposes a rather arbitrary, non-utilitarian constraint on behaviour (Farmer and Randall 1998).

Top-level Ethical Norms: Science and Religion

Current efforts to develop a common environmental ethic begin with nature; nature is the source of value, where we need to look for answers to human ethics regarding environment (Wallace and Norton 1992; Lovelock 1987). The problem with this approach, and why it will be impossible to find the type of compromise necessary to establish a common environmental ethic, is that not everyone will agree that ethics originates in nature, or even with humans. An ethic rooted in nature is evolutionary and relativistic; it is a low-level ethics. It is incompatible with an ethic that comes from outside both humans and nature, one that is absolute, holding at all times and in all circumstances—a top-level ethic. An ethic rooted in relativism is empty and incompatible with one that is absolute (Bloom 1987; Johnson 1995). Top-level ethical norms are determined at the foundational level, originating with one's fundamental beliefs.

We live in the age of science. While science has given us material wealth and products, the likes of which our ancestors could not even dream of, it also influences how we view the world. In many ways, science has become the religion of modern day. What is different about today's science, compared to that of the past, is that it is no longer based on a shared religious view of the world.[3] Science is rooted in what Johnson (1995, 1997) calls "naturalism" or "materialism;" indeed, as Johnson argues, science is by definition the religion of naturalism. Today's science is founded upon a philosophy that has rejected Christianity as a worldview—the new worldview seeks to exorcise God as an explanation in science. This is most evident in the new physics and in evolutionary biology, which together have provided an explanation for the existence of both the universe and life on earth that requires no Creator. As Davies (1983) puts it: "... the creation of matter, so long considered the result of divine action, can now (perhaps) be understood in ordinary scientific terms" (p.32).

Attempts to invoke a divine or teleological explanation in science are usually ridiculed, and many scientists are reluctant to rely on divine explanations for fear that, at some future date, a "scientific" explanation may materialise. There is "... plenty of scope for divine explanations, but that is a purely negative attitude, invoking 'the God-of-the-gaps' only to risk retreat at a later date in the face of scientific advance" (Davies 1983, p.70). While there is no adequate explanation as to *why* the universe exists (Hawking 1988, pp.174-75), neither Hawking nor Davies would accept design as an explanation for the "why" of the Universe. Nonetheless, even after more than a century of attempting to eliminate God as an explanation for the existence of the Universe (Craig 1999; Hawking and Penrose 1996; Smith 1993) and life on earth (Johnson 1993; Moreland 1994; Milton 1997), science has not succeeded—science cannot explain everything. It has succeeded only in reducing God to a "God-of-the-gaps," a device used by some to intimidate those whose science begins with the proposition that God created all things.

If science has succeeded in eliminating miracles and divine intervention as scientific explanations, one might expect faith in God to be inversely correlated with scientific training. But this has not been the case. Rather, empirical evidence indicates that religious faith is directly proportional to scientific training, with those in psychology, anthropology, sociology and evolutionary biology expressing least faith in a Creator (Stark et al. 1996; Fukuyama 1999, p.239). Further, both evolution and claims of widespread loss of species are increasingly being challenged (Goldschmidt 1940; Mann 1991; Johnson 1993; Moreland 1994; Bailey 1995; Behe 1996; Milton 1997; van Kooten 1998; Jones 1999). One might be tempted to sweep this issue under the carpet in a book of this nature, but the volume of scientific literature in opposition to evolutionary notions (and the threat of species loss) is impossible to ignore. Because the challenge has become a threat, Gould (1999) wrote an interesting treatise that seeks to reconcile science (Darwinism) and religion. He fails because he provides a much too narrow definition of religion; he rules out miracles and divine intervention (pp.84-85), which is anathema to the Christian faith (as the incarnation and resurrection of Christ, and hence salvation itself, are ruled out as impossible) as well as most other faiths. That is, Gould permits only a compromise that accepts his ground motive, which is rooted in nature.

With notable exceptions, the traditional view is that neoclassical economics is silent on the role of ethics, particularly top-level ethics.[4] Rather, neoclassical economics is considered to be a science (which it is) that accepts the (low-level) utilitarian ethical norm as a practical starting point. It says nothing about the role of high-level ethical norms, although one might expect it to do so given that economics seeks to explain human behaviour. It is this weakness, among others, that have caused some to reconsider economics by modifying the neoclassical framework. This is discussed in the next section, where top-level norms are shown to be important to the development of appropriate economic policies, including ones to preserve biodiversity.

Re-evaluating Economics' View of Economic Man

In developing policies to address market failure with respect to the provision of nature, it is necessary to have a proper view of economic man, one that explicitly recognises humans' limits and fallibilities, and the human need and desire for social interaction. Such a view of economic man is rooted as much in sociology and psychology as in economics, and emphasises economic and social institutions. In this section, I present a modified view of economic man that sheds light on both ethical norms and efforts to protect biodiversity.

Institutions are defined as "... humanly devised constraints that structure human interaction. They are either formal or informal: formal institutions consist of formal constraints, e.g., policy rules, regulations, laws, constitutions, contracts, property rights, bargaining agreements, [while] informal institutions concern informal constraints, e.g., norms of behaviour, conventions, self-imposed codes of conduct" (CPB 1997, p.42). Included in the definition of institutions are "... a set of moral, ethical behavioural norms which define the contours that constrain the way in which the rules and regulations are specified and enforcement is carried out" (North 1994, p.8). The New Institutional Economics (NIE) evolved in response to the fundamental need to include explicitly institutions into economic analysis. However, while descending out of the "old" institutional economics associated with Veblen and Commons, the NIE was as much a response by neoclassical economists to perceived weaknesses in the assumptions underlying mainstream economics (North 1990; Acheson 1994; Pejovich 1995; Furubotn and Richter 1997). While the NIE is "a science of institutions," its practitioners emphasise that economics is still a "science of choices."

Neoclassical economics assumes that humans are rational economisers who have perfect knowledge. Markets are perfectly competitive, homogeneous goods are traded and prices contain all relevant information. Where market failure occurs, governments can help society attain economic efficiency (correct the failure) through appropriate regulations or market-based incentives. Again the assumption is that economic agents are rational and that governments act only in the best interests of society.

The NIE differs from neoclassical economics in some fundamental ways.

- The NIE takes the position that economic agents are rationally bounded, while information is costly to obtain. Agents do not have perfect information but are often opportunistic, acting in their own self interest with guile—people are only weakly rational and weakly moral, often withholding information when it is in their interests to do so (Acheson 1994, p.8). Bounded rationality and opportunism cause transaction costs (CPB 1997, p.46). Transactions take place even though information is incomplete or distorted. Further, people do not always have exclusive rights to what is traded. This then leads to a great deal of uncertainty and incomplete contracting.
- There are costs to using markets because of market imperfections and outright market failure. Provision of nature (protecting biodiversity) is one form of market failure.
- It is the case in many transactions (including ones that deal with provision of nature) that price is not the sole consideration. There exist many forms of social and legal ties among people, and nonmarket (or beyond market) transactions take place, especially within the same organisation.
- Governments are organisations made up of economic agents who act in their own self interest (with guile) and not always (or even generally) for the good of society (Shleifer 1998; Shleifer and Vishny 1998).
- Finally, a key assumption of the NIE is that institutions have a strong impact on the economic system and that institutions are often the result of political processes.

It would be narrow to think that the new approach to economics focuses only on the evolution of institutions, property rights, transaction costs, and uncertainty (a form of market failure relevant for biodiversity), or that there is some grand unified theory. Rather, the NIE might be looked upon as one approach to what might more properly be termed psychological and socio-political economics (PSPE). PSPE goes beyond monistic (monetary) valuation to include directly and explicitly higher social values within the preference function of an economic agent, including inter-personal relations, the well-being of others, and the interaction between humans and nature. While the economics literature does not often discuss higher values, collectivism, bounded rationality and stewardship (only money counts), there is in principle no reason why factors other than consumption cannot be taken into the decision calculus (other things besides money also count) (Berns et al. 1999).

Markets and Social Capital

As noted in Chapter 1, disagreements about sustainability relate to differing views about whether it is natural capital or a combination of natural and human-made capital that is to be kept intact over time. Strong sustainability does not permit substitutability between natural and human forms of capital, while weak sustainability allows for the demise of some natural capital as long as investments in other forms of capital (say, growing trees, development of wind farms for generating electricity) offset such losses. What is forgotten is the role of social capital (Fukuyama 1999; Berns et al. 1999). Social capital refers to social norms (such as trust, responsibility, initiative, work ethic, etc.) that substitute for complete contracts, because complete contracting is not always possible.

A market transaction that involves the purchase and sale of an item at the time of exchange is an example of a complete contract. With complete contracts all contingencies are covered. Incomplete contracting occurs because the parties to the contract know that unforeseen circumstances will arise, some of which may be dealt with in a court of law (increasing transaction costs) but others that can only be resolved through negotiation or some other means. Social norms reduce transaction costs associated with contingencies that cannot be dealt with via markets (such as moral hazard, free riding and adverse selection), reducing the uncertainty of incomplete contracts. Clearly, social norms have economic value and therefore constitute social capital.

Two corollaries follow:
1. A reduction in social capital will result in greater reliance on markets.
2. The greater the cultural diversity of a civil society, the greater will be the reliance on markets in place of imperfect contracts, and the court system where imperfect contracts are unavoidable. In contrast, the more homogenous is a society, the more it will rely on cultural norms and tradition in resolving uncertainty related to imperfect contracts, and markets are relied upon to a lesser extent (CPB 1997).

It is of little surprise, therefore, that a reduction of social capital leads to reliance on markets and to increasing globalisation. One effect of globalisation is to increase the homogeneity of ecosystems as a result of bio-invasions (see Chapter 6).

It is not clear whether markets enhance or destroy social norms, with arguments having been made in both directions. What is clear from empirical evidence, however, is that economic growth has provided greater consumption opportunities for the masses, and this has been accompanied by increased individual freedoms. This in turn has resulted in two distinguishing features of post-modernism, namely, the rejection of all forms of authority and the throwing off of many norms (Bern et al. 1999, p.39). Markets increasingly replaced social norms, and norms themselves became a product of the increasing reliance on markets—a product of evolutionary processes and thus increasingly relativistic.

Bounded Rationality and Need for Higher Norms

Bounded rationality implies that people no longer have fixed preferences (as in the standard neoclassical theory), but suffer from preference drift and reference drift (Berns et al. 1999). Preference drift refers to the phenomenon that, once an aspiration level has been attained, the person is disappointed and immediately seeks some higher or alternative goal; after making a lifetime choice and attaining one's goals, a person may wish that they had made an alternative life choice. Reference drift, on the other hand, refers to the influence that society has on one's preferences, of which "keeping-up-with-the-Jones" is only a part. Social interaction plays an important role in determining one's preferences (utility function), while moral and relational preferences help individuals discover their *fundamental* personal preferences.

Norms are determined either endogenous to the economic system or come from outside it. Low-level norms are endogenous to the cultural-economic system, with such norms both influencing and being influenced by the cultural-economic system. Norms are relativistic with people no longer trusting the norms of others, thus reducing social capital. There are no top-level norms because the idea that such norms exist is ruled out by the fact that norms are grounded in nature—they are relativistic by definition as nature itself is continually evolving.

This is not true of top-level norms; they are determined outside nature and outside the cultural-economic system. When individuals are rationally bounded, top-level norms that are external to the cultural-economic system are important, because they result in persons being less vulnerable to being misled (Berns et al 1999, pp.42-3). Thus, there is room for Christian and other religious ground motives as a source of higher norms, ones that are absolute. These top-level norms will often be in conflict with endogenous, low-level norms, because the latter are relative. Agreement concerning a universal environmental ethic cannot be based on low-level norms. Agreement based on top-level norms is also unlikely primarily because the debate has not reached (and probably never will reach) that level of recognition—it is mired in low-level norms because of the desire artificially to separate science from religion.

Norms and Protection of Biodiversity

As already noted, increasing opportunities for consumption have resulted in greater personal freedom, and the evolution of relativistic norms. While on the positive side post-modernism rejects many values associated with consumption (i.e., places greater value on such things as biodiversity), it also embraces relativism. When norms are endogenous and relative, there is no reason to suppose that they will favour protection of biodiversity at all times. At some times and in some places (such as today in the western developed countries), norms may favour ecosystems; at other times or places (e.g., ex-Soviet Union, some developing countries), norms might favour materialistic output over biodiversity. One does not known what the outcome of an evolutionary process will be.

It is only when norms are external to nature, when they are absolute, that there is hope for the protection of biodiversity. Top-level norms provide the conditions under which exploitation of biological (and other natural) resources can take. For example, Christian norms regarding consumption and exploitation of nature are quite explicit: such norms place great emphasis on living a life of moderation, helping the poor, and looking after (being stewards of) creation or species (e.g., Schaeffer 1970; Hay 1989; Beisner 1997; Grizzle and Barrett 1998).

Policy needs to focus on creating appropriate social and economic institutions that encourage the development of social capital, including discouraging consumerism and unbounded individual freedom. The establishment of boundaries on individual freedoms originates with religion. Moral universalism owes its origin to religion, and it is religion, and particularly Christianity, that "... bequeathed the idea of the universal equality of human rights [and] secular doctrines like liberalism and socialism" (Fukuyama 1999, p.237). It is also in religion that one must seek a universal environmental ethic, because it can never be found in the spontaneous order that results from social cooperation (p.236). Universal ethics can only be found in religion, and, while "... the aspiration toward moral universalism may be unrealised by any actual religion, ... it is nonetheless an inextricable part of the moral universe created by religion" (p.237). While the implication may not be to rebuild hierarchical (religious) authority, habits of honesty, reciprocity, trust and constraint need to be re-established (p.244).

While institutions do not develop higher norms directly, the lessons of PSPE are valuable in enabling society to construct economic and social institutions that prevent erosion of habits of honesty, reciprocity and trust, perhaps even encouraging them (see, e.g., Hart et al. 1997; Shleifer 1998; Shleifer and Vishny 1998). In addition to establishing moral universalism through greater reliance on top-level rather than low-level norms, therefore, we should begin with a revised model of economic man and use it to recommend economic policies that are both more humane and cognisant of the role and importance of the environment.

Conclusions

I have argued that compromise concerning a universal earth ethic is improbable. However, this does not imply that nothing can be done to protect the world's ecosystems, and species in particular. My conclusions are rather conventional, partly because the notions developed in this chapter (in particular those of the previous section) need further development. Nonetheless, I argue that there are two touchstones upon which it may be possible to develop policy.

First, it is important to recognise that there are limits to what can and cannot be done in the real world of politics. These limits exist because humans do matter more than other life forms (at least for most people), humans are concerned about preserving biodiversity but are not willing to make "significant" sacrifices to do so, and, thus, not all species or even ecosystems can be saved. It also needs to be recognised that, contrary to what often seems to be implied, humans never make decisions about whether or not to eliminate all of the earth's ecosystem functions, or even some significant component thereof—choices are always incremental. In this regard, it is important to distinguish between ecosystem functions and their content (form or makeup). An ecosystem can lose a significant proportion of its original species, having been replaced by exotics (Chapter 6), but it can continue providing all of its natural functions, including scenic and other values. Only the trained biologist might detect that the ecosystem is not what it once was. On a choice between humans and nature that does not involve loss of an ecosystem's function, but perhaps loss of its "originalness," this view would come down on the side of humans.

Second, people are willing to accept certain (limited) constraints to protect nature—a safe minimum standard. Voluntary constraints are probably inadequate, so they will need to take the form of institutional constraints or economic incentives. It is here that questions about the role of markets versus other means of implementing constraints come to the fore. Where social capital has been eroded, greater reliance on markets will be required. Alternatively, one can rely on government provision of nature, or direct intervention. While many environmentalists have called for a greater role for government, the empirical evidence and PSPE strongly suggest that government may do more to contribute to the demise of nature and biodiversity than to its protection.

What can be done? On the one hand, we need to heed Fukuyama's (1999) call to increase social capital, which implies a role for religious organisations such as churches, and on education more generally. On the other hand, we need to rely to a greater extent on markets for protecting nature. Several examples illustrate the direction that this can take.

First, funding to protect nature needs to be incorporated into the political budget-making process of all countries. In this way, tradeoffs can be made between funds directed at protecting ecosystems and other things like education, health care, social programs and defence.

Second, the most valuable and productive resource available to society is humans themselves (Simon 1996). Rather than taxing this resource, society needs to tax consumption since it is consumption that is "bad" and not work per se. The progressive income tax should be replaced by a progressive consumption tax that heavily penalises the use of nature. It is important to penalise activities that result in CO_2 emissions or ones that result in destruction of forest ecosystems (e.g., a heavy tax on palm oil will reduce incentives to convert tropical forests in Indonesia to palm tree plantations).

Finally, governments should be held more accountable to the electorate and given less discretion over a host of things that have a negative impact on nature. The reason is that governments are often corrupt or the object of lobbying (rent seeking) that have both a direct (e.g., subsidies to cut forests) and indirect (e.g., government waste) negative impact on nature protection and the environment.

Notes

1. Beisner (1997) makes perhaps the most radical claims about the stewardship role. He argues that the biblical mandate to subdue the earth requires making it into a "garden," similar to the Garden of Eden. Budiansky (1995, pp.27-31) also points out that wilderness was historically seen as something devoid of value and to be avoided: "To love nature, man first had to invent a nature worth loving" (p.29). The early nature movement was interested in a managed nature, not the foreboding threat and fear associated with true (unmanaged) wilderness. Technology has made wilderness into a garden, because without such technology few would venture into the wilderness.
2. Secular and non-secular approaches need not necessarily be in opposition to each other.
3. Prior to Darwin, a Christian view of how the world worked was held even by those who were not Christians, because they took the existence of God as a creator and even upholder of the world for granted. "The leading philosophers contemporary with Darwin, John Herschel, William Whewell, and John Stuart Mill, were equally adamant in their conviction that the Origin of Species was just one mass of conjecture" (Moreland 1994, p.290 quoting David L. Hull, Darwin and his Critics, p.7).
4. As a reviewer of an earlier version of this chapter notes: "I don't think [neoclassical] economics is an ethical system—it's supposed to be a-ethical."

11 Implications for Democratic Theory: A Normative Analysis
LESLEY JACOBS

In this chapter, the challenges to the theory and practice of democracy posed by certain dimensions of the broader multidisciplinary debate about the concept of biodiversity and its implications are examined. In particular, it examines what kind of good biodiversity is and what the present generation owes to future generations in terms of the preservation and promotion of biodiversity. This focus distinguishes the present discussion from most other philosophical work on biodiversity.

For the most part, political philosophers have asked how concerns about the conservation of biodiversity can be expressed in the language of contemporary theories of justice, not how well democratic theory can accommodate the demands of biodiversity. The main idea is that modern theories of justice have given scant regard to what we owe future generations; nor have they paid much attention to goods that are not material and discernibly instrumental for individuals. This discussion about justice is still in its infancy and its remains unclear where it will lead. It is worth noting, however, that a number of distinguished philosophers have recently questioned the very idea that concern with biodiversity and other environmental considerations can even be properly viewed as problems of justice. For Derek Parfit (1984, 1996), for example, any serious theory of justice is person-affecting in the sense that it addresses how the distribution of benefits and burdens in society affect the interests of persons.

Policies pertaining to biodiversity are distinctive not only because they affect persons, but they actually affect what persons there will be, that is, who will be born. This raises what Parfit calls the *Non-Identity Problem* (1984, p.359; 1996, p.314).[1] The logic is that under one policy, one set of persons will be born, under a different one, another set will be born. But in that case, it is not intelligible to prefer one policy over another because it has an adverse effect on the interests of such a person. In other words, arguments about biodiversity, in so far as they affect future generations, cannot be fit into the person-affecting rubric of theories of justice. From a very different philosophical perspective, Ronald Dworkin (1993) reaches a similar conclusion:

> "... the problem of justice between generations [is that] the idea that each generation of people must in fairness leave the world fit for habitation ... for generations of descendants whose identity is in no way yet fixed ... is misleading because our concern for the future is not concern for the rights or interests of specific people. ... Our concern for future generations is not a matter of justice at all but of our instinctive sense that human flourishing as well as human survival is of sacred importance" (pp.77-78).

I assume in this chapter that, even if the conservation of biodiversity is not a problem of justice, it still has considerable implications for democratic theory. Intuitively, even though democracy and justice are often conflated ideals, common sense suggests that they are distinct. Most of us appreciate that democratic governments can make and implement unjust laws. Indeed, the relation between democracy and the requirements of social justice are complex and contingent. A democratic government's right to rule, and our corresponding duty to obey, is a function of that government making laws and public policy that conform with the requirements of social justice (see Jacobs 1997). The more general point is this: What we do now about the conservation of biodiversity is an important collective decision that must be made, regardless of what we think justice requires. Democracy is fundamentally a forum for collective decision making. It is most readily contrasted in North America to market mechanisms for decision making. In discussions about concerns for future generations, there is an important choice between acting upon policies formulated by democratic governments or leaving it to the market to decide. This is a choice faced not only in the context of biodiversity but also other fields involving future generations, such as genetic testing (see, e.g., Glover 1992, p.127).[2]

There is no shortage of proponents of market solutions to concerns about biodiversity (see Ferguson 1997, 1999). Without intending to dismiss these proponents, I shall proceed on the assumption that at least a significant amount of the collective decision making about biodiversity should and will be made by governments. What I intend to show is that taking the conservation of biodiversity seriously has significant implications for the theory and practice of democratic governance.

Unlike with some philosophers, the problem posed by a specific issue, like conservation of biodiversity, is not treated merely as the application of a theoretical artifice. Instead, what is significant about the conservation of biodiversity is that it poses not simply a challenge to the application of democratic theory but provides insight into what is the best theory of democracy and how that theory can be refined in practice. Democracy as a forum for collective decision making is distinctive because of the core idea of "rule of the *demos* or people." In the history of political thought, it was ordinarily contrasted to aristocracy, understood as "rule by the few," and monarchy, meaning "rule by the one." An elementary distinction can be drawn between direct and indirect democracy. Direct democracy is any form of government in which all political decisions are made directly by the people who are subject to them. Indirect democracy is any form of government in which the people choose representatives to make political decisions on their behalf. The latter has dominated most modern thinking about democracy, principally because direct democracy has not seemed a feasible alternative for large industrial societies. As illustrated below, the conservation of biodiversity generates two distinct problems for any theory of indirect democracy. The first problem, denoted the *problem of scope*, has to do with what kind of goods can play a legitimate role in democratic decision making, that is to say, what kind of goods should concern representatives in their capacity as collective decision-makers. The second problem, denoted the *problem of constituency*, has to do with who are the legitimate constituents of representatives in an indirect democracy. Do those constituents include future persons?

Two Broad Approaches to Democracy

For our purposes, it is possible to distinguish between two broad approaches to the idea of indirect democracy.[3] Both approaches focus on the fact that democratic government is a particular type of political procedure for making, implementing and administering collective decisions that are binding on all citizens. They differ with regard to what it is that makes particular collective decision making procedures democratic. The first approach subscribes to what is referred to as *convergent procedural democracy*. Here the main idea is that democratic governments are those that rule in the interests of the people, or *demos*, or what is often called the public interest or common good. The practical problem of democratic politics is to develop a decision-making procedure that makes collective decisions that serve the public interest. Competing theories of convergent procedural democracy offer different accounts of what form of government produces decisions that converge with or promote that particular goal or outcome. The second approach subscribes to *fair procedural democracy*. According to this second approach, democratic government is characterised not so much by a concern to promote a particular outcome or goal, such as the public interest, but rather by a concern for making collective decisions in a manner that treats all citizens fairly. The essence of fair procedural democracy is the idea of political equality, not the public interest or common good.

Convergent procedural democracy and fair procedural democracy reflect very different ways of thinking about democratic government. These differences are not, however, unique to abstract philosophical differences about the nature of democracy. Analogous distinctions also underlie more concrete discussions of public institutions. Consider the case of courts administering criminal justice. There are at least two very different ways to look at the courts in this regard. One way is to ask what is the ideal goal or outcome of the courts in their administration of criminal justice. The ideal outcome seems simple enough: find innocent people not guilty, and find guilty people guilty. The problem for the administration of criminal justice by the courts is a practical one of designing trial procedures that promote this goal. Trials by a jury of one's peers and putting the onus of proof on the prosecution to establish guilt beyond a reasonable doubt are rules which might be defended because they appear to promote the ideal outcome of declaring innocence or guilt. The rules are outcome oriented: Are the outcomes the correct ones? Convergent procedural democracy reflects a very similar way of thinking about how government should make collective decisions.

An alternative is to say that it does not make much sense to talk about the ideal outcome of the administration of criminal justice by the courts, since it is inevitable that the courts are not always going to achieve this outcome, no matter how perfect the rules or procedures might be. Instead, we should think about trials as a kind of game, where the concern is whether the rules or procedures are fair, not whether they promote any particular outcome. The rights of the accused, on this view, should be judged not by how well they function to produce decisions (finding the guilty at fault and the innocent not-guilty), but rather by how well they ensure a fair match between the defendant and the crown. This alternative way of thinking about the courts administering criminal justice, with its emphasis on people being treated fairly, is similar to how democratic decision making is regarded by fair procedural democracy.

Which is the better approach to democracy? This general question is fundamental to modern democratic theory. The tendency among democratic theorists, historically, has been to work within the framework of convergent procedural democracy. Recently, however, the more innovative work on democratic theory has been in the development of the critique of convergent procedural democracy and the refinement of fair procedural democracy. The concept of biodiversity and the demand that it be conserved has implications for this broad debate.

The Problem of Scope

Fundamental to convergent procedural democracy is the proposition that democratic governance is driven by an emphasis on the common good or public interest. Criticism of this approach often questions that proposition. Sometimes the very idea of the common good is probed for its coherence and intelligibility. A different line of criticism questions the usefulness of that idea in societies where there is incredible diversity and difference. In other words, whilst some sort of notion of the common good may be helpful in homogeneous political communities, it is deeply problematic in the type of heterogeneous political culture of North America.[4] The reasoning is that, while convergent procedural democracy may be an attractive approach to governance in homogeneous community, in societies where there is a politics of difference, fair procedural democracy is the better approach (see Jacobs 1996).

What sort of good is biodiversity? Can it be included in the fold of the public interest or common good? Biodiversity can be characterised as an intrinsic good where an intrinsic good is understood to be something of which it is always better to have more of it. Justice and having a liberal education are two other familiar examples of intrinsic goods. They are, almost as a matter of stipulative definition, things that it is always better to have more of.[5] Intrinsic goods can be contrasted to instrumental goods. Instrumental goods are those for which, at some point, it is no longer better to have more of them. Money is an example of an instrumental good. Presumably, there is some level of wealth at which point it is no longer better to have more money. Intrinsic goods, like instrumental goods, are not necessarily *absolute goods*. An absolute good is something that, all things considered, is always better to have more of than of anything else. There are very compelling reasons to be sceptical about the existence of any absolute good; it is hard to imagine anything, including biodiversity, that could not be sacrificed at the margins for significant gains in some other good.[6]

Consider why biodiversity is characterised as an intrinsic good. Although there is widespread disagreement about the precise definition of biodiversity, it is nonetheless the case that it refers at some level to a degree of diversity and difference between genetic structures, biological entities, ecosystems and habitation, and so on (see, e.g., Wood 1997, p.253). The goodness of biodiversity is, therefore, a function of that diversity, howsoever it is conceived or defined. Logically, then, an increase in that diversity necessarily entails an increase in goodness. Hence, it is always better to have more of it than less of it. The upshot of this characterisation of biodiversity as an intrinsic good is that, although it can be traded off for other goods, it cannot be replaced by them. An increase in biological resources *per se* cannot, for example, replace or be a surrogate for biodiversity.

Not only is biodiversity an intrinsic good, it also relies for its human-centred, anthropocentric value on its contribution to the lives of future people. This distinguishes biodiversity from other intrinsic goods, like justice, which derive at least a significant part of their value from the important role they play in the lives of people in the here and now.

Convergent procedural democracy holds that the valid scope of democratic decision making is restricted to concern for the public interest. The *Problem of Scope* arises because, although the conservation of biodiversity appears to be within the valid scope of democratic decision making, it involves a kind of goodness that is beyond the realm of the public interest. The problem stems not from the fact that biodiversity is future looking, but from the combination of that feature and its being an intrinsic good.

Concerns about future people are commonly captured in conceptions of the public interest through discounting mechanisms. In effect, these mechanisms hold that, while the welfare of future people should count in calculations of the public interest, they count less than the welfare of existing persons. Various mechanisms and models exist for calculating the exact rate of discounting the welfare of future people. Even assuming what Rawls (1971, p.294) describes as the moral arbitrariness of our "temporal position," this practice of discounting the welfare of future generations can be justified on the grounds of the opportunity costs to current generations and the uncertainty about the precise character of the welfare of future generations.[7] Although the details surrounding the idea of discounting are exceedingly complex and involve sophisticated welfare economics, the current characterisation of biodiversity as an intrinsic good will likely undermine any attempt to discount it, and thus accommodate it within the folds of the public interest or common good. Discounting presupposes what Sen (1979; 1984, p.468) calls welfarism: the view that judgements about the goodness of a state of affairs must be based exclusively on the welfare levels of individuals in that state of affairs (see also Jacobs 1993, pp.14-6). Significantly, in order to aggregate individual welfare functions, welfarism requires that those functions be exchangeable. Because it is an intrinsic good, biodiversity is not exchangeable in this required sense and, thus, concerns about its conservation cannot be discounted in a way that enables it to be included in a calculation of the public interest or common good.[8]

The Problem of Constituency

The argument in the previous section is designed to put pressure on convergent procedural democracy by showing that biodiversity is a type of good that cannot be captured by an approach to democratic decision making that concentrates on the public interest or common good. The reasoning is that, in order to take the concern for biodiversity seriously, fair procedural democracy holds more promise because it does not restrict the scope of democratic decision making to some idea of the common good or public interest. The problem of democratic government, within this approach, is to design a political decision making procedure that treats all members of the state fairly in the process of making, implementing and administering public policy. What distinguishes democratic government from other forms of government, like aristocracy or monarchy, is that the concern lies with treating fairly all members of the state, and not just the majority or a small minority.

For representatives in a system of fair procedural democracy, the conservation of biodiversity poses a serious problem to this formulation of democracy. The common assumption is that who counts as members of the state is reasonably straightforward. The problems posed by immigrants, refugees, *et cetera*, to this assumption are familiar ones (see Galloway 1994). A concern based on biodiversity involves a claim that future members of the state should be given consideration in fair democratic decision making. The trouble for representatives is whether the constituents they are required to consider and represent as a matter of fairness include only those members at present alive or also those who will be members in the future. Moreover, if the circle of constituents is expanded to include future members, how far into the future does this expansion extend? Does it extend to one or two generations, or to fifty (see Barry 1989)? The challenges posed by expanding the circle of constituents to include future members constitutes the problem of constituency.

The problem of constituency does not, I think, defeat fair procedural democracy as an approach to democratic decision making. It does, however, demand a refinement in that approach. Among proponents of fair procedural democracy, there are two distinct schools of thought about when decisions can be said to be fair. Pure proceduralists hold that a democratic decision is fair provided that the decision is an outcome of a set of fair rules of procedure (Ely 1980; Dahl 1989). Revisionists hold that, while in most instances decisions are fair provided they are the outcome of fair procedures, in some instances even decisions of fair procedures are unfair because they violate our intuitive sense of fair outcomes (see Dworkin 1988, 1990). To use the trial analogy again, pure proceduralists hold that a trial is fair provided the rules of procedure are fair and were complied with. Revisionists allow that sometimes a trial can conform to fair procedures but nonetheless convict an innocent person, in which case the outcome is an affront to our sense of fairness and should be overturned.

Despite this disagreement, there is still a consensus among pure proceduralists and revisionists that fair procedures matter. What are the rules that make a democratic political decision-making procedure fair? Fair procedural democracy fixates on the idea that fair procedures give equal consideration to the interests of all constituents. This is the relevant sense of the claim that the essence of democratic government is political equality. Who is the best judge of a person's interests? This is a poignant question because it puts a finger on the basic assumption of much of modern democratic theory, namely, that individuals are generally the best judges of what is in their own interests. When there is disagreement about what is in your best interest, your view, not the government's or anyone else's, should prevail. Although this assumption is intuitively appealing, it is problematic principally because it is easy to imagine people believing that something that is morally debased or repugnant is nevertheless in his or her best interests.

The problem of constituency reinforces the argument that, despite its initial appeal, democratic governments cannot rely exclusively on people to judge what is in their own best interests. The reason is, of course, that future people do not exist to inform us of their own judgements of what is in their own best interests. How then do representatives in a system of fair procedural democracy judge those interests? The most compelling response seems to be the following principle: "What will future generations say about what we have done to their world?" (Gutmann and Tompson 1996, p.161). This principle encourages representatives to think about the future from the perspective of trying to justify to those future people the decisions and policies they make. This does not require that current policies be optimal for those future people, but it does restrict significantly the range of possibilities. Ironically, this perspective is also instructive for democratic decision making that affects the interests of our contemporaries, where the judgement of the representative about what is in their best interests diverges from their own judgement.

Conclusions

In this chapter, it was argued that two dimensions of the multi-disciplinary debate around the conservation of biodiversity—what type of good biodiversity is and what the present generation owes to future generations in terms of promoting and preserving biodiversity—have interesting and important implications for the theory and practice of democracy. The arguments put forward here have been designed to validate further the view that fair procedural democracy is the preferred approach to democratic government. This conclusion, whilst bold, is offered tentatively and is intended more to provoke a normative research agenda focused on the relationship between democracy and the conservation of biodiversity than to bring closure to the matter.

Notes

1. Parfit's argument is extended to the case of biodiversity, but important complexities are neglected.
2. See also the discussion on this choice that is pervasive in the final report of the (Canadian) Royal Commission on Reproductive Technologies (1994).
3. The distinction here between approaches to democracy draws on Jacobs (1997, Chapter 2).
4. A similar observation is made in Chapter 10 of this volume with respect to social capital—that there is less social capital in a heterogeneous society. However, there it is argued that markets have a greater role as a consequence.
5. Examples of intrinsic bads are probably more familiar. Slavery would be considered an extrinsic bad to the extent that less slavery is generally thought to be better.
6. Why then are absolute goods sometimes taken so seriously? There are likely two main reasons. The first is a failure by some to appreciate the plurality and diversity of goods. Once you concede that goods are diverse and pluralistic, the impossibility of absolute goods is stark. The second reason is that it is sometimes mistakenly inferred from the fact that two goods are incommensurable, that at least one of them is therefore absolute.
7. For the claim that this moral arbitrariness undermines the entire practice of discounting, see Parfit (1984, pp. 480-86); also see Gutmann and Thompson (1996, pp.156-58) for an accessible summary.
8. This point is analogous to that of Sen (1984, pp.193-95), who points out that the commitment to welfarism in social discounting mechanisms means that they are unable to capture some of the moral concerns we have about the well-being of future generations, such as the inviolability of their rights.

References

Acheson, J.M., 1994. Welcome to Nobel Country: A Review of Institutional Economics. Chapter 1 in *Anthropology and Institutional Economics* (pp.3-42) edited by J.M. Acheson. Lanham, MD: University Press of America.

Adam, P., 1987. *New South Wales Rainforests: The Nomination for the World Heritage List*. Sydney: National Parks and Wildlife Service.

Adam, P., 1992. The End of Conservation on the Cheap, *National Parks Journal* 36(3): 19-22.

Adler, T., 1995. Providing the Data to Protect Biodiversity, *Science News* 148:326.

Aiken, S.R., 1994. Peninsular Malaysia's protected areas' coverage, 1903-92: creation, rescission, excision, and intrusion. *Environmental Conservation* 21: 49-56.

Aldous, P., 1993. Tropical deforestation: not just a problem in Amazonia. *Science* 259: 1390.

Allen, E. A., 1999. *Exotic Insect Interceptions from Wooden Dunnage and Packing Material*. Victoria, BC: Canadian Forest Service. (www.pfc.cfs.nrcan.gc.ca/health/exotics.htm, viewed September 15, 1999).

Altieri, M.A., D.K. Letourneau and J.R. Davis, 1983. Developing Sustainable Agroecosystems, *BioScience* 33: 45-49.

Ando, A., J. Camm, S. Polasky and A. Solow, 1998. Species Distributions, Land Values, and Efficient Conservation, *Science* 279: 2126-28.

Anonymous, 1992. *National Forest Policy Statement: a New Focus for Australia's Forests*. Canberra: Australian Government Publishing Service.

Anonymous, 1995. *National Forest Conservation Reserves: Commonwealth Proposed Criteria*. Canberra: Commonwealth of Australia.

ANZECC (Australian and New Zealand Environment and Conservation Council, State of the Environment Reporting Task Force), 1998. *Core Environmental Indicators for Reporting on the State of the Environment*. Canberra: ANZECC Secretariat.

Awimbo, J.A., D.A. Norton and F.B Overmars, 1996. An Evaluation of Representativeness for Nature Conservation, Hokitika Ecological District, New Zealand, *Biological Conservation* 75: 177-86.

Bailey, R. (editor), 1995. *The True State of the Planet*. New York: The Free Press.

Barnard, P., C.J. Brown, A.M. Jarvis and A. Robertson, 1998. Extending the Namibian Protected Area Network to Safeguard Hotspots of Endemism and Diversity, *Biodiversity and Conservation* 7: 531-47.

Barrett, G.W., H.A. Ford and H.F. Recher, 1994. Conservation of Woodland Birds in a Fragmented Varied Landscape, *Pacific Conservation Biology* 1: 245-56.

Barry, B., 1989. *Theories of Justice*. Berkeley, CA: University of California Press.

Barzetti, V. (editor), 1993. *Parks and Progress: Protected Areas and Economic Development in Latin America and the Caribbean*. Washington DC: IUCN.

Baskin, Y. 1994. Ecologists Dare to Ask: How much does Biodiversity Matter? *Science* 264: 202-203.

Bean, M.J. and D.S. Wilcove, 1997. The Private-land Problem, *Conservation Biology* 11: 1-2.

Beardsley, K. and D. Stoms, 1993. Compiling a Map of Areas Managed for Biodiversity in California, *Natural Areas Journal* 13: 177-90.

Behe, M.J., 1996. *Darwin's Black Box. The Biochemical Challenge to Evolution*. New York: The Free Press.

Beisner, E.C., 1997. *Where Garden Meets Wilderness*. Grand Rapids, MI: Wm. B. Eerdmans Publishing Co.

Beissinger, S.R., E.C. Steadman, T. Wohlgenant, G. Blate and S. Zack, 1996. Null Models for Assessing Ecosystem Conservation Priorities: Threatened Birds as Titers of Threatened Ecosystems in South America, *Conservation Biology* 10: 1343-52.

Bennett, A.F. and L.A. Ford, 1997. Land Use, Habitat Change and the Conservation of Birds in Fragmented Rural Environments: A Landscape Perspective from the Northern Plains, Victoria, Australia, *Pacific Conservation Biology* 3: 244-61.

Benson, D.H. and J. Howell, 1990. Sydney's Vegetation 1788-1988: Utilization, Degradation and Rehabilitation, *Proceedings of the Ecological Society of Australia* 16: 115-27.

Benson, J., 1991. The Effect of 200 Years of European Settlement on the Vegetation and Flora of New South Wales, *Cunninghamia* 2: 343-70.

Berger, J. and C. Cunningham, 1994. Active Intervention and Conservation: Africa's Pachyderm Problem, *Science* 263: 1241-42.

Berghdal, D.R., 1988. Impact of Pinewood Nematode on North America: Present and Future, *Journal of Nematology* 20: 260-65.

Berns, G., L. Bovenberg, E. van Damme, F. van der Duyn Schouten, F. van den Heuvel, T. van de Klundert, N. Noorderhaven and H. Weigand, 1999. Economisering van de samenleving (The Economisation of Society). Tilburg, NL: Centrum voor Wetenschap en Levensbeschouwing. May. 63pp. (In Dutch)

Blockstein, D.E. and H.B. Tordoff, 1985. Gone Forever. A Contemporary Look at the Extinction of the Passenger Pigeon, *American Birds* 39: 845-51.

Bloom, A., 1987. *The Closing of the American Mind*. New York: Simon and Schuster.

Bloom, D.E., 1995. International Public Opinion on the Environment. *Science* 269: 354-58.

Bond, W.J., 1993. Keystone Species. In *Biodiversity and Ecosystem Function* (pp. 237-253) edited by E-D. Schultze and H.A. Mooney. Berlin: Springer-Verlag.

Braithwaite, W., L. Belbin, J. Ive and M. Austin, 1993. Land Use Allocation and Biological Conservation in the Batemans Bay Forests of New South Wales, *Australian Forestry* 56: 4-21.

Bright, C., 1998. *Life out of bounds. Bioinvasion in a Borderless World*. New York: W.W. Norton &Company.

Bromley, D. W., 1999. *Sustaining Development. Environmental Resources in Developing Countries*. Cheltenham, UK: Edward Elgar.

Brown, G.M. and J.F. Shogren, 1998. Economics of the Endangered Species Act, *Journal of Economic Perspectives* 12 : 3-20.

Budiansky, S., 1995. *Nature's Keepers. The New Science of Nature Management*. New York: The Free Press.

Bulte E.H., M. Joenje and H.P.G. Jansen, 2000. Socially optimal Forest Stocks in the Atlantic Zone of Costa Rica, *Canadian Journal of Forest Research* (In press).

Bulte, E.H. and G.C. van Kooten, 1996. A Note on Ivory Trade and Elephant Conservation, *Environment and Development Economics* 1: 433-43

Bulte, E.H. and G.C. van Kooten, 1999a. The Ivory Trade Ban and Elephant Numbers: Theory and Application to Zambia, *American Journal of Agricultural Economics* 81: 453-66.

Bulte, E.H., and G.C. van Kooten, 1999b. Species Valuation, Extinction and Declining Marginal Utility of Preservation: Minke Whales in the Northeast Atlantic, *Environmental and Resource Economics* 14: 119-30.

Bulte E.H., D.P. van Soest, G.C. van Kooten and R. Schipper, 2000. Trading off Forests and Agriculture in Humid Costa Rica: Investing in Forest Conservation under Uncertainty. Mimeograph. Tilburg University, The Netherlands.

Burbidge, A.A. and N.L. McKenzie, 1989. Patterns in the Modern Decline of Western Australia's Vertebrate Fauna: Causes and Conservation Implications, *Biological Conservation* 50: 143-98.

Burkey, T.V., 1995. Extinction Rates in Archipelagos: Implications for Populations in Fragmented Habitats, *Conservation Biology* 9: 527-41.

Burney, D.A., 1993. Recent animal Extinctions: Recipes for Disaster. *American Scientist* 81: 530-41.

Castle, E.N., 1993. A Pluralistic, Pragmatic and Evolutionary Approach to natural Resource Management, *Forest Ecology and Management* 56: 279-95.

Caufield, C., 1982. *Tropical Moist Forests. The Resource, the People, the Threats.* London: Earthscan.

Cavalier-Smith, T., 1987. Eukaryotes with no Mitochondria, *Nature* 326: 332-33.

Cavalier-Smith, T., 1991. The Evolution of Cells. In *Evolution of Life. Fossils, Molecules, and Culture* (pp. 271-304) edited by S. Osawa and T. Honjo. Berlin: Springer-Verlag.

Chapin III, F.S., B.H. Walker, R.J. Hobbs, D.U. Hooper, J.H. Lawton, O.E. Sala and D. Tilman, 1997. Biotic Control over the Functioning of Ecosystems, *Science* 277: 500-09.

Chatelain, C., L. Gautier and R. Spichiger, 1996. A Recent History of Forest Fragmentation in Southwestern Ivory Coast, *Biodiversity and Conservation* 5: 37-53.

Chen, B. and D.H. Wise, 1999. Bottom-up Limitation of Predaceous Arthropods in a Detritus-based Terrestrial Food Web, *Ecology* 80: 761-72.

Coase, R.H., 1960. The Problem of Social Cost, *Journal of Law and Economics* 3: 1-44.

Cobb, J.B. Jr., 1988. A Christian View of Biodiversity. Chapter 55 in *Biodiversity* edited by E.O. Wilson with F.M. Peter. Washington: National Academy Press.

Cohen, J.E., 1995. Population Growth and Earth's Human Carrying Capacity, *Science* 269: 341-46.

Cole, D.N. and P.B. Landres, 1996. Threats to Wilderness Ecosystems: Impacts and Research Needs, *Ecological Applications* 6: 168-84.

Common, M. 1995. *Sustainability and Policy.* Cambridge, UK: Cambridge University Press.

Costanza, R., R. d'Arge, R. de Groot, S. Farber, M. Grasso, B. Hannon, K. Limburg, S. Naeem, R.V. O'Neill, J. Paruelo, R.G. Raskin, P. Sutton and M. van den Belt, 1997. The Value of the World's Ecosystem Services and Natural Capital, *Nature* 387: 253-61.

Cowling, R.M., R.L. Pressey, A.T. Lombard, P.G. Desmet and A.G. Ellis, 1999. From Representation to Persistence: Requirements for a Sustainable Reserve System in the Species-rich Mediterranean-climate Deserts of Southern Africa, *Diversity and Distributions* In press.

Cox, T.R., 1983. The "Worthless Lands" Thesis: Another Perspective, *Journal of Forest History* 27: 144-45.

CPB (Netherlands Bureau for Economic Policy Analysis), 1997. *Challenging Neighbours. Rethinking German and Dutch Economic Institutions.* Berlin: Springer.

Craig, W.L., 1999. Naturalism and Cosmology. The Fundamental Question. Unpublished paper. February, 19pp.

Csuti, B., S. Polaski, P.H.Williams, R.L. Pressey, J.D. Camm, M. Kershaw, A.R. Kiester, B. Downs, R. Hamilton, M. Huso and K. Sahr, 1997. A Comparison of Reserve Selection Algorithms using Data on Terrestrial Vertebrates in Oregon, *Biological Conservation* 80: 83-97.

Dahl, R., 1989. *Democracy and Its Critics*. New Haven, CT: Yale University Press.

Daily, G., P. Dasgupta, B. Bolin, P. Crosson, J. du Guerny, P. Ehrlich, C. Folke, A.M. Jansson, B.-O. Jansson, N. Kautsky, A. Kinzig, S. Levin, K.-G. Mäler, P. Pinstrup-Andersen, D. Siniscalco and B. Walker, 1998. Food Production, Population Growth, and the Environment, *Science* 281: 1291-92.

Daily, G.C. (editor), 1997. *Nature's Services. Societal Dependence on Natural Ecosystems*. Washington, DC: Island Press.

Dargavel, J., 1998. Politics, Policy and Process in the Forests, *Australian Journal of Environmental Management* 5: 25-30.

Davis, K. and M.S. Bernstam (editors), 1991. *Resources, Environment, and Population. Present Knowledge, Future Options*. New York: Oxford University Press.

Davis, M.B., 1986. Climatic Instability, Time Lags, and Community Disequilibrium. In *Community Ecology* (pp. 269-84) edited by J. Diamond and T.J. Case. New York: Harper & Row.

Davis, P., 1983. *God and the New Physics*. New York: Simon and Schuster.

de Ruiter, P.C., A.-M. Neutel and J.C. Moore, 1995. Energetics, Patterns of Interaction Strengths, and Stability in Real Ecosystems, *Science* 269: 1257-60.

Demsetz, H., 1967. Toward a Theory of Property Rights, *American Economic Review* 57: 347-73.

Diamond, J.M., 1989. The Present, Past and Future of Human Caused Extinctions, *Philosophical Transactions of the Royal Society*, Series B 325: 469-77.

Dick, R., 1997. NPWS State Reserve System (SRS) Program—Past, Present and Future. Unpublished internal report of the New South Wales National Parks and Wildlife Service, Sydney.

Dobson, A.P., J.P. Rodriguez, W.M. Roberts and D.S. Wilcove, 1997. Geographic Distribution of Endangered Species in the United States, *Science* 275: 550-53.

Dodson, A.P., A.D. Bradshaw and A.J.M. Baker, 1997. Hopes for the Future: Restoration Ecology and Conservation Biology, *Science* 277: 515-22.

Doherty, L., 1998a. Carr "Betrayal" Threatens New Forest War, *Sydney Morning Herald*, November 12, p.5.

Doherty, L., 1998b. Carr's Gamble Faces Early Test at Blockades, *Sydney Morning Herald*, November 13, p.4.

Dooyeweerd, H., 1979. *Roots of Western Culture. Pagan, Secular and Christian Options*. Toronto: Wedge Publishing Foundation.

Dooyeweerd, H., 1980. *In the Twilight of Western Thought*. Nutley, NJ: The Craig Press.
Drake, J. A., H.A. Mooney, F. di Castri, R.H. Groves, F.J. Kruger, M. Rejmanek and M. Williamson (editors), 1989. *Biological Invasions: A Global Perspective*. SCOPE 37. Chichester, England: Wiley.
Dworkin, R., 1988. What is Equality? Part IV: Political Equality, *University of San Francisco Law Review* 22: 1-30.
Dworkin, R., 1990. Equality, Democracy, and Constitution: We the People in Court, *Alberta Law Review* 28: 325-416.
Dworkin, R., 1993. *Life's Dominion*. NewYork: Alfred Knopf.
Economic Commission for Europe/FAO, 1989. *Outlook for the Forest and Forest Products Sector of the USSR*. ECE/TIM/48. New York: United Nations Food and Agricultural Organization. 75pp.
Edwards, S.R., 1995. Conserving Biodiversity. Chapter 7 in *The True State of the Planet* (pp. 211-65) edited by R. Bailey. New York: The Free Press.
Edwards, V.M. and B.M.H. Sharp, 1990. Institutional Arrangements for Conservation on Private Land in New Zealand, *Journal of Environmental Management* 31: 313-26.
Ehrenfeld, D., 1988. Why Put a Value on Biodiversity. Chapter 24 in *Biodiversity* edited by E.O. Wilson with F.M. Peter. Washington: National Academy Press.
Ehrlich, P.R., 1988. The Loss of Biodiversity: Causes and Consequences. Chapter 2 in *Biodiversity* (pp. 21-27) edited by E.O. Wilson with F.M. Peter. Washington: National Academy Press.
Ehrlich, P.R. 1993. Biodiversity and Ecosystem Function: Need we Know More. In *Biodiversity and Ecosystem Function* (pp. vii-ix) edited by E.-D. Schultz and H.A. Mooney. Berlin: Springer-Verlag, Berlin.
Ehrlich, P.R. and E.O. Wilson, 1991. Biodiversity Studies: Science and Policy, *Science* 253: 758-62.
Elton, C.S., 1958. *The Ecology of Invasions by Animals and Plants*. London: Methuen.
Ely, J.H., 1980. *Democracy and Distrust*. Cambridge: Harvard University Press.
Emery, K.A., 1985. *Rural Land Capability Mapping*. Sydney: Soil Conservation Service of New South Wales (now Department of Land and Water Conservation).
EPA (Environment Protection Authority), 1997. *New South Wales State of the Environment 1997*. Sydney: EPA.
Estades, C.F. and S.A. Temple, 1999. Deciduous-forest Bird Communities in a Fragmented Landscape Dominated by Exotic Pine Plantations, *Ecological Applications* 9: 573-85.
Estes, J.A., M.T. Tinker, T.M. Williams and D.F. Doak, 1998. Killer Whale Predation on Sea Otter Linking Oceanic and Nearshore Ecosystems, *Science* 282: 473-76.

Fahrig, L., 1997. Relative Effects of Habitat Loss and Fragmentation on Population Extinction, *Journal of Wildlife Management* 61: 603-10.

Faith, D.P., 1992. Conservation Evaluation and Phylogenetic Diversity, *Biological Conservation* 61: 1-10.

FAO, 1993. *Forest Resources Assessment 1990*. Paper 112. Rome: Food and Agricultural Organization of the United Nations.

FAO, 1997. *State of the World's Forests 1997*. Rome: Food and Agricultural Organization of the United Nations.

Farmer, M.C. and A. Randall, 1998. The Rationality of a Safe Minimum Standard, *Land Economics* 74(August): 287-302.

Farrier, D., 1995. Policy Instruments for Conserving Biodiversity on Private Land. In *Conserving Biodiversity: Threats and Solutions* (pp. 337-59) edited by R.A. Bradstock, T.D. Auld, D.A. Keith, R.T. Kingsford, D. Lunney and D.P. Sivertsen. Sydney: Surrey Beatty and Sons.

Feeney, A. 1989. The Pacific Northwest's Ancient Forests: Ecosystems under Siege. In *Audubon Wildlife Report 1989/1990* (pp. 93-153) edited by W.J. Chandler, L. Labate and C. Wille. San Diego, CA: Academic Press.

Ferguson, J., 1997. The Expanses of Sustainability and the Limits of Privatarianism, *Canadian Journal of Political Science* 30(June): 285-306.

Ferguson, J., 1999. *What Sustains Sustainability?* Montreal-Kingston: McGill-Queen's Press.

Ferrier, S. and G. Watson, 1997. *An Evaluation of the Effectiveness of Environmental Surrogates and Modelling Techniques in Predicting the Distribution of Biological Diversity*. Canberra: Environment Australia.

Ferrier, S., 1997. Biodiversity Data for Reserve Selection: Making Best Use of Incomplete Information. In *National Parks and Protected Areas: Selection, Delimitation and Management* (pp. 315-29) edited by P.J. Pigram and R.C. Sundell. Armidale: University of New England, Centre for Water Policy Research.

Filip, G.M. and J.J. Morrell, 1996. Importing Pacific Rim Wood: Pest Risks to Domestic Resources. *Journal of Forestry* 94(10): 22-26.

Finkel, E., 1998a. Ecology: Software helps Australia Manage Forest Debate, *Science* 281: 1789-91.

Finkel, E., 1998b. Australia—Forest Pact Bypasses Computer Model, *Science* 282: 1968-69.

Franklin, J.F., 1995. Scientists in Wonderland: Experiences in Development of Forest Policy, *BioScience* Supplement S74-S78.

French Ministry of Agricultural and Fisheries, 1995. Sustainable Forest Management in France. Paris: Countryside and Forest Department, April. 72pp.

Fukuyama, F., 1999. *The Great Disruption. Human Nature and the Reconstitution of Social Order*. New York: The Free Press.

Furubotn, E.G. and R. Richter, 1997. *Institutions and Economic Theory. The Contribution of the New Institutional Economics*. Ann Arbor, MI: University of Michigan Press.

Galloway, D., 1994. Strangers and Members: Equality in an Immigration Setting, *The Canadian Journal of Law and Jurisprudence* 7(1): 149-72.

Gayton, D., 1990. *The Wheatgrass Mechanism. Science and Imagination and the Western Canadian Landscape*. Saskatoon, SK: Fifth House Publishers.

Glover, J., 1992. Future People, Disability, and Screening. In *Justice between Age Groups and Generations: Philosophy, Politics, and Society, Sixth Series* edited by P. Laslett and J. Fishkin. New Haven: Yale University Press.

Glowka, L., F. Burhenne-Guilmin, H. Synge, J. McNeely. and L. Gundling, 1994. A Guide to the Convention on Biological Diversity. Gland, Switzerland: World Conservation Union (IUCN) Environmental Policy and Law Paper No. 3.

Goldschmidt, R., 1940. *The Material Basis of Evolution*. Yale, CT: Yale University Press.

Gottschalk, K.W., 1990. Economic Evaluation of Gypsy Moth Damage in the United States of America. In *Proceedings, Division 4, IUFRO 19th World Congress* (pp. 236-246) edited by Canadian IUFRO World Congress Organizing Committee. Montreal, PQ.

Gould, S.J., 1999. *Rock of Ages. Science and Religion in the Fullness of Life*. New York: Ballantine.

Graetz, R.D., M.A. Wilson and S.K. Campbell, 1995. Landcover Disturbance over the Australian Continent: A Contemporary Assessment. Canberra: Department of the Environment, Sports and Territories Biodiversity Series Paper No. 7.

Graham, R.W. and E.C. Grimm, 1990. Effects of Global Climate Change on the Patterns of Terrestrial Biological Communities, *Trends in Ecology and Evolution* 5: 289-292.

Green, G.M. and R.W. Sussman, 1990. Deforestation History of the Eastern Rain Forests of Madagascar from Satellite Images, *Science* 248: 212-15.

Griffith, B., J.M. Scott, J.W. Carpenter and C. Reed. 1989. Translocation as a Species Conservation Tool: Status and Strategy, *Science* 245: 477-80.

Grime, J.P., 1997. Biodiversity and Ecosystem Function: The Debate Deepens, *Science* 29(August): 1260-61.

Grizzle, R.E. and C.B. Barrett, 1998. The One Body of Christian Environmentalism, *Zygon* 33(June): 233-53.

Groombridge, B. (editor), 1992. *Global Biodiversity. Status of the Earth's Living Resources*. London: Chapman and Hall.

Grumbine, R.E., 1992. *Ghost Bears: Exploring the Biodiversity Crisis*. Washington DC: Island Press.

Gutmann, A. and D. Thompson, 1996. *Democracy and Disagreement*. Cambridge: Harvard University Press.

Haack, R.A. and J.W. Byler, 1993. Insects and Pathogens: Regulators of Forest Ecosystems. *Journal of Forestry* 37: 32-7.

Haeckel, E., 1866. *Generelle Morphologie II. Algermeine Entwicklungsgeschichte der Orgamismen.* Berlin: Reimer.

Hagenbaugh, B., 1999. Clinton Battles Invasive Pests. Reuters News Service. February 3.

Hall, C.M., 1988. The "Worthless Lands Hypothesis" and Australia's National Parks and Reserves. In *Australia's Ever Changing Forests* (pp. 441-56) edited by K.J. Frawley and N.M. Semple. Canberra: Australian Defence Force Academy.

Hall, J. P. and B. Moody, 1994. *Forest Depletions Caused by Insects and Diseases in Canada 1982-1987.* Information Report ST-X-8. Ottawa, ON: Forest Insect and Disease Survey. Natural Resources Canada.

Hansen, A.J. and D.L. Urban, 1992. Avian Response to Landscape Pattern: The Role of Species Life History, *Landscape Ecology* 7: 163-80.

Harris, C.R., 1977. Towards a Historical Perspective, *Proceedings of the Royal Geographical Society of Australasia, South Australian Branch* 78: 55-71.

Harris, M., 1998. *Lament for an Ocean.* Toronto: McClelland and Stewart.

Harris, P. and M. Maw, 1984. *Hypericum perforatum* L., St. John's-wort (Hypericaceae). In *Biological Control Programmes against Insects and Weeds in Canada 1969-1980* (pp. 171-78) edited by J.S. Kellerher and M.A. Hulme. Slough, Bucks, UK: Commonwealth Agricultural Bureau.

Hart, O., A. Shleifer and R.W. Vishny, 1997. The Proper Scope of Government: Theory and an Application to Prisons, *Quarterly Journal of Economics* CXII(November): 1127-61.

Hawking, S.W., 1988. *A Brief History of Time.* Toronto: Bantam Books.

Hawking, S.W. and R. Penrose, 1996. *The Nature of Space and Time.* Princeton, NJ: Princeton University Press.

Hay, Donald A., 1989. *Economics Today. A Christian Critique.* Leicester UK: Apollos.

Henderson, N., 1992. Wilderness and the Nature Conservation Ideal: Britain, Canada and the United States Contrasted, *Ambio* 21: 394-99.

Hengeveld, R., 1989. *Dynamics of Biological Invasions.* New York: Chapman & Hall.

Hitchcock, P., 1981. The Establishment of National Parks, *National Parks Journal* 25(4): 14-20.

Hogan, G.D. and B. Wilson, 2000. Recent Trends in Forest Management: The Plantation Experience. In *Environmental Considerations: Genetically Modified Trees.* Proceedings of an OECD Workshop, September 12-15, 1999 held in Trondheim, Norway (In press).

Holden, C., 1996. Endangered Species List Updated, *Science* 274: 183.

Holden, C., 1997. NIH to Explore St. John's Wort, *Science* 278: 391.

Holling, C.S., 1973. Resilience and Stability of Ecological Systems, *Annual Review of Ecology and Systematics* 4: 1-23.

Holling, C.S., 1986. The Resilience of Terrestrial Ecosystems: Local Surprise and Global Change. In *Sustainable Development of the Biosphere* (pp. 297-317) edited by W.C. Clark and R.E. Munn. Cambridge, UK: Cambridge University Press.

Holloway, J.K., 1964. Projects in Biological Control of Weeds. In *Biological Control of Insect Pests and Weeds* (pp. 650-70) edited by P. de Bach. London: Chapman and Hall.

Howarth, R.B. and R.B. Norgaard, 1993. Intergenerational Changes and the Social Discount Rate, *Environmental and Resource Economics* 3: 337-58.

Howarth, R.B. and R.B. Norgaard, 1995. Intergenerational Choices under Global Environmental Change. In *Handbook of Environmental Economics* (pp. 111-38) edited by D.W. Bromley. Oxford, UK: Basil Blackwell.

Hubbell, S.P., R.B. Foster, S.T. O'Brien, K.E. Harms, R. Condit, B. Wechsler, J. Wright and S. Loo de Lao, 1999. Light-gap Disturbances, Recruitment Limitation and Tree Diversity in a Neotropical Forest, *Science* 283: 554-57.

Hubbes, M., 1999. The American Elm and Dutch Elm Disease. *The Forestry Chronicle* 75(2): 265-73.

Huffaker, C.B., 1967. A Comparison of the Status of Biological Control of St. John's-wort in California and Australia, *Mushi* 39: 51-73.

Hughes, J.B., G.C. Daily and P.R. Ehrlich, 1997. Population Diversity: Its Extent and Extinction, *Science* 278: 689-92.

Humble, L.A., E.A. Allen and J.D. Bell, 1998. *Exotic Wood-boring Beetles in British Columbia: Interceptions and Establishments*. Victoria, BC: Canadian Forest Service. (web site: www.pfc.cfs.nrcan.gc.ca/biodiversity/exotics/, viewed September 15, 1999)

Huston, M.A., 1993. Biological Diversity, Soils, and Economics, *Science* 262: 1676-80.

Huston, M.A., 1997. Hidden Treatments in Ecological Experiments: Re-evaluating the Ecosystem Function of Biodiversity, *Oecologia* 110: 449-60.

Innis, R., 1999. Takings and Endangered Species Protection, *Choices*, Third Quarter, pp.10-16.

Jacobs, L., 1993. *Rights and Deprivation*. Oxford: Oxford University Press.

Jacobs, L., 1996. How is a Democratic Politics of Difference Possible? Paper presented at the conference on "Democracy, Pluralism, and Citizenship" at the Ritz-Carlton Hotel, Montreal, November.

Jacobs, L., 1997. *The Democratic Vision of Politics*. Saddle Creek, NJ: Prentice-Hall.

JANIS (Joint ANZECC/MCFFA National Forest Policy Statement Implementation Sub-committee), 1997. *Nationally Agreed Criteria for the Establishment of a Comprehensive, Adequate and Representative Reserve System for Forests in Australia.* Canberra: Commonwealth of Australia.

Johansson-Stenman, O., 1998. The Importance of Ethics in Environmental Economics, *Environmental and Resource Economics* 11: 429-42.

Johnson, P.E., 1993. *Darwin on Trial.* 2nd Edition. Downers Grove, IL: InterVarsity Press. (1st Edition, 1991, Regnery Gateway, Washington DC)

Johnson, P.E., 1995. *Reason in the Balance. The Case against Naturalism in Science, Law and Education.* Downers Grove, Illinois: InterVarsity Press.

Johnson, P.E., 1997. *Defeating Darwinism by Opening Minds.* Downers Grove, Illinois: InterVarsity Press.

Jokimäki, J. and E. Huhta, 1996. Effects of Landscape Matrix and Habitat Structure on a Bird Community in Northern Finland: A Multiscape Approach, *Ornis Fennica* 73: 97-113.

Jones, L., with L. Fredricksen, 1999. Crying Wolf? Public Policy on Endangered Species in Canada. Fraser Institute Critical Issues Bulletin. Vancouver, BC: The Fraser Institute. 60pp.

Kaiser, J., 1998. Sea Otter Declines Blamed on Hungry Killers, *Science* 282: 390-91.

Kaiser, J., 1999. Battle over a Dying Sea, *Science* 284: 28-30.

Kay, J.J., 1991. A Non-equilibrium Thermodynamic Framework for Discussing Ecosystem Integrity, *Environmental Management* 15: 483-95.

Kay, J.J., 1993. On the Nature of Ecological Integrity: Some Closing Comments. In *Ecological Integrity and the Management of Ecosystems* (pp. 201-212) edited by S. Woodley, J. Kay and G. Francis. Delray, FL: St. Lucie Press.

Kay, J.J. and E.D. Schneider, 1992. Thermodynamics and Measures of Ecological Integrity. In *Ecological Indicators* (pp. 159-182) edited by D.H. McKenzie, D. Hyatt and V.J. McDonald. London: Elsevier.

Keith, D.A., 1995. Involving Ecologists and Local Communities in Survey, Planning and Action for Conservation in a Rural Landscape: An Example from the Bega Valley, New South Wales. In *Nature Conservation 4—The Role of Networks* (pp. 385-400) edited by D.A. Saunders, J.L. Craig and E.M. Mattiske, Sydney, AU: Surrey Beatty and Sons.

Keith, D.A. and M. Bedward, 1999. Native Vegetation of the South East Forests Region, Eden, New South Wales, *Cunninghamia* (in press).

Kershaw, M., G.M. Mace and P.H. Williams, 1995. Threatened Status, Rarity, and Diversity as Alternative Selection Measures for Protected Areas: A Test using Afrotropical Antelopes, *Conservation Biology* 12: 324-34.

Khan, M.L., S. Menon and K.S. Bawa, 1997. Effectiveness of the Protected Area Network in Biodiversity Conservation: A Case-study of Meghalaya State, *Biodiversity and Conservation* 6: 853-68.

Kiester, A.R., J.M. Scott, B. Csuti, R.G. Noss, B. Butterfield, K. Sahr and D. Whiter, 1996. Conservation Prioritization using GAP Data, *Conservation Biology* 10: 1332-42.

Kimmins, J.P., 1996a. The Health and Integrity of Forest Ecosystems: Are They Threatened by Forestry? *Ecosystems Health* 2: 5-18.

Kimmins, J.P., 1996b. Importance of Soil and Role of Ecosystem Disturbance for Sustained Productivity of Cool Temperate and Boreal Forests, *Soil Science Society of America Journal* 60: 1643-54.

Kingsford, R.T., 1995. Ecological Effects of River Management in New South Wales. In *Conserving Biodiversity: Threats and Solutions* (pp. 144-61) edited by R.A. Bradstock, T.D. Auld, D.A. Keith, R.T. Kingsford, D. Lunney and D.P. Sivertsen. Sydney: Surrey Beatty and Sons. pp. 144-61.

Kirkpatrick, J.B., 1987. Forest Reservation in Tasmania, *Search* 18: 138-42.

Klein, R.G., 1992. The Impact of Early People on the Environment: The Case of Large Mammal Extinctions. In *Human Impact on the Environment: Ancient Roots, Current Challenges* (pp. 13-34) edited by J.E. Jacobsen and J. Firor. Boulder, CO: Westview Press.

Knight, R.L., 1999. Private Lands: The Neglected Geography, *Conservation Biology* 13: 223-24.

Kruess, A. and T. Tscharntke, 1994. Habitat Fragmentation, Species Loss, and Biological Control, *Science* 264: 1581-84.

Lambert, J. and J. Elix, 1996. Community Involvement: Incorporating the Values, Needs and Aspirations of the Wider Community in Bioregional Planning. In *Approaches to Bioregional Planning, Part 1* (pp. 59-65) edited by R. Breckwoldt. Canberra: Department of the Environment.

Landres, P.B., J. Verner and J.W. Thomas, 1988. Ecological Uses of Vertebrate Indicator Species: A Critique, *Conservation Biology* 2: 316-17.

Landsberg, J., C.D. James, S.R. Morton, T.J. Hobbs, J. Stol, A. Drew and H. Tongway, 1997. *The Effects of Artificial Sources of Water on Rangeland Biodiversity*. Canberra: CSIRO Wildlife and Ecology.

Laurance, W.F., L.V. Ferreira, J.M. Rankin de Merona and S.G. Laurance, 1998. Rain Forest Fragmentation and the Dynamics of Amazonian Tree Communities, *Ecology* 79: 2032-40.

Laurance, W.F., S.G. Laurance, L.V. Ferreira, J.M. Rankin de Merona, C. Gascon and T.E. Lovejoy, 1997. Biomass Collapse in Amazonian Forest Fragments, *Science* 278: 1117-18.

Lawton, J.H. and V.K. Brown, 1993. Redundancy in Ecosystems. In *Biodiversity and Ecosystem Function* (pp. 255-70) edited by E.-D. Schultze and H.A. Mooney. Berlin: Springer-Verlag.

Lawton, J.H. and R.M. May (editors), 1995. *Extinction Rates*. Oxford, UK: Oxford University Press.

Lawton, J.H., S. Naeem, L.J. Thompson, A. Hector and M.J. Crawley, 1998. Biodiversity and Ecosystem Function: Getting the Ecotron Experiment in its Correct Context, *Functional Ecology* 12: 843-56.

Leader-Williams, N., J. Harrison and M.J.B. Green, 1990. Designing Protected Areas to Conserve Natural Resources, *Science Progress* 74: 189-204.

Leakey, L. and R. Lewin, 1995. *The Sixth Extinction*. London: Weidenfeld and Nicholson.

Levin, M.D., 1983. Value of Bee Pollination to US Agriculture, *Bulletin of the Entomological Society of America* 29: 50-51.

Liebhold, A.M., W.L. MacDonald, D. Bergdahl, and V.C. Mastro, 1995. Invasion of Exotic Forest Pests: A Threat to Forest Ecosystems. *Forest Science Monograph* 30.

Linnaeus, C., 1735. *Systema Naturae sive Regna Tria Naturae Systemice Proposita per Classes, Ordines, Genera and Species*. Leyden.

Lombard, A.T., A.O. Nicholls and P.V. August, 1995. Where Should Nature Reserves be Located in South Africa? A Snake's Perspective, *Conservation Biology* 9: 363-72.

Lombard, A.T., C. Hilton-Taylor, A.G. Rebelo, R.L. Pressey and R.M. Cowling, 1999. Reserve Selection in the Succulent Karoo, South Africa: Coping with High Compositional Turnover, *Plant Ecology* (in press).

Lovejoy, T.E., 1997. Biodiversity: What is It? In *Biodiversity II. Understanding and Protecting Our Biological Resources* (pp. 7-14) edited by M.L. Reaka-Kulda, D.E. Wilson and E.O. Wilson. Washington, DC: Joseph Henry Press.

Lovelock, J., 1987. *Gaia: A New Look at Life on Earth*. Oxford, UK: Oxford University Press.

Lunney, D. and T. Leary, 1988. The Impact on Native Mammals of Land-use Changes and Exotic Species in the Bega District, New South Wales, Since Settlement, *Australian Journal of Ecology* 13: 67-92.

Lunney, D. and A. Matthews, 1997. The Changing Roles of State and Local Government in Fauna Conservation Outside Nature Reserves: A Case Study of Koalas in New South Wales. In *Conservation Outside Nature Reserves* (pp. 97-106) edited by P. Hale and D. Lamb. Brisbane: Centre for Conservation Biology, University of Queensland.

Lunney, D. and C. Moon, 1988. An Ecological View of the History of Logging and Fire in Mumbulla State Forest on the South Coast of New South Wales. In *Australia's Ever Changing Forests* (pp. 23-61) edited by K.J. Frawley and N.M. Semple. Canberra: Australian Defence Force Academy.

MacArthur, R.H., 1972. *Geographical Ecology*. New York: Harper & Row.

MacArthur, R.H. and E.O. Wilson, 1967. *The Theory of Island Biogeography*. Princeton, NJ: Princeton University Press.

MacKinnon, K., A. Irving and M.A. Bachruddin, 1994. A Last Chance for Kutai National Park—Local Industry Support for Conservation, *Oryx* 28: 191-98.
Maehr, D.S., 1990. The Florida Panther and Private Lands, *Conservation Biology* 4: 167-70.
Malakoff, D., 1998. Death by Suffocation in the Gulf of Mexico, *Science* 281: 190-92.
Mann, C., 1991. Extinction: Are Ecologists Crying Wolf? *Science* 253: 736-38.
Mann, C. and M.L. Plummer, 1995. *Noah's Choice*. New York: Alfred A. Knopf.
Margules, C.R., 1989. Introduction to Some Australian Developments in Conservation Evaluation, *Biological Conservation* 50: 1-11.
Margules, C.R. and M.P. Austin, 1994. Biological Models for Monitoring Species Decline: The Construction and Use of Data Bases, *Philosophical Transactions of the Royal Society of London B* 344: 69-75.
Margules, C.R., A.O. Nicholls and R.L. Pressey, 1988. Selecting Networks of Reserves to Maximize Biological Diversity, *Biological Conservation* 43: 63-76.
Margules, C.R., R.L. Pressey and A.O. Nicholls, 1991. Selecting Nature Reserves. In *Nature Conservation: Cost-effective Biological Surveys and Data Analysis*. (pp. 90-97) edited by C.R. Margules and M.P. Austin. Melbourne: CSIRO.
Mark, A.F., 1985. The Botanical Component of Conservation in New Zealand, *New Zealand Journal of Botany* 23: 789-810.
Marshall, E., 1997. Yellowstone Opens the Gates to Biotech, *Science* 277: 1027.
Matson, P.A., W.J. Parton, A.G. Power and M.J. Swift, 1997. Agricultural Intensification and Ecosystem Properties, *Science* 277: 504-08.
May, R.M., 1973. *Stability and Complexity in Model Ecosystems*. Princeton, NJ: Princeton University Press.
May, R.M., 1977. Thresholds and Breakpoints in Ecosystems with a Multiplicity of Stable States, *Nature* 269: 471-77.
May, R.M., J.H. Lawton and N.E. Stork, 1995. Assessing Extinction Rates. In *Extinction Rates* (pp. 1-24) edited by J.H. Lawton and R.M. May. Oxford, UK: Oxford University Press.
McMichael, D.F., 1973. Further Case Studies in Selecting and Allocating Land for Nature Conservation. In *Nature Conservation in the Pacific* (pp. 53-6) edited by A.B. Costin and R.H. Groves. Canberra: Australian National University Press.
McMichael, D.F., 1990. The Selection of Land for Nature Conservation Purposes in New South Wales, *Australian Zoologist* 26: 78.

McNamara, D.G. and I.M. Smith, 1993. Pine Wood Nematode-European Reaction to an Exotic Pest. In *Plant Health and the European Single Market.* Proceedings of an International Symposium held at the University of Reading on March 30-April 1, 1993. (pp. 167-73) edited by D. Ebbels. Surrey, UK: British Crop Protection Council.

McNaughton, S.J., 1977. Diversity and Stability of Ecological Communities: A Comment on the Role of Empiricism in Ecology, *American Naturalist* III: 515-25.

McNeely, J. and K. Miller (editors), 1984. *National Parks Conservation and Development: The Role of Protected Areas in Sustaining Society.* Proceedings of the World Congress of National Parks. Washington, DC: Smithsonian Institution Press.

McNeely, J.A., K.R. Miller, W.V. Reid, R.A. Mittermeir and T.B. Werner, 1990. *Conserving the World's Biological Diversity.* Washington, DC: The World Bank.

Menge, B.A., E.L. Berlow, C.A. Blanchette, S.A. Navarrete and S.B. Yamada, 1994. The Keystone Species Concept: Variation in Interaction Strengths in a Rocky Intertidal Habitat, *Ecological Monographs* 64: 249-87.

Mercer, D. and J. Peterson, 1986. The Revocation of National Parks and Equivalent Reserves in Tasmania, *Search* 17: 134-40.

Miller, G.H., J.W. Magee, B.J. Johnson, M.L. Fogel, N.A. Spooner, M.T. McCulloch and L.K. Ayliffe, 1999. Pleistocene Extinction of *Genyornis newtoni*: Human Impact on Australian Megafauna. *Science* 283: 205-08.

Miller, K.R., 1996. *Balancing the Scales: Guidelines for Increasing Biodiversity's Chances through Bioregional Management.* Washington, DC: World Resources Institute.

Mills, L.S., M.E. Soulé and D.F. Doak, 1993. The Keystone-species Concept in Ecology and Conservation, *BioScience* 43: 219-24.

Milton, R., 1997. *Shattering the Myths of Darwinism.* Rochester, VT: Park Street Press.

Mittermeier, R.A., N. Myers, J.B. Thomsen, G.A.B. da Fonseca and S. Olivieri, 1998. Biodiversity Hotspots and Major Tropical Wilderness Areas: Approaches to Setting Conservation Priorities, *Conservation Biology* 12: 516-20.

MLO, 1997. *Canada's Report on the Montreal Process Criteria and Indicators for the Conservation and Sustainable Management of Temperate and Boreal Forests.* Ottawa. ON: Montreal Process Liaison Office.

Mlot, C., 1997. Population Diversity Crowds the Ark, *Science News* 152: 260.

Moffat, A.S., 1998. Global Nitrogen Overload Problem Grows Critical, *Science* 279: 988-89.

Monastersky, R. 1994. Earthmovers. Humans Take Their Place Alongside Wind, Water, and Ice, *Science News* 146: 432-33.

Mooney, H.A. and J.A. Drake (editors.), 1986. *Ecology of Biological Invasions of North America and Hawaii.* Ecological Studies 58. New York: Springer-Verlag.

Moore, N.W., 1987. *The Bird of Time: The Science and Politics of Nature Conservation—A Personal Account.* Cambridge, UK: Cambridge University Press.

Moreland, J.P. (editor), 1994. *The Creation Hypothesis. Scientific Evidence for an Intelligent Designer.* Downers Grove, IL: Intervarsity Press.

Morris, D.W., 1995. Earth's Peeling Veneer of Life, *Nature* 373: 25.

Mosquin, T. and P.G. Whiting, 1992. Canada Country Study of Biodiversity: Taxonomic, and Ecological Census Economic Benefits, Conservation Costs and Unmet Needs. (Draft version 1.1). Canadian Centre for Biodiversity, Canadian Museum of Nature, Ottawa. 282 pp.

Myers, N., 1987. The Extinctions Spasm Impending: Synergisms at Work, *Conservation Biology* 1: 14-21.

Myers, N., 1988a. Threatened Biotas: Hotspots in Tropical Forests, *The Environmentalist* 8: 178-208.

Myers, N., 1988b. Tropical Forests and Their Species. Going, Going...? In *Biodiversity* (pp. 28-35) edited by E.O. Wilson. Washington, DC: National Academy Press.

Myers, N., 1990. The Biodiversity Challenge: Expanded Hotspots Analysis, *The Environmentalist* 10: 243-56.

Myers, N., 1995a. The World's Forests: Need for a Policy Appraisal, *Science* 268: 823-24.

Myers, N., 1995b. Environmental Unknowns, *Science* 269: 358-60.

Naeem, S., 1998. Species Redundancy and Ecosystem Reliability, *Conservation Biology* 12: 39-45.

Naeem, S. and S. Li, 1997. Biodiversity Enhances Ecosystem Reliability, *Nature* 390: 507-09.

Naeem, S., L.J. Thompson, S.P. Lawler, J.H. Lawton and R.M. Woodfin, 1994. Declining Biodiversity can Alter the Performance of Ecosystems, *Nature* 368: 734-37.

Naeem, S., L.J. Thompson, S.P. Lawler, J.H. Lawton and R.M. Woodfin, 1995. Empirical Evidence that Declining Species Diversity may Alter the Performance of Terrestrial Ecosystems, *Proceedings of the Royal Society of London* (B) 347: 249-62.

Nash, S., 1991. What Price nature? *BioScience* 41: 677-80.

Nealis, V.G. and S. Erb, 1993. *A Sourcebook for Management of Gypsy Moth.* Sault Ste. Marie, ON: Forestry Canada, Ontario Region, Great Lakes Forestry Centre.

Nee, S. and R. M. May, 1997. Extinction and the Loss of Evolutionary History, *Science* 278: 692-94.

Nepstad, D.C., A. Verissimo, A. Alencar, C. Nobre, E. Lima, P. Fefebvre, P. Schlesinger, C. Potter, P. Moutinho, E. Mendoza, M. Colhrane and V. Brooks, 1999. Large-scale Impoverishment of Amazonian Forest by Logging and Fire, *Nature* 398: 505-08.

Newmark, W.D., 1987. A Land Bridge Perspective on Mammalian Extinctions in Western North American Parks, *Nature* 325: 430-2.

NFDP, 1999. *National Forestry Database Program.* Canadian Council of Forest Ministers. Natural Resources Canada. Canadian Forest Service (web site: www.nrcan.gc.ca/cfs/proj/iepb/nfdp/, viewed September 10, 1999)

Nicholls, A.O. and C.R. Margules, 1993. An Upgraded Reserve Selection Algorithm, *Biological Conservation* 64: 164-69.

Niemela, P. and W.J. Mattson, 1996. Invasion of North American Forests by European Phytophagous Insects. *BioScience* 46(10): 741-753.

Noble, I.R. and R. Dirzo, 1997. Forests as Human-dominated Ecosystems, *Science* 277: 522-25.

Norse, E.A., 1990. *Ancient Forests of the Pacific Northwest.* Washington, DC and Covelo, CA: Island Press.

North, D.C., 1990. *Institutions, Institutional Change and Economic Performance.* Cambridge, UK: Cambridge University Press.

North, D.C., 1994. Economic Performance Through Time, *American Economic Review* 84(June): 359-68.

Norton, B.G. and M.A. Toman, 1997. Sustainability: Ecological and Economic Perspectives, *Land Economics* 73(November): 553-68.

Norton, B.W., 1999. Is there a Universal Earth Ethic? A Reflection on Biodiversity Values. Centre for Biodiversity Research, UBC, Vancouver. Mimeograph.

Norton, G.A. and J.D. Mumford, 1993. Decision Analysis Techniques. In *Decision Tools for Pest Management* (pp.43-68) edited by G.A. Norton and J.D. Mumford. Wallingford, UK: CAB International.

Noss, R.F., 1990. Indicators for Monitoring Biodiversity: A Hierarchical Approach, *Conservation Biology* 4: 355-64.

Nozick, R., 1974. *Anarchy, State, and Utopia.* New York: Basic Books.

NPWS (National Parks and Wildlife Service), 1999. NSW Biodiversity Strategy. New South Wales NPWS, Sydney.

O'Brien, S.J., 1994. Genetic and Phylogenetic Analysis of Endangered Species, *Annual Review of Genetics* 28: 467-89.

Oedekoven, K., 1980. The Vanishing Forest, *Environmental Policy and Law* 6: 184-85.

Olson, S.L. and H.F. James, 1982. Fossil Birds from the Hawaiian Islands: Evidence for Wholesale Extinction by Man before Western Contact, *Science* 217: 633-35.

Orr, L., S.D. Cohen, and R.L. Griffin, 1993. *Generic Non-Indigenous Pest Risk Assessment Process*. Riverdale, MD: US Department of Agriculture, Animal and Plant Health Inspection Service, Planning and Risk Analysis Systems, Policy and Program Development.

OTA, 1993. *Harmful Non-Indigenous Species in the United States*. OTA-F-565. Washington, DC: US Congress. Office of Technology Assessment.

Paine, R.T., 1966. Food Web Complexity and Species Diversity, *American Naturalist* 100: 65-75.

Paine, R.T., 1969. A Note on Trophic Complexity and Community Stability, *American Naturalist* 103: 91-93.

Pan, D., G. Domon, S. de Blois and A. Bouchard, 1999. Temporal (1958-1993) and Spatial Patterns of Land Use Changes in Haut-Saint-Laurent (Quebec, Canada) and Their Relation to Landscape Physical Attributes, *Landscape Ecology* 14: 35-52.

Parfit, D., 1984. *Reasons and Persons*. Oxford: Oxford University Press.

Parfit, D., 1996. Acts and Outcomes: A Response to Boonin-Vail, *Philosophy and Public Affairs* 25: 308-17.

Parr, J.W.K., N. Mahannop and V. Charoensiri, 1993. Khao Sam Roi Yot - One of the World's Most Threatened Parks, *Oryx* 27: 245-49

Patrick, R., 1997. Systematics: A Keystone to Understanding Biodiversity. *Biodiversity II. Understanding and Protecting Our Biological Resources* (pp. 213-16) edited by M.L. Reaka-Kudla, D.E. Wilson and E.O. Wilson. Washington, DC: Joseph Henry Press.

Pauly, D. and V. Christensen, 1995. Primary Production Required to Sustain Global Fisheries, *Nature* 374: 255-57.

Pauly, D., V. Christensen, J. Dalsgaard, R. Froese and F. Torres Jr., 1998. Fishing Down Marine Food Webs, *Science* 279: 860-63.

Pejovich, S., 1995. *Economic Analysis of Institutions and Systems*. Dordrecht: Kluwer Academic Publishers.

Perrings, C. (co-ordinator), 1995. Economic Values of Biodiversity. In *Global Biodiversity Assessment* (Published for the United Nations Environment Programme) (pp. 823-914) edited by V.H. Heywood and R.T. Watson. New York: Cambridge University Press.

Perrings, C., 1998. Resilience in the Dynamics of Economy-Environment Systems, *Environmental and Resource Economics* 11: 503-20.

Pezzey, J.C.V., 1997. Sustainability Constraints versus "Optimality" versus Intertemporal Concern, and Axioms versus Data, *Land Economics* 73(November): 448-66.

Pimentel, D. and C.A. Edwards, 1982. Pesticides and Ecosystems, *BioScience* 32: 595-600.

Pimentel, D., L. Larch, R. Zuniga and D. Morrison, 1999. *Environmental and Economic Costs Associated with Non-Indigenous Species in the United States.* Ithaca: College of Agriculture and Life Sciences, Cornell University. (web site: www.news.cornell.edu/releases/Jan99/species_costs.html, viewed August 20, 1999)

Pimm, S.L., 1984. The Complexity and Stability of Ecosystems, *Nature* 307: 321-26.

Pimm, S.L. 1998. Extinction. In *Conservation Science and Action* edited by W.J. Sutherland. Oxford, UK: Blackwell Science.

Pimm, S.L., M.P. Moulton and L.J. Justice, 1995a. Bird Extinctions in the Central Pacific. In *Extinction Rates* (pp. 75-87) edited by J.H. Lawton and R.M. May. Oxford, UK: Oxford University Press.

Pimm, S.L., G.J. Russell, J.L. Gittleman and T.M. Brooks. 1995b. The Future of Biodiversity, *Science* 269: 347-50.

Polis, G.A. and K.O. Winemiller, 1996. *Food Webs: Integration of Patterns and Dynamics.* New York: Chapman & Hall.

Power, M.E., 1995. The Keystone Cops Meet in Hilo, *Trends in Ecology and Evolution* 10: 182-84.

Power, M.E., D. Tilman, J.A. Estes, B.A. Menge, W.J. Bond, L.S. Mills, G. Daily, J.C. Castilla, J. Lubchenko and R.T. Paine, 1996. Challenges in the Quest for Keystones, *BioScience* 46: 609-20.

Powledge, F., 1998. Biodiversity at the Crossroads, *BioScience* 48: 347-52.

Prendergast, J.R., R.M. Quinn, J.H. Lawton, B.C. Eversham and D.W. Gibbons, 1993. Rare Species, the Coincidence of Diversity Hotspots and Conservation Strategies, *Nature* 365: 335-37.

Pressey, R.L., 1994. Ad hoc Reservations: Forward or Backward Steps in Developing Representative Reserve Systems? *Conservation Biology* 8: 662-68.

Pressey, R.L., 1997. Priority Conservation Areas: Towards an Operational Definition for Regional Assessments. In *National Parks and Protected Areas: Selection, Delimitation and Management.* (pp. 337-57) edited by J.J. Pigram and R.C. Sundell. Armidale, Australia: University of New England, Centre for Water Policy Research.

Pressey, R.L., 1998. Algorithms, Politics and Timber: An Example of the Role of Science in a Public, Political Negotiation Process over New Conservation Areas in Production Forests. In *Ecology for Everyone: Communicating Ecology to Scientists, the Public and the Politicians* (pp. 73-87) edited by R. Wills and R. Hobbs. Sydney: Surrey Beatty & Sons.

Pressey, R.L. and A.O. Nicholls, 1989. Application of a Numerical Algorithm to the Selection of Reserves in Semi-arid New South Wales, *Biological Conservation* 50: 263-78.

Pressey, R.L. and A.O. Nicholls, 1989. Efficiency in Conservation Evaluation: Scoring vs. Iterative Approaches, *Biological Conservation* 50: 199-218.

Pressey, R.L. and K.H. Taffs, 1999. Priority Conservation Areas: A Definition for the Real World Applied to Western New South Wales, *Biological Conservation*. Submitted.

Pressey, R.L. and S.L. Tully, 1994. The Cost of ad hoc Reservation: A Case Study in Western New South Wales, *Australian Journal of Ecology* 19: 375-84.

Pressey, R.L., S. Ferrier, T.C. Hager, C.A. Woods, S.L. Tully and K.M. Weinman, 1996. How Well Protected are the Forests of North-eastern New South Wales?—Analyses of Forest Environments in Relation to Tenure, Formal Protection Measures and Vulnerability to Clearing, *Forest Ecology and Management* 85: 311-33.

Pressey, R.L., I.R. Johnson and P.D. Wilson, 1994. Shades of Irreplaceability: Toward a Measure of the Contribution of Sites to a Reservation Goal, *Biodiversity and Conservation* 3: 242-62.

Pressey, R.L., T.C. Hager, K.M. Ryan, J. Schwarz, S Wall, S. Ferrier and P.M. Creaser, 1999a. Terrestrial Reserves in New South Wales: Gaps, Biases, and Priorities to Minimize Further Loss of Native Vegetation, *Biological Conservation*, Submitted.

Pressey, R.L., C.J. Humphries, C.R. Margules, R.I. Vane-Wright and P.H. Williams, 1993. Beyond Opportunism: Key Principles for Systematic Reserve Selection, *Trends in Ecology and Evolution (TREE)* 8: 124-28.

Pressey, R.L., G.L. Whish, T.W. Barrett and M.E. Watts, 1999b. Effectiveness of Conservation Decisions: An Extended Set of Measures Applied to North-eastern New South Wales, *Conservation Biology*. Submitted.

Prober, S. and K. Thiele. 1993. Surviving in Cemeteries—The Grassy White Box Woodlands, *National Parks Journal* 37(1): 13-15.

Prober, S.M., 1996. Conservation of the Grassy White Box Woodlands: Rangewide Floristic Variation and Implications for Reserve Design, *Australian Journal of Botany* 44: 57-77.

Pullan, R.A., 1983. Do National Parks have a Future in Africa? *Leisure Studies* 2: 1-18.

Rabinowitz, A., 1995. Helping a Species go Extinct: The Sumatran Rhino in Borneo, *Conservation Biology* 9: 482-88.

RACAC (Resource and Conservation Assessment Council), 1996. *Draft Interim Forestry Assessment Report*. Sydney: RACAC.

Raeburn, P., 1995. *The Last Harvest. The Genetic Gamble that Threatens to Destroy American Agriculture*.New York: Simon & Schuster.

Randall, A., 1988. What Mainstream Economists have to Say About the Value of Biodiversity. Chapter 25 in *Biodiversity* edited by E.O. Wilson. Washington: National Academy Press.

Randall, A., 1991a. The Value of Biodiversity, *AMBIO* 20: 64-7.

Randall, A., 1991b. Thinking About the Value of Biodiversity. Columbus, OH: Department of Agricultural Economics and Rural Sociology, Ohio State University. Mimeograph.

Randall, A. and M.C. Farmer, 1995. Benefits, Costs, and the Safe Minimum Standard of Conservation. Chapter 2 in *The Handbook of Environmental Economics* (pp.26-44) edited by D.W. Bromley. Cambridge MA: Basil Blackwell.

Raup, D.M. and J.J. Sepkoski, 1984. Periodicity of Extinctions in the Geological Past, *Proceedings of the National Academy of Science, USA* 81: 801-05.

Raup, D.M., 1986. Biological Extinction in Earth History, *Science* 231: 1528-33.

Raup, D.M., 1992. Large-body Impact and Extinction in the Phanerozoic, *Paleobiology* 18: 80-88.

Raven, P.H. and E.O. Wilson, 1992. A Fifty-year Plan for Biodiversity Surveys, *Science* 258: 1099-1100.

Rawls, J. 1971. A *Theory of Justice*. Cambridge: Harvard University Press.

Ray, G.C. and J.F. Grassle, 1991. Marine Biological Diversity, *BioScience* 41: 453-57.

Reaka-Kudla, M.L., D.E. Wilson and E.O. Wilson (editors), 1997. *Biodiversity II. Understanding and Protecting Our Biological Resources*. Washington, DC: Joseph Henry Press.

Rebelo, A.G., 1997. Conservation. In *Vegetation of Southern Africa* (pp. 571-90) edited by R.M. Cowling, D.M. Richardson and S.M. Pierce. Cambridge, UK: Cambridge University Press.

Recher, H.F., 1990. Response to Conserving What?—The Basis for Nature Conservation Reserves in New South Wales 1967-1989, *Australian Zoologist* 26: 83-4.

Reed, P., 1990. An Historical Perspective on: Conserving What?—The Basis for Nature Conservation Reserves in New South Wales 1967-1989, *Australian Zoologist* 26: 85-91.

Reed, R.A., J. Johnson-Barnard and W.L. Baker, 1996. Contribution of Roads to Fragmentation in the Rocky Mountains, *Conservation Biology* 10: 1098-1106.

Regier, H.A., 1992. Indicators of Ecosystem Integrity. In *Ecological Indicators. Vol. I* (pp. 183-200) edited by D.H. McKenzie, D.E. Hyatt and J.V. McDonald. London: Elsevier.

Reid, W.V., 1998. Biodiversity Hotspots, *Trends in Ecology and Evolution* 13: 275-80.

Ricciardi, A. and J. Rasmussen, 1999. Extinction Rates of North American Freshwater Fauna, *Conservation Biology* 13(October): 1220-22.

Richter, W., 1997. Restoring ecosystems, *Science* 278: 997.

Ride, W.L.D., 1975. Towards an Integrated System: A Study of Selection and Acquisition of National Parks and Nature Reserves in Western Australia. In *A National System of Ecological Reserves in Australia* (pp. 64-85) edited by F. Fenner. Canberra: Australian Academy of Science.

Rodriguez, J.P. and F. Rojas-Saurez, 1996. Guidelines for the Design of Conservation Strategies for the Animals of Venezuela, *Conservation Biology* 10: 1245-52.
Roush, W., 1994. Population: The View from Cairo, *Science* 265: 1164-67.
Roush, W., 1997. Putting a Price on Nature's Bounty, *Science* 276: 1029.
Royal Commission on Reproductive Technologies, 1994. *Proceed With Care.* (Final Report) Ottawa: Minister of Supply and Services Canada.
Runte, A., 1972. Yellowstone: It's Useless, So Why not a Park? *National Parks and Conservation Magazine* March, pp. 4-7.
Runte, A., 1979. *National Parks: The American Experience.* Lincoln, Nebraska: University of Nebraska Press.
Runte, A., 1983. Reply to Sellars, *Journal of Forest History* 27: 135-41.
Rylands, A.B., 1991. Priority Areas for Conservation in the Amazon, *Trends in Ecology and Evolution* 5: 240-41.
Saetersdal, M., J.M. Line and H.J.B. Birks, 1993. How to Maximise Biological Diversity in Nature Reserve Selection: Vascular Plants and Breeding Birds in Deciduous Woodlands, Western Norway, *Biological Conservation* 66: 131-38.
Sagoff, M., 1988. *The Economy of the Earth.* Cambridge: Cambridge University Press.
Sagoff, M., 1994. Should Preferences Count? *Land Economics* 70(May): 127-44.
Sailer, R.I. , 1983. History of Insect Introductions. In *Exotic Plant Pests and North American Agriculture* (pp. 15-38) edited by C.L. Wilson and C.L. Graham. New York: Academic Press.
Saunders, D., A. Beattie, S. Eliott, M. Fox, B. Hill, M. Maliel, R.L. Pressey, D. Veal, J. Venning and C. Zammit, 1996. Biodiversity. In *Australia—State of the Environment, 1996* (pp.4.1-4.59). Melbourne: CSIRO.
Saunders, D., C. Margules and B. Hill, 1998. *Environmental Indicators for National State of the Environment Reporting—Biodiversity.* Canberra: Environment Australia.
Saunders, D.A., R.J. Hobbs and C.R. Margules, 1991. Biological Consequences of Ecosystem Fragmentation, *Conservation Biology* 5: 18-32.
Schaeffer, F. A., 1970. *Pollution and the Death of Man. The Christian View of Ecology.* Wheaton, IL: Tyndale House Publishers.
Schaeffer, F.A., 1982. *A Christian Manifesto.* Hants, UK: Pickering and Inglis Ltd.
Schindler, D.W., 1991. Comments on the Sustainable Biosphere Initiative, *Conservation Biology* 5: 550-51.
Schipper, R.A., H.G.P. Jansen, B.A.M. Bouman, H. Hengsdijk and A. Nieuwenhuyse, 1999. Integrated Biophysical and Socio-economic Land Use Analysis at the Regional Level. In *Tools for Land Use Analysis at Different Scales, with Case Studies for Costa Rica* edited by B. Bouman, H. Jansen, H. Hengsdijk and A. Nieuwenhuyse. Dordrecht: Kluwer Academic Publishers, In Press.

Schonewald-Cox, C. and M. Buechner, 1991. Housing Viable Populations in Protected Habitats: The Value of a Coarse-grained Geographic Analysis of Density, Patterns and Available Habitat. In *Species Conservation: A Population-biological Approach* (pp. 213-26) edited by A. Seitz and V. Loeschche. Basel: Binkhaüser Verlag.

Scudder, G.G.E., 1991. Threatened and Endangered Invertebrates of the South Okanagan. In *Community Action for Endangered Species*, (pp. 47-58) edited by S. Rautio. Vancouver, BC: Federation of British Columbia Naturalists.

Scudder, G.G.E., 1993. Biodiversity over Time. In *Our Living Legacy: Proceedings of a Symposium on Biological Diversity* (pp. 109-26) edited by M.A. Fenger, E.H. Miller, J.A. Johnson and E.J.R. Williams. Vancouver, BC: Royal British Columbia Museum.

Sedjo, R. A., 1992. Property Rights, Genetic Resources, and Biotechnological Change, *Journal of Law and Economics* 35(April): 199-213.

Sellars, R.W., 1983. National Parks: Worthless Lands or Competing Land Values? *Journal of Forest History* 27: 130-34.

Sen, A., 1979. Utilitarianism and Welfarism, *Journal of Philosophy* 76: 463-88.

Sen, A., 1984. Approaches to the Choice of Discount Rates for Social Benefit-Cost Analysis. In *Resources, Values and Development*. Oxford: Basil Blackwell.

Sepkoski, J.J., 1992. Phylogenetic and Ecological Patterns in the Phanerozoic History of Marine Biodiversity. In *Systematics, Ecology, and the Biodiversity Crisis* (pp. 77-100) edited by N. Eldridge. New York: Columbia University Press.

Shleifer, A., 1998. State versus Private Ownership. Department of Economics, Harvard University, Cambridge MA. Mimeograph. 32pp.

Shleifer, A. and R.W. Vishny, 1998. *The Grabbing Hand*. Cambridge, MA: Harvard University Press.

Shogren, J.F. 1998. A Political Economy in an Ecological Web, *Environmental and Resource Economics* 11: 557-570

Shogren, J.F. and J. Tschirhart, 1999. The Endangered Species Act at Twenty-five, *Choices*, Third Quarter, pp.4-9.

Short, J., S.D. Bradshaw, J. Giles, R.I.T. Prince and G.R. Wilson, 1992. Reintroduction of Macropods (Marsupialia: Macropodoidea) in Australia: A Review, *Biological Conservation* 62: 189-204.

Shukla, J., C. Noble and P. Sellers, 1990. Amazon Deforestation and Climate Change, *Science* 247: 1322-25.

Sierra Club of Western Canada. 1993. Ancient Rainforests at Risk. Final Report of the Vancouver Island Mapping Project. Victoria, BC: Sierra Club of Western Canada.

Simon, J.L., 1996. *The Ultimate Resource 2*. Princeton, NJ: Princeton University Press.

Simpson, R.D. and R.A. Sedjo, 1996a. Investments in Biodiversity Prospecting and Incentives for Conservation. Discussion Paper 96-14. Washington DC: Resources for the Future.

Simpson, R.D. and R.A. Sedjo, 1996b. Valuation of Biodiversity for Use in New Product Research in a Model of Sequential Search. Discussion Paper 96-27. Washington DC: Resources for the Future.

Simpson, R.D., R.A. Sedjo and J.W. Reid, 1996. Valuing Biodiversity for Use in Pharmaceutical Research, *Journal of Political Economy* 104: 163-85.

Sinclair, A.R.E. and P. Arcese, 1995. Serengeti in the Context of Worldwide Conservation Efforts. In *Serengeti II: Dynamics, Management and Conservation of an Ecosystem.* (pp 31-46) edited by A.R.E. Sinclair and P. Arcese. Chicago: University of Chicago Press.

Sinclair, A.R.E. and M.P. Wells, 1989. Population Growth and the Poverty Cycle in Africa: Colliding Ecological and Economic Processes? In *Food and Natural Resources.* (pp. 439-84) edited by D. Pimentel and C. Hall. New York: Academic Press.

Sinclair, A.R.E., D.S. Hik, O.J. Schmitz, G.G.E. Scudder, D.H. Turpin and N.C. Larter, 1995. Biodiversity and the Need for Habitat Renewal, *Ecological Applications* 5: 579-87.

Sinclair, A.R.E., R.P. Pech, C.R. Dickman, D. Hik, P. Mahon and A.E. Newsome. 1998. Predicting Effects of Predation on Conservation of Endangered Prey, *Conservation Biology* 12: 564-75.

Singleton, G.R. 1989. Population Dynamics of an Outbreak of House Mice (*Mus domesticus*) in the Mallee Wheatlands of Australia, *Journal of Zoology, London* 219: 495-515.

Sisk, T.D., A.E. Launer, K.R. Switky and P.R. Ehrlich, 1994. Identifying Extinction Threats: Global Analyses of the Distribution of Biodiversity and the Expansion of the Human Enterprise, *BioScience* 44: 592-604.

Sivertsen, D., 1993. Conservation of Remnant Vegetation in the Box and Ironbark Lands of New South Wales, *Victorian Naturalist* 110: 24-9.

Sivertsen, D., 1994. The Native Vegetation Crisis in the Wheatbelt of NSW, *Search* 25: 5-8.

Sivertsen, D., 1997. Assessment of Native Vegetation Loss in the Wheatbelt of NSW. In *Ecology at the Cutting Edge–Information Technologies for Managing Biodiversity and Ecological Processes* (pp. 84-97) edited by B. Diekman, E. Higginson, F. Sutton and H. Webb. Sydney: Nature Conservation Council of New South Wales.

Skole, D. and C. Tucker. 1993. Tropical Deforestation and Habitat Fragmentation in the Amazon: Satellite Data from 1978 to 1988, *Science* 260: 1905-10.

Smith, F.D.M., G.C. Daily and P.R. Ehrlich, 1995. Human Population Dynamics and Biodiversity Loss. Chapter 11 in *The Economics and Ecology of Biodiversity Decline* (pp.125-42) edited by T.M. Swanson. Cambridge, UK: Cambridge University Press.

Smith, F.D.M., R.M. May, R. Pellew, T.H. Johnson and K.R. Walter, 1993. How Much Do We Know about the Current Extinction Rate? *Trends in Ecology and Evolution* 8: 375-78.

Smith, Q., 1993. The Concept of a Cause of the Universe, *Canadian Journal of Philosophy* 23: 1-24.

Solow, A.R. and S. Polasky, 1999. The Endangered Species Act as a Tool to Conserve Biological Diversity, *Choices*, Third Quarter, pp. 17-21.

Soulé, M., M. Gilpin, W. Conway and T. Foose. 1986. The Millenium Ark: How Long a Voyage, How Many Staterooms, How Many Passengers? *Zoo Biology* 5: 101-13.

Soulé, M.E. and M.A., Sanjayan, 1998. Conservation Targets: Do They Help? *Science* 279: 2060-1.

Soulé, M.E. 1991. Conservation: Tactics for a Constant Crisis, *Science* 253: 744-50.

Sousa, W.P. 1984. The Role of Disturbance in Natural Communities, *Annual Review of Ecology and Systematics* 15: 353-91.

Specht, R.L., E.M. Roe and V.H. Boughton, 1974. Conservation of Major Plant Communities in Australia and New Guinea, *Australian Journal of Botany* Supplement No. 7.

Stark, R., L.R. Iannaccone and R. Finke, 1996. Religion, Science, and Rationality, *American Economic Review* 86(May): 433-37.

Steadman, D.W. 1991. Extinction of Species: Past, Present and Future. In *Global Climate Change and Life on Earth*. (pp. 156-69) edited by R.L. Wyman. London: Routledge, Chapman and Hall.

Steadman, D.W. 1995. Prehistoric Extinctions of Pacific Island Birds: Biodiversity Meets Zooarcheology, *Science* 267: 1123-31.

Stern, P.C. 1993. A Second Environmental Science: Human-Environmental Interactions, *Science* 260: 1897-99.

Stoms, D.M., F.W. Davis, K.L. Driese, K.M. Cassidy and M.P. Murray, 1998. Gap Analysis of the Vegetation of the Intermountain Semi-Desert Ecoregion, *Great Basin Naturalist* 58: 199-216.

Stone, R. 1993. Déjà Vu Guides the Way to New Antimicrobial Steroid, *Science* 259: 1125.

Stone, R. 1999. Coming to Grips with the Aral Sea's Grim Legacy, *Science* 284: 30-33.

Stork, N.E. and C.J.C. Lyal. 1993. Extinction or Co-extinction Rates, *Nature* 366: 307.

Strom, A., 1983. Nature Conservation in the Western Division, *National Parks Journal* 27(6): 23-4.

Strom, A.A., 1979a. Impressions of a Developing Conservation Ethic, 1870-1930. *Parks and Wildlife* 2(3-4): 45-53.

Strom, A.A., 1979b. Some Events in Nature Conservation over the Last Forty Years, *Parks and Wildlife* 2(3-4): 65-73.

Strom, A.A., 1990. Response to: Conserving What? - The Basis for Nature Conservation Reserves in New South Wales 1967-1989, *Australian Zoologist* 26: 94-6.

Stuart, A. 1991. Mammalian Extinctions in the Late Pleistocene of Northern Eurasia and North America, *Biological Reviews* 66: 453-562.

Swanson, T.M. 1994. The Economics of Extinction Revisited and Revised: A Generalised Framework for the Analysis of the Problems of Endangered Species and Biodiversity Losses, *Oxford Economic Papers* 46: 800-21.

Swanson, T.M., 1995. Why does Biodiversity Decline? The Analysis of Forces for Global Change. Chapter 1 in *The Economics and Ecology of Biodiversity Decline* (pp. 1-9) edited by T.M. Swanson. Cambridge, UK: Cambridge University Press.

Swanson, T.M., and E.B. Barbier, 1992. *Economics for the Wilds*. London: Earthscan.

Temple, S.A., 1977. Plant-Animal Mutualism: Coevolution with Dodo Leads to Near Extinction of Plant, *Science* 197: 885-86.

Terborgh, J., 1974. Preservation of Natural Diversity: The Problem of Extinction Prone Species, *BioScience* 24: 715-22.

Thackway, R. and I.D. Cresswell (editors), 1996. *Interim Marine and Coastal Regionalisation for Australia: an Ecosystem-based Hierarchical Classification of Coastal and Marine Environments. Stage 1–the Inshore Waters*. Canberra: Australian Nature Conservation Agency.

Thirgood, J.V., 1981. *Man and the Mediterranean Forest. A History of Resource Depletion*. London: Academic Press.

Tibbetts, J., R. Collins, J. Humbach, R. Marzulla, F.L. Smith, J.R. Schubel, R.J. Lyman, M. Permar and W. Travis, 1995. Private Rights Versus Public Interests: Who Decides the Fate of the Coast? *Coastal Management* 23: 1-17.

Tilman, D. 1996a. Biodiversity: Population Versus Ecosystem Stability, *Ecology* 77: 350-63.

Tilman, D. 1996b. The Benefits of Natural Disasters. *Science* 273: 1518.

Tilman, D. and J.A. Downing, 1994. Biodiversity and Stability in Grasslands, *Nature* 367: 363-65.

Tilman, D., C.L. Lehman and C.E. Bristow, 1998. Diversity-Stability Relationships: Statistical Inevitability or Ecological Consequence, *American Naturalist* 151: 277-82.

Tilman, D., C.L. Lehman and K.T. Thompson, 1997a. Plant Diversity and Ecosystem Productivity: Theoretical Considerations, *Proceedings of the National Academy of Sciences* 94: 1857-61.

Tilman, D., S. Naeem, J. Knops, P. Reich, E. Siemann, D. Wedin, M. Ritchie and J.H. Lawton, 1997b. Biodiversity and Ecosystem Properties, *Science* 278: 1866-67.

Tilman, D., D. Wedin and J. Knops, 1996. Productivity and Sustainability Influenced by Biodiversity in Grassland Ecosystems, *Nature* 379: 718-20.

Tisdell, C., 1990. Economics and the Debate about Preservation of Species, Crop Varieties and Genetic Diversity, *Ecological Economics* 2: 77-90.

TNC (The Nature Conservancy), 1997. *Designing a Geography of Hope: Guidelines for Ecoregion-based Conservation in The Nature Conservancy*. Arlington, Virginia: TNC.

Tolba, M.K., D.A. El-Kholy, E. El-Hinnawi, M.W. Holdgate, D.F. McMichael and R.E, Munn (editors), 1992. *The World Environment 1972-1992: Two Decades of Challenge*. London: Chapman and Hall.

USDA, 1991. *Pest Risk Assessment of the Importation of Larch from Siberia and the Soviet Far East*. Misc. Publications No. 1495. Washington, DC: US Department of Agriculture, Forest Service.

USDA, 1998a. *Pest Risk Assessment of the Importation of Into the United States of Unprocessed Pinus and Abies Logs from Mexico*. General Technical Report FPL-GTR-104. Washington, DC: US Department of Agriculture, Forest Service.

USDA, 1998b. *Importation of Logs, Lumber and Other Unmanufactured Wood Articles*. Final supplement to the environmental impact statement. Riverdale, MD: US Department of Agriculture, Marketing and Regulatory Programs, Animal and Plant Health Inspection Service.

van Kooten, G.C., 1995. Can Nonmarket Values be used as Indicators of Forest Sustainability? *The Forestry Chronicle* 71(Nov/Dec): 1-10.

van Kooten, G.C., 1998. Economics of Conservation Biology: A Critical Review, *Environmental Science and Policy* 1: 13-25.

van Kooten, G.C., 1999. Preserving species without an endangered species act: British Columbia's Forest Practices Code. Chapter 4 in *Topics in Environmental Economics* (pp.63-82) edited by M. Boman, R. Brännlund and B. Kristrom. Dordrecht, Netherlands: Kluwer Academic Publishers.

van Kooten, G.C. and E.H. Bulte, 1999. How Much Primary Coastal Temperate Rain Forest Should Society Retain? Carbon Uptake, Recreation and Other Values, *Canadian Journal of Forest Research* 29(12): 1879-90.

van Kooten, G.C. and E.H. Bulte, 2000. *The Economics of Nature: Managing Biological Assets*. Oxford, UK: Blackwell Publishers.

van Kooten, G.C., R. Sedjo and E.H. Bulte, 1999. Tropical Deforestation: Issues and Policies. Chapter 5 in *International Yearbook of Environmental and Resource Economics 1999/2000* (pp.198-249) edited by H. Folmer and T. Tietenberg. Aldershot, UK: Edward Elgar.

Vane-Wright, R.I., C.J. Humphries and P.H. Williams, 1991. What to Protect? Systematics and the Agony of Choice, *Biological Conservation* 55: 235-54.

Vincent, J.R., 1992. The Tropical Timber Trade and Sustainable Development, *Science* 256: 1651-55.

Vitousek, P., P.R. Ehrlich, A.H. Ehrlich and P. Matson, 1986. Human Appropriation of the Products of Photosynthesis, *BioScience* 36: 368-74.

Vitousek, P.M. and D.U. Hooper, 1993. Biological Diversity and Terrestrial Ecosystem Biochemistry. In *Biodiversity and Ecosystem Function* (pp. 3-14) edited by E.-D. Schultz and H.A. Mooney. Berlin: Springer-Verlag.

Vitousek, P.M., H.A. Mooney, J. Lubchenko and J.M. Melillo, 1997. Human Domination of Earth's Ecosystems, *Science* 277: 494-99.

Walker, B.H., 1991. Biodiversity and Ecological Redundancy, *Conservation Biology* 6: 18-23.

Wallace, R.R. and B.G. Norton, 1992. Policy Implications of Gaian Theory, *Ecological Economics* 6(October): 103-18.

Wallner, W.E., 1996. Invasive Pests (Biological Pollutants) and US Forests: Whose Problem, Who Pays? *EPPO Bulletin* 26: 167-80.

Wallner, W.E., 1997. Global gypsy - the moth that gets around. In *Exotic Pests of Eastern Forests*, Proceedings of a Conference held in Nashville, Tennessee on April 8-10, 1997. Nashville, TN: Tennessee Exotic Pest Plant Council and USDA Forest Service. (web site www.webriver.com/tn-eppc/sympos.htm, viewed August 3, 1999)

Wallner, W.E., 1999. Pest Risk Assessment and International Forest Resources. In *Biological Pollution: An Emerging Global Menace*. St. Paul, MN: American Phytopathological Society Press. (in Press)

Webb, L.J., 1966. The Identification and Conservation of Habitat-types in the Wet Tropical Lowlands of North Queensland, *Proceedings of the Royal Society of Queensland* 78: 59-86.

Westwood, A.R., 1991. A Cost Benefit Analysis of Manitoba's Integrated Dutch Elm Disease Management Program 1975-1990. *Proceedings of the Entomological Society of Manitoba* 47: 44-59.

White, P.S., 1997. Biodiversity and the Exotic Species Threat. In *Exotic Pests of Eastern Forests*, Proceedings of a Conference held in Nashville, Tennessee on April 8-10, 1997. Nashville, TN: Tennessee Exotic Pest Plant Council and USDA Forest Service. (web site www.webriver.com/tn-eppc/sympos.htm, viewed August 3, 1999)

Whitehouse, J.F., 1990. Conserving What?—The Basis for Nature Conservation Reserves in New South Wales 1967-1989, *Australian Zoologist* 26: 11-21.

Wiens, J.A., 1989. *The Ecology of Bird Communities. Volume 2. Processes and Variations*. Cambridge, UK: Cambridge University Press.

Wiens, J.A., 1994. Habitat Fragmentation: Island vs. Landscape Perspective on Bird Conservation, *Ibis* 137(Supplement 1): S97-S105.

Wilcove, D.S., 1994. Turning Conservation Goals into Tangible Results: The Case of the Spotted Owl and Old-growth Forests. In *Large-scale Ecology and Conservation Biology* (pp. 313-29) edited by P.J. Edwards, R.M. May and N.R. Webb. Oxford, UK: Blackwell.

Wilcove, D.S. and R.F. Whitcomb, 1983. Gone with the Tree, *Natural History* 9/83: 82-91.
Williams, J.D., M.L. Warren, K.S. Cummings, J.L. Harris and R.J. Neves. 1992. Conservation Status of Freshwater Mussels of the United States and Canada, *Fisheries* 18: 6-22.
Williams, N., 1998a. Overfishing Disrupts Entire Ecosystems, *Science* 279: 809.
Williams, N., 1998b. Study Finds 10% of Tree Species under Threat, *Science* 281: 1426.
Williams, P., D. Gibbons, C. Margules, A. Rebelo, C. Humphries and R. Pressey, 1996. A Comparison of Richness Hotspots, and Complementarity Areas for Conserving Diversity of British birds, *Conservation Biology* 10: 155-74.
Williamson, M., 1996. *Biological Invasions*. New York: Chapman & Hall.
Williamson, M. and and A. Fitter, 1996. The Varying Success of Invaders. *Ecology* 77: 1661-66.
Wilson, B., G.C. van Kooten, I. Vertinsky and L.M. Arthur (editors), 1998. *Forest Policy: International Comparisons*. Wallingford, UK: CABI Publishing.
Wilson, C.L. and C.L. Graham (editors), 1983. *Exotic Plant Pests and North American Agriculture*. New York: Academic Press.
Wilson, E.O., 1985. The Biological Diversity Crisis, *BioScience* 35: 700-06.
Wilson, E.O. (editor), 1988. *Biodiversity*. Washington, DC: National Academy Press.
Winston, M.L. and C.D. Scott, 1984. The Value of Bee Pollination to Canadian Agriculture, *Canadian Beekeeping* 11: 134.
Woinarski, J.C.Z., G. Connors and B. Oliver, 1996. The Reservation Status of Plant Species and Vegetation Types in the Northern Territory, *Australian Journal of Botany* 44: 673-89.
Wood, P., 1997. Biodiversity as the Source of Biological Resources, *Environmental Values* (3): 251-68.
Woodward, F.I., 1993. How Many Species are Required for a Functioning Ecosystem? In *Biodiversity and Ecosystem Function* (pp. 271-91) edited by E.-D. Schultz and H.A. Mooney. Berlin: Springer-Verlag.
World Commission on Environment and Development (WCED). 1987. *Our Common Future*. Oxford, UK: Oxford University Press.
World Trade Organization, 1998. *Annual Report 1997*. Geneva. Switzerland: World Trade Organization.
Young, M.D. and N. Gunningham. 1997. Mixing Instruments and Institutional Arrangements for Optimal Biodiversity Conservation. In *Conservation Outside Nature Reserves* (pp.123-35) edited by P. Hale and D. Lamb. Brisbane: Centre for Conservation Biology, University of Queensland.

Index

adverse selection, 154
Africa, 9, 11, 13, 32, 35–6, 39, 50, 71, 109, 125, 133, 171, 173, 182, 189–90, 193
African elephant, 133
agriculture, 11, 19, 24, 46, 48–51, 55, 70–1, 73, 76–7, 84, 86, 93, 126–30, 134, 140–1
alteration of river flows, 64
Amazon, 29, 35, 99, 191–3
ambrosia beetles, 74
anthropocentric analysis, 123
anthropocentric view, 143
Aral Sea, 20, 194
areas dedicated to nature conservation, 5, 35, 38, 44, 59, 60, 124, 170
Asian water buffalo, 43
Australia, 5, 9, 13, 32, 36, 42–3, 50, 57, 59, 70–1, 108–9, 170–2, 176–82, 188, 190–5

background rate of extinction, 12, 131
Bering Strait, 9
bilogical invasion, 69, 84–5
biodiversity conservation, 6, 100, 125
Biodiversity Convention, 14, 16, 111, 120

biodiversity hotspots, 35–6, 43, 61–2
Biodiversity Treaty, 111
biological invasion (bio-invasion), 69, 84–5
biological redundancy, 116
blackfooted ferret, 116
bounded rationality, 154
Brazil, 18
Britain, 35–6, 50, 178
British Columbia, 1, 11, 29, 35, 40, 44, 69, 71, 74, 170, 179–80, 192, 196
Bruntland Commission (see World Commission on Environment and Development)
bumblebees, 38
burrowing owl, 37, 41

Canada, 11, 18, 23, 32, 38, 50, 74, 76–81, 178, 180, 184–7, 191–2, 198
canine distemper, 39
carbon sink, 126–7, 130, 137
Carolina parakeet, 14
Central America, 18, 37
charismatic species, 32
chestnut blight, 70
China, 32, 38, 72, 74, 99

200 *Conserving Nature's Diversity*

civil society, 154
clear-cutting of tropical forests, 1, 6, 18, 109, 131–2
climate change (see also global warming), 21, 29, 41, 44, 60, 83
collective decision making, 161–3
Colombia, 118
common good, 121, 163–4, 166
compensation for spillover benefits, 134, 136–7
compound of commercial value, 96
conservation organisations, 32, 100
conservation planning, 32, 57, 60–4, 104
contingent valuation, 98
contingent valuation method, 98
contractarian, 149
control costs, 80, 82
Convention on International Trade in Endangered Species (CITEs), 86, 134
Costa Rica, 5, 31, 117–20, 125–30, 137, 140, 172, 191
costs of control measures, 79

Darwinism, 151, 180, 184
DDT, 20
Deep Ecology, 143–4, 146, 150
defensive expenditures, 95
demand for biodiversity, 110
democratic theory, 160–8
    and convergent procedural democracy, 163–4, 166
    and fair procedural democracy, 163–4, 166–8
    and problem of constituency, 162, 167–8
    and problem of scope, 162
desertification, 19–20
discounting and discount rates, 101, 127, 134–6, 139, 141–2, 165, 169
dodo bird and extinction, 42
Dutch elm disease, 70, 80–1

Earth Charter, 143–5
Earth Summit, 16, 34
economic costs, 75–6, 78–9, 82–3, 131–3
economic development, 1
economic efficiency, 26, 61–2, 88–9, 119–20, 138–40, 147–8, 153
economic losses, 75, 79, 82
economic valuation (see also contingent valuation method), 91, 123–4
ecosystem cycle, 26–8
ecosystem disruption, 21
ecosystem function, 7, 21, 24–6, 42, 116, 121, 158
ecosystem services, 21, 23–4, 110, 125
Ecotron experiments, 25
Ecuador, 17
effects on biodiversity, 84
elephants, 10, 32, 125, 133–8
elm trees, 81
embedding problem (see also contingent valuation method), 98

endangered species, 2, 6
Endangered Species Act (ESA), USA, 2, 140, 144–8, 172, 192, 194
Endangered Species Committee, 144
England, 35, 54, 81, 175–6, 188
environmental and ecological impacts, 84
environmental catastrophe, 20, 94
environmental ethic, 146, 148, 150, 156–7
environmental threshold, 40, 100, 114
establishment of exotic species (see also exotic species), 50–52, 59, 69–70, 72, 74–5, 80, 84–5, 102, 157
ethical norms, 145, 150–1, 155–7
Europe, 10–11, 43, 71–4, 80, 82, 107–9, 175
European and Mediterranean Plan Protection Organisation, 82, 197
European rabbit, 13, 71
existence values, 110
exotic organisms, 72–3
exotic pests, 68–9, 76–8, 83–6
exotic plants, 11, 69–71
exotic species (see also biological invasion), 1, 4, 11, 13, 20, 42, 68–79, 82–7
 non–native species, 4
 pathogens, 69–71, 73–4, 83
 policy response, 85
exterminating species, 9, 31
extinction event, 12, 15

extinction of species (see also species loss), 1, 4, 9–18, 30, 32–4, 39–44, 90, 98, 107, 116, 119, 131–2, 137, 149
extinction rates, 4, 11–2, 14
Exxon Valdez oil spill, 99

flagship species, 32, 134
Florida, 70, 183
forest pests, 74
forestry, 20, 68, 70, 73, 76–7, 86–7, 127
France, 79, 108, 176
free riding, 154
frequency of extinctions (see also species loss), 10
functional ecosystem, 7, 21, 24, 25–6, 42, 116, 121, 158

gap analysis, 35, 43
General Agreement on Tarifs and Trade (GATT), 82
giant panda, 32, 90
global warming, 21, 29, 41, 44, 60, 83
globalisation, 68, 72, 85–6, 155
grazing, 48, 50, 52–3, 55, 63, 134, 149
Great Auk, 11
green accounting, 94–5
ground sloth, 10
gypsy moth, 70, 79–80

habitat constant, 39
habitat degradation, 21
habitat destruction, 31

habitat fragmentation, 16, 33
  connectivity of habitat patches, 33
habitat loss, 2, 13–4, 39, 53, 60, 115
  habitat conversion, 1, 131–2
habitat renewal, 13, 39, 43
Hawaii, 9–10, 42–3, 116, 185
Heisenberg's uncertainty principle, 98
horse chestnut tree, 116
hotspots, 35, 61–2
human health, 70, 73, 76–7, 80, 144

ice age, 10, 41
incomplete contracting, 153
India, 32
indicator species, 32
Indonesia, 9, 159
insects, 35, 41, 69–70, 74, 79, 83
inspection and quarantine, 77
instrumental goods, 165
instrumental value, 143–5, 147, 149
integrated conservation and development protects ICDP, 103
intellectual property, 111
intergenerational equity, 89, 101, 139
intergenerational fairness, 7, 161
international compensation, 129
International Convention on Biological Diversity, 16, 20
International Plant Protection Convention (IPPC), 86
international trade, 68, 82, 134

International Union for the Conservation of Nature (IUCN), 32
International Whaling Commission, 137
intrinsic good, 164–66
intrinsic value, 110, 143–4, 146
introduced species, 69–70, 73–4, 84
invasion of exotic species, 4, 75
  economic costs (damages), 75–9, 82–3, 131–3
  pathway for the introduction of, 71, 85
  risk assessment, 85, 87
  risk management, 64
investment in biodiversity, 134, 137–8
IPPC, 86
ivory ban (see also elephants), 39, 135
ivory billed woodpecker, 14
Ivory Coast, 18, 134, 173

Japan, 81, 108–9

kangaroos, 9
Kenya, vii, 134–6
keystone species, 25, 116
Kudzu, 71

Lake Victoria, 13
land conversion, 2, 106
larch, 82
loss of biodiversity, 1, 2, 16, 30, 83

low–level ethical norms, 145, 150, 152

Madagascar, 9–10, 17–8, 177
mainstream economics, 8, 146, 151–3
maintenance of viable populations, 69, 137
major episodes of extinction, 12, 15
Malaysia, 50, 170
mangroves, 18
marginal valuation, 22, 51, 77, 91, 93, 104, 106, 113, 115, 121, 125, 127–9, 133, 137–8, 141–2
market failure (see also policy failure), 91, 106, 124–5, 152–3
  Coase Theorem, 111, 173
  externalities, 7, 23, 90–1, 94, 111
marsupial, 9
Mauritius, 42
Melaleuca quinquenervia, 70
milkweed butterflies, 37–8
minimal viable population (MVP), 19, 52
minke whales, 137
monetary valuation (see contingent valuation method)
moral hazard, 154
moral responsibility, 124

NAFTA, 74
National Forest Policy Statement, 57, 170, 180

National Parks and Wildlife Service, 58, 60, 66, 170, 174, 186
Native Vegetation Conservation Bill, 59, 66
natural area, 5, 35, 38, 44, 59–60, 124, 170
natural disturbance, 27–8, 83
  fire, 10, 28, 70, 84
naturalism, 150
nature conservation, 45–6, 48, 51, 53, 56, 60–6, 123–4, 139–40
Neanderthal man, 10
net primary productivity (NPP), 21
New Caledonia, 10
New Guinea, 29, 99, 194
New Institutional Economics (NIE), 152–3, 177
New South Wales, 45–66, 170–5, 180–3, 186–97
New South Wales Biodiversity Strategy, 58
New South Wales Department of Land and Water Conservation, 55, 58, 175
New South Wales Fauna Protection Panel, 56
New Zealand, 9–10, 31–2, 42, 50, 82, 87, 108–09, 170, 175, 183
Nigeria, 18
nonrival goods, 95
nonuse values (see contingent valuation method), 127, 136–7

204 *Conserving Nature's Diversity*

North America, 4, 9–13, 22, 28, 32, 37, 40, 42, 68, 70–4, 79–82, 107–09, 161, 164, 171, 185–6, 190–1, 195, 198
North American Free Trade Agreement (NAFTA), 74

oak, 79
Okanagan Valley, British Columbia, 35, 40
old–growth forests, 18, 20, 32, 38, 58, 125, 138
Ontario, 79–80, 185
open–access resource, 106
optimal forest stocks, 126, 129
option value, 78, 101–2, 121, 126, 130
Oregon, 36, 174

Panama, 118
passenger pigeon, 13–4
pathogens, 69–71, 73–4, 83
pharmaceutical value, 96, 112, 117, 121, 127, 131–2, 137–8
pine shoot beetle, 74
pine wood nematode, 81–2
poaching, 17, 38, 134–5
policy failure (see also market failure), 1, 56, 124–5
population growth, 6, 83
population viability analysis (see also minimum viable population), 33, 41
post–modernism, 155–6
poverty, 1, 6
prairie dog, 116
Precautionary Principle, 7

preservation benefits, 127
property rights, 89, 106–7, 111, 119–21, 152–3
   intellectual property, 111
protected areas, 5, 35, 38, 44, 59–60, 124, 170
   areas of conservation, 33
   nature reserves, 5
   reserve networks, 34
   reserves, 34–60, 63, 65, 67, 101, 136
psychological and socio–political economics (PSPE), 154, 157–8
public good, 1, 114
public land, 5, 45–6, 48, 55–6

Quebec, 80–1, 187
Queen Charlotte Island, 35

rabbits, 71
rainforest (see old-growth forests)
re–colonisation of a species, 53
red fox, 13
redundancy hypothesis, 25
reservation (see also protected areas), 36, 45–6, 48, 50, 52, 56–9, 67
reserve selection
   complementarity, 36–7, 41, 43
   criteria, 59–61
   irreplaceability, 36, 53, 57, 60
   location, 35, 44
   reservation bias, 48, 60
resilience, 7, 28, 60
resource rent, 76–7, 106–7, 121

responses to conservation on the cheap, 64–5
rhino horn, 38
risk assessment, 85, 87
risk management, 64
risk of extinction, 17
Rule of Law, 7
rule of ten, 69
Russia, 108

safe minimum standard (SMS) (see also Precautionary Principle), 7, 102, 147, 149, 158, 190
sage thrasher, 41
Scotch Broom, 71
Scotland, 29–30, 35
self–organisation, 29
Serengeti National Park, 38, 193
shipping containers (see also biological invasion), 69, 71, 74, 86
Siberia, 82–3, 196
social capital, 154–56, 158, 169
South Africa, 36, 182
Southeast Asia, 37–8
Southern England, 81
species loss, 2, 6, 8, 20, 31, 43, 122, 131–2, 151
   causes of extinction, 1, 11–2, 18
   centres of extinction, 14
   and co–extinctions, 13
   eradication, 10, 22, 80–2
   extinction rates, 4, 9, 11–2, 14, 16–7, 38, 90, 131
   population, 17
   processes of extinction, 15

species–area relation, 2, 14, 131, 142
Strathcona Provincial Park, British Columbia, 38
sustainable development, 5–6
   strong sustainability, 5, 37

Tanzania, 38
technological change, 7
temperate rainforests (see also old–growth forest), 18, 20, 38, 58, 125, 138
threatened and endangered species, 2–3, 6, 32, 34–5, 41, 84, 90, 93, 97–8, 136, 138, 196
tiger, 32
tiger salamander, 41
top–level ethical norms, 145, 150, 152, 155–6
tourism, 70, 78, 82, 126–7, 134
trade, 6, 13, 39, 68, 71–5, 82, 84–6, 101, 134–6, 144
trade liberalisation, 72, 86
tragedy of the commons (see also open–access resource), 106–7
transaction costs, 148, 153–4
tropical deforestation, 1, 6, 18, 109, 126, 131–2
tropical forests, 17–8, 37–8, 109, 116, 130–1, 159

umbrella species, 32
uncertainty, 73, 84–5, 98, 101–2, 126, 130–2, 153–5, 166

United States, 1–3, 14, 22–3, 50, 69–82, 84, 87, 108, 112, 174, 177–8, 187–8, 190, 196, 198
universal earth ethic, 145–6, 157
US National Institute of Health, 22
US National Park Service, 118
utilitarian, 7, 124, 139, 143, 148–9, 152

value of the marginal species, 113
Vancouver Island, 35, 38, 192
Venezuela, 61, 118, 191
voluntary conservation agreement, 65

water buffalo, 43
welfarism, 166, 169
willingness to pay (WTP) (see also contingent valuation method), 23, 137

Winnipeg, Canada, 81
wood packaging, 69, 74
wood–boring beetle, 69, 74
woody plant, 71, 74
woolly rhino, 10, 31
World Commision on Environment and Development (WCED), 17, 22, 40, 198
world trade (see also GATT), 72–3
World Wildlife Fund, 32

Yellowstone National Park, 22, 50, 118, 183, 191
Yukon, 31

Zambia, 134–6, 172
zoning, 49